Tomart's Price Guide To
Garage Sale GOLD

Edited by Bob Welbaum

Color Photography by Tom Schwartz

Masthead designed by Fred Blumenthal

Wallace-Homestead Book Company
Radnor, Pennsylvania

Prices listed are based on the experience of the authors and a national panel of dealers and collectors. They are presented as a guide for information purposes only. No one is obligated in any way to buy, sell, or trade according to these prices. Condition, rarity, demand and the reader's desire to own determine the actual price paid. No offer to buy or sell at the prices listed is intended or made. Buying and selling is conducted at the reader's risk. Neither the author nor publisher assumes any liability for any losses suffered for use of, or any typographic errors contained in, this book. The numeric code system used in this book is not consistent with some collectible guides published by Tomart Publications.

All value estimates are presented in U.S. dollars. The dollar sign is omitted to avoid needless repetition.

© Copyright 1992, Tomart Publications

All Rights Reserved

Published by Tomart Publications, Dayton, Ohio 45439-1944

Also published in 1992 in Radnor, Pennsylvania, by Wallace-Homestead,
a division of Chilton Book Company

Library of Congress Catalog Card Number: 91-65432

ISBN: 0-87069-655-6   Manufactured in the United States of America

3 4 5 6 7 8 9 0   1 0 9 8 7 6 5 4

TABLE OF CONTENTS

COLOR PLATES

HERE'S A BOOK WHERE EVERY ITEM HAS EXCEPTIONAL VALUE...COLLECTIBLES YOU CAN FIND

Tomart Publications has become known as a publisher of definitive price guides on contemporary collectibles. For many years we looked on generalist price guides with mixed emotions. Too often they reported random auction results without sufficient descriptions or background. We cringed at the inaccurate information in the categories of our greatest expertise. Yet collectors, dealers, and casual book store browsers tend to buy "price guides" which cover many subjects rather than one which covers the subject completely. The sales figures would command any publisher's attention.

It became obvious Tomart needed to publish a broader based price guide, but another "me too" antique or flea market price guide wasn't our style.

In contemplating the book which was to become *Garage Sale Gold* one thought kept recurring. In press interviews and speaking engagements someone invariably asked: "What is the most valuable _____ item?" You can insert Disney, Radio Premium, Space Adventure, or what have you. There seemed to be a fascination with the big buck items.

It's always a tough question, because there is rarely a single item which stands clear cut above the rest. Collectible markets are dynamic and constantly changing. A Disney animation cel may be hot among Disney art collectors, but totally avoided by lovers of Disney ceramics, dolls or watches. A debate would likely ensue just to pinpoint a group of the most valuable items in any given Disney collectible category.

So a list of items, rather than a single item, is the answer to any questions seeking to identify the "most" valuable collectible in any given area. Yet coming up with a price guide of the most valuable contemporary collectibles sounded like an intriguing idea.

Once an editorial direction was established, a decision had to be made on how to identify the most valuable items in collectible areas where Tomart hadn't already done a definitive guide. The answer was obvious. Ask the top experts in each field.

But would they do it?

We started calling around and found there was sufficient support. Getting all these experts to stick to deadlines was another matter, but the result is something new.

Every item in this book is one of exceptional value. Some are just a few years old. Yet these everyday items can easily be worth more than many prize antiques. And the best part is readers have an excellent chance of finding these top collectibles in their attic or garage...or at sales they routinely attend. The "Where to Buy and Sell" section even provides a sales outlet for these extra special finds.

It was a learning experience to put this book together. Hopefully you too will find it educational and fun to read.

More importantly, by spreading the job among the experts, the values in this book tend to be more accurate.

Tom Tumbusch
Publisher

INTRODUCTION

Art takes many unsuspecting forms. Everyday objects - cars, toys, magazines, political buttons, cereal boxes - are insignificant discards in our ever increasingly disposable society. Yet to some, the work of industrial designers, product creators, and commercial artists has always been appreciated and collected, not as art, but because the item has a certain appeal.

It's doubtful many of these savers of popular culture icons ever attended an art appreciation course. Nor is it likely the "art world" is anxious to embrace the variety of expressions cherished by collectors. The instinct to save items of special appeal is a personal adventure. Interest can cool if a field becomes too crowded. Heaven forbid it should mature into a formal hobby with the attendant investors the publicity attracts.

Most of the items found in this book were never designed to be collected. Some of the most collectible failed in the market place. Others were extremely successful, but highly disposable. Virtually all have some unique appeal...or some connection with real or fictitious characters who have succeeded in capturing a national interest.

Demand, not age, creates value.

Exposure and availability spur demand. At no time in the history of man has this been more true than the period since 1950 when television sets became available for every home. Unquestionably a more materialistic society resulted. TV soon reached 98% of all households in the United States. Magazines and newspapers never came close to such penetration. Radio once had the reach, but never the impact of television. The '50s were a revolution of information and visual images.

TV programs provided new forms of entertainment and re-runs of old movies. Film studios feared the tube would put them out of business until they understood how to make the medium work for rather than against them. Hollywood's knee jerk reaction resulted in 3-D, Cinerama, stereophonic sound, and CinemaScope. (Over 40 years later movie theaters continue to set new box office records.)

Television expanded the reach of its new heroes. Actors, sports stars, entertainers and news reporters became as familiar as members of our own family. We wanted to be like them and associated with them. The amount of merchandise produced to satisfy this want mushroomed. The visual images were so strong they stayed with us. The desire to retain or regain items from these periods triggered a wave of "nostalgia" collecting. Such collecting is now highly predictable, and many collectors have learned what will be valuable in the future. The time frame for an item becoming collectible has telescoped down to a matter of days (or even hours) rather than years.

Everyone has some souvenirs of post-1950 popular culture. Once they are no longer treasured, there are collectors willing to buy them.

Garage Sale Gold is an aid to help determine the value of items which have "made the charts" among collectors, and to help those who frequent garage and yard sales make the trip a bit more rewarding.

This book has been written by 38 individual experts in the covered fields. Writing styles vary. At times information overlaps from section to section...i.e. the same item may appear more than once in the book. Rarely were the value estimates exactly the same. After due consideration, it was decided to let these conflicts stand. They are reflective of forces in the market where a Beatles collector, for example, values a lunch box higher than a lunch box collector. These contrasts also mirror different experiences and perceptions of value as they vary from one dealer or collector to another. Collectible values are indeed subjective, and the true value of any item is what a ready buyer is willing to pay...no more, no less.

Each author has also identified the condition criteria and grading for the values listed. Sometimes an apparent conflict is merely one expert describing a mint condition item, another the same item in very fine to near-mint

Condition is everything to the true collector willing to pay the top price. It is difficult to describe condition once you have seen exceptional pristine examples. The standards are often very personal. A bright shinny penny from the bank is the best there is until you've seen a penny in a proof set. A person who has seen neither can honestly believe a mint penny is any one with the current year's date. Then there are those who repair and repolish in an attempt to upgrade condition. Each collector and dealer eventually learns what is truly worth a top price, and set their own standards for condition accordingly. Knowledge of how individual sellers grade condition will avoid disappointment when you buy. Avoiding lower grade items when you collect will prevent disappointment when you want to sell.

HOW TO USE THIS BOOK

Garage Sale Gold is designed to be an authoritative and easy to use reference guide. It uses a classification system to create a standard identification number for each individual item. In addition to being an aid to identification, this system provides a framework into which future items may be added.

The format is a classification system - one similar to the yellow pages of a telephone book. The listings are divided into alphabetically arranged categories. All categories are listed in the Table of Contents.

Individual items are listed within the categories. Each item has been assigned a reference code number consisting of two letters and three numbers. Use of these numbers in dealer and distributor ads and collector's correspondence is encouraged. Permission for such use to conduct buying, selling and trading in lists, letters or ads is hereby granted. All rights for reporting values in newsletters or advisory services require written permission from Tomart Publications, 3300 Encrete Lane, Dayton, OH 45439-1944.

The identity code numbers also serve to match the correct listing to a nearby photo. Unfortunately, not all items can be depicted. Some items in this volume have been previously listed in other publications by Tomart. This book utilizes a code system which is inconsistent with other Tomart guides.

Occasionally items were applicable to two or more categories. For example, a Mickey Mouse watch could have been listed under "Disney" or under "Watches." In such cases a classification decision was made based on the category best suited for the item. Extensive cross-references will also be found at the end of most categories.

HOW TO GET MORE INFORMATION

The most valuable items identified by the experts are included in this book, but this is just a small number of the items available in each category. In each case, a cutoff point was established for the "most valuable." If items were made before 1950, they too were excluded even though they were sometimes more valuable. The goal of *Garage Sale Gold* was to focus on the most sought after and valuable collectibles of the '50s, '60s, '70s, and '80s...things people would have a good chance of finding.

Other items almost as valuable and older pieces worth more are covered in specialized and more complete price guides. Space does not permit a list of the best guides available, but collectors in each field are quick to advise the "must have" guide they use most. Definitive guides are more expensive to produce...especially ones with a lot of photos. They cost more, but save time, are easier to use, and pay back more in the long run. Usually the cost can be recouped on one or two items.

GARAGE SALE GOLD II

There are many contemporary collectible subjects not included for lack of a knowledgeable expert. Others aren't included because of missed deadlines. So there is a strong possibility of a *Garage Sale Gold II* sometime in the future. If you are an expert in a modern collectible subject, and would like to participate, contact Tomart Publications, 3300 Encrete Lane, Dayton, OH 45439-1944 for consideration.

ACTION FIGURES   by T. N. Tumbusch

An action figure is an articulated replica of a fictional character, usually molded in plastic but sometimes in die-cast metal. This category also includes accessory sets, vehicles, playsets, and other toys which were sold for use with or in conjunction with the figures.

Collecting action figures is growing fast. Some of the greatest popular culture icons from films, TV, and the comics are reproduced in interesting and intriguing ways. They can be found in any flea market or toy show, and usually cost less than older collectible items such as antique toys or robots. What's more, action figures are popular toys which are still being made, and the toy industry doesn't show any signs of stopping. The quality of these miniature sculptures is constantly improving, and they are, in a way, contemporary art.

In 1964, Hasbro, then known as Hassenfield Bros., Inc., was the first company to fully develop action figures — G.I. Joe Action Soldiers. There were vehicles and accessories from the start.

Action figures seem to be designed with the collector in mind. The common statement found on every action figure package is "Collect Them All!"...and many kids did. Some were so intrigued they bought one to play with and one to keep mint in the sealed package.

Price ranges are divided into three categories: "Complete No Package," "Mint in Package," and "Mint in Mint Package."

"Complete No Package" refers to loose items with all weapons, decals, and other items found in the original bubble pack or box. Figures, accessories, vehicles, playsets, etc. without all the original items are therefore worth less than the value listed for "loose" but complete items.

"Mint in Package" means the unopened figure on a card or in a box which is at least in fine condition with no tears, prominent creases, battered corners, or price sticker damage. The figure will of course be mint, but collectors value the card or box as much, if not more, than the contents. Figures, vehicles, playsets and other accessories may have been opened, decals applied, and assembled — but still complete and undamaged — in a fine or better original box. The phrase "Mint in Package" can be misleading. This is frequently interpreted by dealers to mean the item inside the package is mint, but the package itself could be re-glued, bent, faded, marred, or covered with adhesive tags which are difficult to remove without damage.

"Mint in Mint Package" means the item is in perfect condition, just like it rolled from the manufacturer's assembly line. The highest values for action figures assume the figure is mint, and is complete in a mint package. No price sticker was ever applied, or if so, it was removed without marks or any trace of adhesive. Particular collectors even want the cardboard inserts in the hanger holes if they are to pay the top price. Boxed items are preferred factory sealed. Mint items were probably original stock, never in circulation, or not used.

AF133   AF135

AF137   AF139

Highly popular lines such as Megos, G.I. Joe, Star Wars and others have been listed in their own sections elsewhere in this book.

For a complete guide to action figure collecting, check out *Tomart's Price Guide to Action Figure Collectibles*. The book lists more than 300 action figure lines, with nearly 4,000 color and b&w photographs. It is regularly updated in *Tomart's Action Figure Digest*. For ordering information, see page 150.

	CNP	MIP	MMP
A-TEAM, THE (Galoob) 1984-85			
AF105 Amy A. Allen	10	20	30
ADVANCED DUNGEONS & DRAGONS (LIN) 1983-84			
AF112 Pulvereye	10	20	30
AF113 Metta Flame	10	20	30
AF114 Mandoom	10	20	30
AF115 Hawkler	12	30	40
AF118 Tiamat, the Five-Headed Dragon	30	85	110

AF105

AF121

AF123

AF125

AF115

AF231

AF234

AF353　　　　AF354

AF254

AF174

AF301

AF226

ADVENTURES OF INDIANA JONES, THE (Kenner) 1982

AF121	Indiana Jones	30	60	100
AF123	Marion Ravenwood	50	120	250
AF125	Sallah	15	30	40
AF128	Belloq in ceremonial robe (mail in premium) on card	10	150	200

BATTLESTAR GALACTICA (Mattel) 1978

AF133	Cylon Commander (gold)	17	32	45
AF135	Baltaar	12	30	42
AF137	Boray	12	28	40
AF139	Lucifer	12	30	42

BEST OF THE WEST (Marx) 1965-76

AF141	Sam Cobra	35	70	85
AF143	Princess Wild Flower	35	70	85
AF145	Chief Cherokee	35	70	85
AF147	Daniel Boone	50	110	150
AF149	Davy Crockett	50	110	150
AF151	Bill Buck	50	110	150
AF153	Joe Gibson	75	150	200
AF155	Johnny West/Thunderbolt set	40	75	95
AF157	Jane West/Flame set	40	75	95
AF159	Circle X Ranch	50	125	200
AF162	Johnny West Ranch	50	125	200
AF165	Fort Apache	60	150	240

BLACK HOLE, THE (Mego) 1980

AF170	V.I.N.Cent	15	35	45
AF172	Maximillian	10	22	30
AF174	Old B.O.B.	30	50	65
AF176	S.T.A.R.	30	45	60
AF178	Humanoid	30	45	60
AF179	Sentry Robot	20	42	50

BONANZA (American Character) 1966

AF201	Ben	40	75	100
AF202	Little Joe	40	75	100
AF203	Hoss	40	75	100
AF204	Outlaw	45	85	115
AF211	Ben's Palomino	25	65	100
AF212	Little Joe's Pinto	25	65	100
AF213	Hoss's Stallion	25	65	100
AF214	Outlaw's Mustang	30	75	115

Action Men and Horses in stable packages AF221-23

AF221	Ben and Palomino	65	175	220
AF222	Little Joe and Pinto	65	175	220
AF223	Hoss and Stallion	65	175	220
AF226	4 in 1 Wagon	35	70	85

CLASH OF THE TITANS (Mattel) 1980

AF231	Perseus	10	15	20
AF232	Calibos	10	17	25
AF233	Thallo	10	16	22
AF234	Charon	12	20	25
AF237	Pegasus	15	25	30
AF239	Kraken	65	80	120

COMIC HEROINES (Ideal) 1967

AF251	Mera, Queen of Atlantis	600	1100	2000
AF252	Batgirl (Barbara Gordon)	600	1100	2000
AF253	Wonder Woman (Diana Prince)	550	900	1800
AF254	Supergirl (Linda Lee Davers)	600	1100	2000

DOCTOR WHO (Denys Fisher Toys) 1976

AF261	Doctor Who	100	150	185
AF262	Leela	100	175	225
AF263	Dalek	100	150	250
AF264	Giant Robot	125	200	275
AF265	Cyberman	150	200	300
AF266	Tardis	175	275	400

DOCTOR WHO (Dapol) 1988

AF280	Commemorative Set	-	120	150

FLINTSTONES IN ACTION, THE (D-Toys) 1985

AF290	The Flintstones' House	50	80	120

HONEY WEST (Gilbert) 1965

AF301	Honey West Figure	85	175	300
AF302	Honey West outfits, ea	15	35	45

I DREAM OF JEANNIE (Remco) 1978

AF314	Bottle playset	55	125	175

INDIANA JONES (Kenner) 1982-83

AF321	12" Indiana Jones	70	150	190

INDIANA JONES & THE TEMPLE OF DOOM (LJN) 1984

AF331	Indiana Jones	20	45	60

AF332	Mola Ram	15	35	50
AF333	Giant Thugee	15	35	50

JAMES BOND (Gilbert) 1965-66

AF341	James Bond	100	150	275
AF342	Oddjob	125	275	350
AF343	Disguise Kit	45	60	80

LINCOLN INTERNATIONAL MONSTERS (Lincoln) 1975

AF351	Count Dracula	40	75	100
AF352	Frankenstein	40	75	100
AF353	Hunchback of Notre Dame	60	100	150
AF354	Phantom of the Opera	60	100	150

LORD OF THE RINGS, THE (Kinckerbocker) 1979

AF371	Gandalf the Grey	10	35	48
AF372	Aragorn	5	30	35
AF373	Frodo	5	30	35
AF374	Samwise	5	30	35
AF375	Gollum	5	30	35
AF376	Ringwraith	10	35	45
AF381	Frodo's Horse	12	40	50
AF382	Charger of the Ringwraith	12	40	50

MAJOR MATT MASON (Mattel) 1967-70

AF401	Major MATT MASON w/Flight Set	45	100	160
AF402	Major MATT MASON w/Moon Suit	55	175	225
AF403	Major MATT MASON w/Cat Trac	35	75	125
AF404	Major MATT MASON w/Space Power Suit Pak	-	200	250
AF405	Talking Major MATT MASON	75	175	225
AF406	Talkin, Flying Major MATT MASON	-	300	350
AF407	Sgt. Storm w/Flight Set	55	125	175
AF408	Sgt. Storm w/Cat Trac	35	100	150
AF409	Captain Lazer (hard plastic)	75	125	175
AF410	Doug Davis (yellow uniform)	45	150	175
AF411	Jeff Long (blue uniform)	75	200	300
AF412	Callisto	75	150	200
AF413	Scorpio (lights up)	500	1000	1200
AF414	Space Mission Team (4-pack)	-	450	600
AF421	Space Probe Pak	35	60	85
AF422	Moon Suit Pak	35	60	85
AF423	Super Power Set	-	200	250
AF424	Space Crawler Action Set w/ Major MATT MASON	-	125	175
AF425	Uni-Tred and Space Bubble	-	100	150
AF426	Firebolt Space Cannon Action Set w/Capt. Lazer	-	150	200
AF427	Firebolt Space Cannon Super Action Set w/Capt. Lazer, Major MATT MASON, and Sgt. Storm	-	250	275
AF430	Star Seeker	65	100	150
AF435	Orbitor w/Or	700	1200	1500
AF437	XRG-1 Reentry Glider	60	100	125
AF440	Space Station	45	85	125
AF445	Astro Trac 4-Unit Space Missile Convoy (Sears Exclusive)	-	550	650
AF460	Talking Command Console	75	90	125

AF806

AF511

MAN FROM U.N.C.L.E., THE (Gilbert) 1965

AF501	Napoleon Solo	75	140	175
AF502	Illya Kuryakin	75	140	175

MARTIAN CHRONICLES, THE (Larami) 1974

AF511-13	*Martian Chronicles* aliens, ea	25	50	80

MARVEL SUPER HEROES SECRET WARS (Mattel) 1984

AF523	Wolverine (black claws)	15	30	50
AF524	Wolverine (silver claws)	10	20	30
AF539	Spider-Man, black costume	10	25	30
AF541	Falcon	20	34	45
AF542	Baron Zemo	10	20	25
AF543	Hobgoblin	20	40	45
AF545	Iceman	18	35	40
AF546	Constrictor	18	35	40
AF547	Electro	18	35	40

MIKE HAZARD (Marx) 1967

AF601	Mike Hazard	100	280	320
AF611	Display stand	375	-	-

NOBLE KNIGHTS, THE (Marx) 1968-72

AF701	The Silver Knight	60	90	115
AF702	The Gold Knight	60	90	115
AF703	The Black Knight	60	170	200
AF711	Valour (black w/silver armor)	80	100	125
AF712	Victor (bay w/gold armor)	80	100	125
AF713	Valiant (grey w/black armor)	80	100	125

OFFICIAL WORLD FAMOUS SUPER MONSTERS (AHI/Remco) 1976

AF731	The Mummy	30	55	90
AF732	Creature from the Black Lagoon	75	125	150
AF733	Count Dracula	30	55	90
AF734	Frankenstein	30	55	90
AF735	Wolfman	30	55	90

AF545   AF546   AF547

AF733

AF440

AF875   AF877

AL110

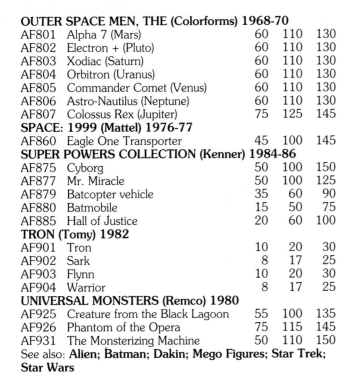

AL170

AL120

Alien/Aliens section, as well as information on 19 other categories of Space Adventure, with 2,000+ b&w and color photos. See page 150 for ordering information.

AL110	18" Alien action figure (Kenner, 1979)	150-350
AL115	Jumbo Alien (Tsukuda Hobbys)	80-120
AL120	Giant jigsaw puzzle (H. G. Toys, 1979)	15-25
AL150	Giant Blaster target set (H. G. Toys, 1979)	40-90
AL155	Target game	20-40
AL170	Board game	15-60
AL180	Movie viewer (Kenner, 1979)	15-75
AL200	Alien mask (25 cast from original mold)	175-300
AL330	Film, Super-8	12-40
AL335	Costume (Ben Cooper)	12-35
AL540	Giger's Alien book, original	50-150
AL541	Same as AL540, reissue	20-40

OUTER SPACE MEN, THE (Colorforms) 1968-70

AF801	Alpha 7 (Mars)	60	110	130
AF802	Electron + (Pluto)	60	110	130
AF803	Xodiac (Saturn)	60	110	130
AF804	Orbitron (Uranus)	60	110	130
AF805	Commander Comet (Venus)	60	110	130
AF806	Astro-Nautilus (Neptune)	60	110	130
AF807	Colossus Rex (Jupiter)	75	125	145

SPACE: 1999 (Mattel) 1976-77

| AF860 | Eagle One Transporter | 45 | 100 | 145 |

SUPER POWERS COLLECTION (Kenner) 1984-86

AF875	Cyborg	50	100	150
AF877	Mr. Miracle	50	100	125
AF879	Batcopter vehicle	35	60	90
AF880	Batmobile	15	50	75
AF885	Hall of Justice	20	60	100

TRON (Tomy) 1982

AF901	Tron	10	20	30
AF902	Sark	8	17	25
AF903	Flynn	10	20	30
AF904	Warrior	8	17	25

UNIVERSAL MONSTERS (Remco) 1980

AF925	Creature from the Black Lagoon	55	100	135
AF926	Phantom of the Opera	75	115	145
AF931	The Monsterizing Machine	50	110	150

See also: **Alien; Batman; Dakin; Mego Figures; Star Trek; Star Wars**

ALIEN/ALIENS   by T.N.Tumbusch

The Alien movies brought back the "hostile monster from outer space" theme, combining suspense and horror with space adventure. The creature from the films was considered so frightening that most of the original merchandise was taken off the shelves. The Kenner version of the alien is one of the most highly-sought pieces. Even when found, the figure is usually missing the plastic dome which covered its head, or is otherwise incomplete.

Space Adventure Collectibles includes a more detailed

ANIMATION ART   by Tom Tumbusch & Ron Stark
with pricing input by Howard
Lowery and Richard Taylor

A cel, short for celluloid, represents the action of usually one character in one frame of an animated film. It takes up to 24 cels per character, photographed on at a time against a painted background, for each second of screen time, or as many as 1440 per minute. Except for some recently produced serigraphed (screen printed) cels, limited edition "gallery" cels and souvenir cels from the Disney Animation Studio Tour in Florida, each is a one-of-a-kind piece of art. Collecting them demands a certain amount of knowledge and expertise.

Originally, cels were traced onto the front of clear celluloid sheets using pen or brush and ink then painted on the reverse with specially prepared gum-based paints. Cels were intended to last long enough to meet production needs. The paints and inks were designed for easy removal, as early cels were washed and reused from film to film. Thus, it is a gift of fortune when old cels remain intact today. Prior to 1940 cels were made of nitrocellulose, an unstable and flammable material. The change to safety cels, made of cellulose acetate, began with Disney's *Fantasia*.

Original master backgrounds are many times more valuable than cels because there were normally thousands of cels used with a single background.

AN340

AN183

AF511   AF511

Disney Animation Art

Cels first became commercially available in 1937 as a result of a licensing agreement between San Francisco art dealer Guthrie Courvoisier and the Disney brothers. Art first offered through the Courvoisier Gallery was from *Snow White and the Seven Dwarfs*. Special set-ups were prepared by a 20 artist unit at the Disney Studios using original and stenciled backgrounds on a variety of art boards and wood veneer. Characters in studio-prepared set-ups were usually cut out of the original cel and adhered directly to the background. These set-ups usually had two small labels: a copyright/"handle with care" notice and a label noting the title of the film. Backs were sealed using a special colored paper and a white label was added stating the art's provenance. Because Courvoisier distributed animation art to many other galleries it is not unusual to see labels from local framers and sellers in addition to those placed by the Studio.

No animation art marketing effort was in effect from 1943 to 1954. Set-ups from films produced during those years were scare and now command high prices.

Beginning in 1955 cels were sold at Disneyland as souvenirs at the Art Corner in Tomorrowland. Featured were cels from *Lady and the Tramp* and later *Sleeping Beauty* as well as other current features and television shows. Prices began at $1.25. A distinctive metallic gold label authenticates the art as having been sold at Disneyland. Over the years five different versions of the label were used. The cels sold in the theme park had inexpensive paperboard mats and no backgrounds. As the program continued, the Studio mass produced litho backgrounds from *Sleeping Beauty*, *101 Dalmatians*, *The Sword in the Stone* and *Mary Poppins* for use in these souvenir set-ups.

101 Dalmatians, released in 1961, was Disney's first feature-length film using the xerographic process. The animation drawings were "copied" onto the cel by machine instead of by hand, giving the characters a softer, sketchier look. Gone was the intricate colored hand inking. And in 1966 the Art Corner was gone as well to make way for a new Tomorrowland. The remaining Art Corner cels were sold at the Emporium on Main Street until the supply ran out. Cels were not offered again at Disneyland until 1973 when the Disney Original Art Program was organized under the Consumer Products Division.

Instead of offering cels in trimmed sizes as before, the Disney Original Art Program offered the art in full size with better mats and featuring a special embossed seal. Later the seal would be changed to a hot stamp version about the size of a silver dollar, and in 1988 the seal was again changed to dime size.

In recent years the Studio has begun to issue Limited Edition cels along with cels from current film releases.

Many outstanding cels were never sold commercially and have no labels or seals. Animator Ward Kimball recalls giving out cels and drawings to the children in his neighborhood.

Very often a cel or original drawing was sent to a young would-be animator just for writing a letter to Walt. Many pieces were sent to relatives or friends of employees as examples of the Studio's work. Cels of virtually every Disney film still exist somewhere. Full cels released through the Disney Original Art Program are sold at the parks in the $100 to $500 range. *Oliver & Company*, *Who Framed Roger Rabbit?*, and *The Little Mermaid* cels were available with printed or photographic backgrounds.

Now that animation art has entered the fine art arena and values have begun to climb, counterfeit cels and backgrounds are more common. It requires a trained eye to recognize a fake. In a single case in 1982, Walt Disney Productions prosecuted an artist for the creation of over 18,000 bogus cels. A supply of equally fake labels was confiscated as well. So collectors should be aware it is possible to get an education the hard way.

Non-Disney

Disney commands virtually all the most valuable categories in post-1950 animation art and backgrounds. Chuck Jones' work for Warner Brothers is preferred by many collectors. Hanna-Barbera's "Flintstones" and "Jetsons," Walter Lantz's Woody Woodpecker, and MGM's Tom and Jerry have their followers. Saturday morning TV cartoons from Jay Ward, Hanna-Barbera, and a host of other studios are also possible to find. There are hundreds of animation subjects in this category which all appeal to someone but the market price is, more often than not, under $100.

Paint chipping and other cel damage is not uncommon. S/R Labs, located at 31200 Via Colinas Ave, Westlake, CA 91361, is a leading source to contact regarding cel restoration.

Each cel should be appraised individually for the best estimate of value, but some general guidelines are provided by examples of sales of the Howard Lowery Gallery, a large West Coast auction house specializing in animation art, and Gifted Images - an East Coast gallery specializing in fine animation art pre-priced for the ready buyer. These have been selected from over 200 dealers in animation art to provide a cross section of what the post-1950 market is like.

AN147

AN148

AN179

AN132

HOWARD LOWERY GALLERY

All of the sales cited in this section are from public auction sales of the past two years. The condition of the cel and paint can dramatically affect the value. The cels described below were all in fine or better condition, without major defects, except as noted.

Disney Studio

Alice in Wonderland - 1951

AN101	full figure of Alice	1265
AN102	full figure of Alice curtsying	1980
AN103	portrait of Alice wearing one of the strange residents of Tulgey Wood	1100
AN104	Alice & her kitten Dinah	1980
AN105	pair: Alice & Caterpillar-as-butterfly	1870
AN106	nearly full figure of Cheshire Cat	3960
AN107	full figure of Queen of Hearts	1430
AN108	full figure of Tweedledum & Tweedledee	1210
AN109	full figure of White Rabbit holding his pocket watch	2310

Aristocats - 1970

AN110	portrait cels of O'Malley & Duchess	495

Chip and Dale - 1960s

AN111	singing	407
AN112	lively full figure	495
AN113	sharing a peanut	880

Cinderella - 1950

AN114	pretty Cinderella	1650
AN115	wide-eyed Cinderella admiring ball gown	2090

Donald Duck - 1950s

AN116	large full figure, in mat as sold at Disneyland	935

"*Duck Tales*" - 1980s

AN117	Huey, Dewey, & Louie w/matched master background	660

Goofy

AN118	cheerful, loose-limbed full figure, 1950s	935
AN119	cowboy from *Two-Gun Goofy*, 1952	550
AN120	from *Holiday for Hen-Pecked Husbands*, 1961, on color print background, w/label, as sold at Disneyland	275

The Jungle Book - 1967

AN121	Baloo & Mowgli	1100
AN122	expressive Baloo & Mowgli	1760
AN123	set: matched Baloo & Mowgli	2805
AN124	full figure of Mowgli dancing w/King Louie over color print background, w/WDP sticker as sold at Disneyland	1540
AN125	matched cels of Baloo & Mowgli, laminated, w/WDP seal, label & Disneyland Disneyana shop certificate	1210

AN126	matched cels of Shere Khan & Mowgli over color print background as sold at Disneyland	1100
AN127	suave Shere Khan	2420

Lady and the Tramp - 1955

AN128	portrait of Lady, painted in evening colors	2200
AN129	full figure of Lady	1650
AN130	full figure of wide-eyed Lady	2860
AN131	Lady picking up her pup Scamp	2640
AN132	Lady & Tramp together	4070
AN133	full figures of Lady & Tramp	1815
AN135	full figures of Jock & Lady	2530
AN136	full figure of Tramp	1760
AN137	full figure of Tramp	1430
AN138	full figure of Tramp	2200
AN140	matched cels of Lady & Peg	2310
AN141	rakish Tramp, large image	1650
AN142	cels of Siamese cats Si & Am	1045
AN143	set of Lady & Tramp being served dinner by Tony	4620

Ludwig Von Drake - 1960s

AN144	2 cels	358
AN145	full figure	275

Mary Poppins - 1964

AN146	penguin waiter from "Jolly Holiday" sequence	770

Mickey's Christmas Carol - 1983

AN147	Scrooge McDuck, laminated, w/Disney seal & cel print of background line overlay	825

"*Mickey Mouse Club*" - 1955-58

AN148	full figure of Mickey dressed as cowboy	1540
AN149	full figure of Jiminy Cricket, w/Disneyland mat & sticker	1045
AN150	full figure of Mickey Mouse as the Sorcerer's Apprentice	1650
AN151	Minnie Mouse, Daisy Duck, & Fiddler Pig, in mat w/WDP label & Art Corner stamp as sold at Disneyland	1100

One Hundred and One Dalmatians - 1961

AN152	wet Pongo sits in pond, with color print background as sold at Disneyland	1100
AN153	Pongo lifting pup from snow, with studio color print background	3850
AN154	Perdita & Pongo on color print background w/gold WDP sticker as sold at Disneyland	1540
AN155	expressive Cruella de Vil w/gold label label on back as sold at Disneyland	1430
AN156	full figure of Cruella de Vil	1980
AN157	portrait of Cruella de Vil w/Disneyland mat & label	2200

Peter Pan - 1953

AN158	expressive Capt. Hook eyeing ruby ring	2255
AN159	flamboyant Capt. Hook	2200

AN160	full figure of scowling Capt. Hook	3520
AN161	full pose of Peter Pan	2420
AN162	full figure of Peter Pan	1650
AN163	full figure of Peter Pan in Indian headdress	1430
AN164	full figure of Peter Pan flying	1430
AN165	full figures of Peter Pan & Capt. Hook	3850
AN166	3 cels of Wendy, John, & Michael Darling	1650

Robin Hood - 1973
| AN167 | full figure cels of Friar Tuck & King Richard | 1100 |
| AN168 | 2 cels of Robin Hood & Maid Marion, 1 w/Disney seal | 1100 |

The Simple Things - 1953 (Mickey Mouse Cartoon)
| AN169 | full figure of Mickey Mouse | 1760 |

Sleeping Beauty - 1959
AN170	Aurora as Briar Rose w/owl	1320
AN171	full figure of Aurora w/3 forest friends, in mat w/gold label as sold at Disneyland	935
AN172	portrait of Aurora as Briar Rose w/gold WDP sticker as sold at Disneyland	1100
AN173	portrait of smiling Aurora, over color print background as sold at Disneyland	1430
AN174	Briar Rose & birds, over color print forest background as sold at Disneyland's Art Corner	1210
AN175	Art Corner	1210
AN176	Princess Aurora w/Prince Phillip	2530
AN177	set: matched Prince Phillip & horse Samson	1320
AN178	Prince Phillip astride Samson, over color print background as sold at Disneyland	2420
AN179	full figure of gloating Maleficent, in matte w/Disney-INA sticker	3300
AN180	Maleficent laughing evilly, over color print background as sold at Disneyland	2860
AN181	Maleficent on color print background w/ gold Disneyland label	2310
AN182	Maleficent as Dragon, impaled on Prince Phillip's sword, on color print background as sold at Disneyland	5060
AN183	3 cels of Maleficent, the Dragon, & Prince Phillip & Aurora, all w/significant paint damage & wear	3960
AN184	cels of Aurora, Fauna, & Merryweather, all in Disneyland Art Corner mats	1870

The Small One - 1978
| AN185 | matched cels of Boy, Small One, & Auctioneer, laminated, w/Disney seal | 358 |

The Sword in the Stone - 1963
| AN186 | portrait of Wart (future King Arthur) | 413 |

Winnie the Pooh and a Day for Eeyore - 1983
| AN187 | full figures of Pooh, Tigger, & Rabbit, laminated, w/Disney seal | 1540 |

| AN188 | 2 expressive portrait cels of Pooh & Tigger | 1650 |

Winnie the Pooh and the Honey Tree - 1966
AN189	full figure of Pooh	935
AN190	cels of Gopher & Pooh, over color print background w/WDP sticker	880
AN191	full figure of sad Eeyore	1320

Hanna-Barbera

Until recently, studios other than Disney had no retail outlet for their animation art. These cels are usually found without any distinctive or standardized packaging.

AN201	Fred & Wilma Flintstone & Barney Rubble on master background, 1960-61	1760
AN202	*Jetsons: The Movie*: George, Elroy, & Astro, 1990	330
AN203	2 cel & master background sets of Punkin Puss & Mush Mouse, 1960s	369

King Features - *Yellow Submarine* - 1968 (Beatles)
AN210	large full-fronts of John Lennon & George Harrison, w/authenticity certificate	4070
AN211	Paul McCartney, George Harrison, & a Blue Meanie	1870
AN212	Beatles w/mayor of Pepperland	3520
AN213	Paul McCartney & submarine, w/authenticity certificate	1760

MGM - *I'm Just Wild About Jerry* - 1960s
| AN220 | Tom & Jerry cels w/matched master background, signed by Chuck Jones | 2145 |

Warner Brothers
AN230	full figure of Bugs Bunny, 1950s	2640
AN231	full figure of Bugs Bunny w/color master background, 1950s	1980
AN232	pair: full figure of Road Runner & Wile E. Coyote, hand-inked, 1960s	1760
AN233	*Rushing Roulette*: 2 hand-inked full figure cels of Wile E. Coyote, 1965	1210

RICHARD TAYLOR - GIFTED IMAGES GALLERY

These listings are the price ranges of actual sales for cels of characters without backgrounds at the Gifted Images Gallery within two years of publication.

Cinderella - 1950
| AN301 | Cinderella, 5"x7" | 800-1000 |
| AN302 | Prince Charming, 5"x7" | 500-850 |

AN311

AN161

AN165   AN149

AN154

AF511

AN132

AF511

AN303	Cinderella & Prince, 6"x9"	1800-2000
AN304	Jaq & Gus (mice), 4"x6"	600-800
AN305	Lucifer, 3"x4"	600-800
AN306	Stepmother, 5"x7"	800-1000
AN307	Anastasia/Drizella, 5"x7"	600-800
AN308	Fairy Godmother, 5"x7"	1200-1500

Alice in Wonderland - 1951
AN310	Alice, 5"x7"	2100-3000
AN311	White Rabbit, 3"x5"	1000-1200
AN312	Mad Hatter, 3"x5"	1500-2000
AN313	March Hare, 4"x6"	1000-1500
AN314	Walrus/Carpenter, 5"x7"	800-1200
AN315	King/Queen of Hearts, 5"x7"	1200-1500
AN316	Tweedledee & Tweedledum, 5"x7"	1200-1500
AN317	Cheshire Cat, 5"x7"	2500-3000

Peter Pan - 1953
AN320	Peter Pan, 5'x7'	2400-2800
AN321	Captain Hook, 5"x7"	2400-3500
AN322	Tinker Bell, 6"x8"	2000-2400
AN323	Mr. Smee, 5"x7"	800-1000
AN324	Lost Boys, 4"x6"	800-1000
AN325	Wendy, John, & Michael, 5"x7"	800-1000

Lady and the Tramp - 1955
AN330	Lady & Tramp, 4"x6"	3000-3500
AN331	Lady, 3"x5"	2000-2500
AN332	Tramp, 4"x6"	2000-2200
AN333	Peg, 4"x6"	1400-1600
AN334	Jock & Trusty, 3"x5"	800-1200
AN335	Si & Am, 3"x5"	800-1200

Sleeping Beauty - 1959
AN340	Briar Rose, 5"x7"	1200-1500
AN341	Princess Aurora, 5"x7"	1600-2000
AN342	Prince Phillip, 5"x7"	700-1000
AN343	Good Fairies, 4"x6"	900-1200
AN344	Maleficent, 5"x7"	1800-2500

101 Dalmatians - 1961
AN350	Pongo, 4"x6"	1000-1200
AN351	Perdita, 4"x6"	1000-1200
AN352	Puppies, 3"-5"	600-800
AN353	Roger & Anita, 6"x8"	600-800
AN354	Cruella De Vil, 5"x7"	1800-2200
AN355	Colonel, Captain, & Sgt. Tibs, 4"x8"	400-600

The Sword in the Stone - 1963
AN360	Arthur/Wart, 5"x7"	800-1000
AN361	Merlin, 5"x7"	1000-1200
AN362	Madam Mim, 4"x6"	400-600

The Jungle Book - 1967
AN370	Mowgli, 5"x7"	800-1000
AN371	Baloo, 5"x7"	1000-1200
AN372	Bagheera, 4"x6"	600-800
AN373	King Louie, 4"x6"	650-850
AN374	Kaa, 3"x5"	400-600
AN375	Shere Khan, 4"x8"	1800-2000

AUTOGRAPHS   by Bob Welbaum

Autographs are one of the most popular types of celebrity souvenirs. Pricing autographs is the most difficult and subjective of any collectible category. Anything that can be written upon can be signed, so some guidelines are in order.

- An autograph on an important document is more valuable than a simple signature. Hank Aaron's autograph would be worth far more on his first professional contract than as a hasty scrawl on a scrap of paper at the clubhouse door.

- An autograph becomes more valuable if it's with a personalized message, especially if the recipient is a celebrity...or an intimate friend.

- Most highly prized is a signed personal letter or document which gives insight into a celebrity's personality or reveals a heretofore unknown fact for posterity. The more personal the circumstances, the more valuable the autograph.

- Do not automatically dismiss autographs which do not appear authentic. Some celebrities had an artistically stylized public signature for publicity purposes; their real signature was much more pedestrian. Walt Disney is a prime example: his genuine autograph occasionally goes unrecognized because it is substantially different from the looping letters so frequently seen on movie screens.

- Also remember this is the age of mechanization. Many genuine looking signatures are actually untouched by human hands (or recreated by underlings). This is especially true for politicians. Virtually all autographs on routine correspondence with government officials are mechanically reproduced with an "autopen."

- Beware of forgeries. Unfortunately autographs are easy to fake. Use some common sense...an authentic "Mao Tse-tung" would probably not be in English. Also be suspicious of a fantastic bargain or rare find. When in doubt, ask the opinion of a dealer or experienced collector.

Because pricing is so subjective, the following are actual selling estimates of autographs offered on the market in the twelve months prior to publication. The estimated values are for excellent condition or better: a clear, unfaded signature with no tears or stains in the signature's vicinity. This should be the minimum acceptable condition for any autograph since 1950.

Individual Autographs
AT120	Lucille Ball & Desi Arnez 8x10 b&w photo signed "Love, Lucy and Desi"	100-150
AT123	Gene Autry Poster, w/bold black marker "Best Wishes, Gene Autry." Limited Edition series of 100 w/certificate of authenticity by The Art Merchant, Hollywood.	100-200
AT135	Marlon Brando, 8x10 photo w/ personalized autograph, about 1950	250-300
AT140	Hopalong Cassidy photo, 5" x 7" high gloss b&w w/autograph & inscription	100-200
AT150	Elvis Presley, 8x10 photo w/	

	personalized autograph, 1957	400-500
AT175	Jackie Gleason glossy 8x10 b&w photo w/personalized autograph	50-75
AT240	Bob Kane (Batman creator) blue pen Batman drawing inscription & autograph, 1989	700-1000
AT260	John F. Kennedy signed personal letter on stationery of "United States Senate/ Committee on Labor and Public Welfare," dated Jul 19, 1956, signed "Jack". (After 1953, Kennedy's senate letters were secretarial signed w/full name; less than complete signatures are probably genuine.)	200-700
AT275	Robert F. Kennedy signed photograph, boldly inscribed to an individual w/ "Best Wishes Robert F. Kennedy"	500-700
AT300	Elsa Lanchester, personalized autograph still from *The Bride of Frankenstein*	100-150
AT305	"Meadowlark" Lemon, 10" 78 RPM official Harlem Globetrotters theme song ("Sweet Georgia Brown") recorded on Tempo label w/pictures of 8 players plus owner. Label is autographed "Meadowlark"	50-75
AT325	Mary Martin Signed Letter, Photo	75-200
AT330	Steve McQueen Autographed matte for glossy b&w photo of McQueen from "Wanted: Dead or Alive" TV series	100-200
AT500	"Sgt. Preston" personalized autographed b&w photo of Paul Sutton (radio voice of Sgt. Preston)	100-200
AT525	Elizabeth Taylor 8x10 full color photo w/personalized autograph, about 1970	100-200
AT750	John Wayne 8x10 b&w photo w/inscription & autograph	200-400

Group Autographs

AT800	Beatles b&w glossy photo w/autographs on back. Included an 8x10 letter on Official Beatles Fan Club letterhead.	800-1200
AT810	Gilligan's Island 8x10 b&w photo autographed by 6 of 7 cast members	100-200
AT840	"Lost in Space" 8x10 color photo of 8 cast members, autographed by 7	100-200
AT845	"M*A*S*H" Script for June 26, 1980 episode "Fellows," cover autographed by main characters	100-200
AT848	"McHale's Navy" 8x10 color cast photo autographed by 3	100-200
AT880	"Star Trek" 8x10 b&w photo of 8 cast members, autographed by 7	100-200
AT890	"Taxi" b&w cast photo autographed by entire cast	200-400

Movie Books

Autographed movie book page sheets, 9" x 12" b&w page from a movie book published around late 1950s which was then used to collect autographs. One side of each page has large single portrait of star & autograph. Reverse has various photos of stars & scenes, some with autographs.

AT910	Ingrid Bergman front; James Garner, Sophia Loren, Audrey Hepburn back	200-400
AT920	Judy Garland front; Debbie Reynolds on back w/unautographed photo of Marilyn Monroe & six other stars, 1954	100-200
AT925	Gone With The Wind front w/8 scenes, 4 star portraits, & 3 Olivia de Havilland autographs.	75-200
AT926	Gone With The Wind front w/Vivien Leigh autograph; scenes from other films & Bette Davis autograph on back	75-200
AT930	Cary Grant front; Hedy Lamarr, Greer Garson back	200-400
AT945	Vivien Leigh autograph w/scenes from	

	Caesar and Cleopatra	75-200
AT960	Marilyn Monroe signed 11" x 14" b&w matte finish full length photo w/ personalized autograph (secretarial signed)	100-200
AT975	Shirley Temple in Heidi	100-200
AT990	John Wayne (western outfit) front; Kirk Douglas as Vincent Van Gogh on back	200-700

AUTOMOBILES

Special Consultant: David Brownell
Editor, *Hemmings Motor News*

Power and style were the major automotive design criteria of the 50s and 60s. The Arab oil embargo of the 70s changed the emphasis to miles per gallon and "average fleet rate." Yet Americans long for their sleek muscle cars from the past...driving up the cost of choice preservation and restoration specimens.

Few have the garage space or resources to own very many of these beauties. Usually it is one special car or two to satisfy most collectors...at least till they find something they like a little better. This makes for an active trade in the cars of yesteryear. And the marketplace is Hemmings Motor News. This international listing of collector cars and parts for sale or wanted is published each month.

Each collector car should be valued individually. Factors such as mileage, special equipment, paint color and quality, original logos and ornamentation, engine horsepower, and many other details weigh in a particular car's value. Below are listings complied from the April 1991 issue of Hemmings Motor News. These are not the highest or the lowest; they are but a sample of the hundreds of listings chosen to be representative of the most valuable cars of the 50s, 60s, 70s, and 80s.

Cadillac Eldorado

First appeared as one of three General Motors' limited edition convertibles in 1953 (along with the Buick Skylark and Oldsmobile Fiesta). Rarity of this first year's edition was assured by a high price tag ($7750) and a low production run (under 600). Although in 1954 the Eldorado resembled Cadillac's standard convertible and the ragtop was joined by a hardtop in 1956 through 1960, comparatively low production rates continued to give the car considerable appeal. Any pre-1967 Eldorado has collectible value, but perhaps the year that has been appreciating the fastest is 1959.

AU000	1953 convertible, 100% complete, needs total restoration	25500
AU001	1953 convertible, older restoration	65000
AU002	1954 convertible, 100% complete, needs total restoration	11500
AU003	1954 convertible, older restoration, show car	42000
AU004	1955 convertible, restored	35000
AU006	1957 Biarritz convertible, cosmetic restoration	37000
AU008	1959 convertible, unrestored,	37950
AU009	1959 Biarritz convertible, 100% complete, needs restoration	45000

Chevrolet

On the other end of the spectrum is Chevrolet. In 1955 General Motors combined a sleek, clean design with a new, compact 265 cubic inch V8 engine to produce a classic muscle car. The powerful, durable Chevys built from 1955 through 1957 have become highly prized.

AU100	1955 convertible, 265 ci V8, restored	25000-45000
AU101	1955 convertible, unrestored	5000
AU102	1955 Bel Air convertible, 265 ci V8, new top	34900
AU103	1955 Bel Air 2 dr hardtop 265 ci V8, completely restored, show car	21500-33500

AU104	1955 Bel Air Nomad, restored	28000
AU105	1955 210 2 dr sedan, unrestored,6 cyl	2775
AU106	1956 convertible, restored	28000-41500
AU107	1956 Bel Air convertible, restored,	50000
AU108	1956 Bel Air hardtop, restored	25900
AU109	1956 Bel Air 4 dr, all original, needs work	4000
AU110	1957 convertible 283 HP, fuel injected, trophy winner	90000-105000
AU111	1957 Bel Air convertible, restored	46000-65000
AU112	1957 Bel Air 2 dr hardtop, restored,	29900
AU113	1957 4 dr, 283 ci V8, runs well	5500

Chevrolet Camaro

Chevrolet's answer to the Mustang, the Camaro debuted in 1967. Customers could virtually design the car themselves! The performance oriented options package, block #Z-28 was the most popular. Chevrolet responded by providing the most famous Camaro model - the Z-28!

AU120	1967 RS convertible, needs restoration, not driveable	3500
AU121	1967 RS convertible, restored, trophy winner	10900
AU122	1967 coupe, restored, good	8500
AU123	1967 Z-28 (1 of 602 made in '67) restored	16500
AU124	1969 Z-11 RS/SS Indy pace car convertible good to excellent	16000
AU126	1972 SS, 62000 mi, good	4500
AU127	1974 Z-28, 33000 mi, good to excellent	9500
AU128	1979 Z-28, full options, 32000 mi, near mint	7500

Chevrolet Corvair

Originally introduced in 1960 with high expectations, the Corvair gained notoriety through Ralph Nader's 1965 book *Unsafe at Any Speed* as a symbol of Detroit's alleged disregard for safety. The last Corvair was produced in 1969.

AU130	1964 Spyder coupe, turbocharged, fresh engine, needs work	1800
AU132	1964 Spyder convertible, turbocharged, show car	12000

Chevrolet Corvette

One of the most successful sports cars of all time, the Corvette was introduced in 1953. This austere convertible with the fiberglass body and "Blue Flame" 6 cylinder engine did not sell well initially. Of a planned 1953-54 production run of 12,300, less than 4000 were made. The line might have been killed outright, but a dazzling smallblock V8 engine and the need to compete with the Thunderbird gave impetus to a critical redesign first sold in 1956.

AU140	1954 restored, show car	40000-50000
AU141	1954 unrestored, fair	10000
AU142	1956 needs restoration, wrong engine	16000
AU143	1956 complete professional restoration	85000
AU144	1956 265 cu 225 hp V8	32000-39000
AU145	1957 fuel injected 283 hp V8	53000
AU146	1958 283 ci 230 hp V8, all new	34500-39000
AU147	1959 283 ci 230 hp V8, fine	19990-34000

The line became the Corvette Sting Ray in 1963 with the controversial split rear window after an extensive redesign to incorporate lessons learned on the race track. The 1963 version was the first of the Corvette coupes and also came as a convertible. In 1968 the name reverted back to simply Corvette, then was changed again to Corvette Stingray (one word) in 1969 and remained that way until another redesign in 1984.

AU150	1963 split window coupe, needs restoration	12000
AU151	1963 split window coupe, near mint	30000
AU152	1964 convertible, excellent	16800
AU154	1966 roadster, rebuilt, excellent	22000
AU156	1967 convertible, excellent	28500
AU158	1969 T-top, excellent	22500

Chrysler 300

This series began with the 300 hp C-300 in 1955, which went on to achieve phenomenal success as a stock racer. Chrysler Corp. had developed an engine with a hemispherically shaped cylinder head, or "hemi," in 1951 to increase operating efficiency. This chassis-engine combination made the 300 the world's most powerful production car. Perhaps the most famous of the line is the 1956 300B. Only about 1100 were made.

AU200	1955 C-300 good but needs interior, 60,000 mi.	15000
AU201	1955 C-300 all options, near mint	45000
AU202	1956 300B 354 ci hemi V8, good	17200
AU204	1957 300C runs well, needs restoration, 46000 mi	12000
AU206	1958 300D coupe, sun damaged, needs paint	12500
AU208	1959 300E convertible, needs top & interior	28000

DeLorean

A gull winged stainless steel body sports car of original design by renowned ex-General Motors auto executive John Z. DeLorean, produced for only two years. DeLorean achieved notoriety by being arrested on drug trafficking charges in October 1982, ostensibly to raise money to keep his Northern Ireland factory in production. Although the jury ultimately returned a "not-guilty" verdict, the company was already doomed. The DMC-12 was the sole model, and only about 5000 were built. The car attained fame by being featured in the movie *Back To The Future*.

AU300	1981, 22000 mi	16900
AU302	1982, 652 original mi, near mint	28500

Ford Fairlane

Although the mid-1950s Chevys are more famous, the Fords of this era are classics in their own right. The 1955 Crown Victoria is considered the most memorable.

AU400	1954 Sunliner convertible, 60000 mi, new engine, excellent	13250
AU402	1955 Sunliner convertible, rare options, near mint	28950
AU403	1955 Crown Victoria, V8, excellent	12900
AU404	1955 Crown Victoria, needs total restoration	4500
AU406	1956 Sunliner convertible	35000

Ford Skyliner

In 1957 Ford introduced a truly innovative idea: a hardtop-convertible. The Skyliner's conventional top could automatically fold up and slide into the trunk. Unfortunately the complex mechanism added cost, weight, and was prone to breakdowns. The biggest drawback was lack of trunk space. The Skyliner was only produced for three years (1957-1959).

AU410	1957 restored, show winner	25000
AU412	1958 runs, top works, needs restoration	6500
AU414	1959 72000 mi, show car	22500

Ford Edsel

The Edsel was a classic marketing blunder. Actually a separate Ford division, the premise was to present a single line with models ranging from the equivalent of a basic Ford up to a Lincoln Continental. This strategy ignored the prestige associated with driving the top-of-the-line. The series became the most celebrated flop in U.S. automotive history (rumor says an Edsel has never been reported stolen), lasting only from 1958 through 1960. Convertibles are the rarest.

AU415	1958 Pacer 4 dr hardtop, driveable	3250
AU416	1959 Corsair convertible, V8, new paint	12900

Ford Mustang

The brainchild of Lee Iacocca, the first Mustang appeared in April, 1964, and was an immediate hit. Offering both style and low price, the car set an all time record for first year sales by a new model. Soon customizers and accessories manufacturers were rushing to cash in with the Carroll Shelby version being the most widely produced. Because of this success the basic design remained unchanged until the Mach 1 appeared in 1969. That year's remake began the evolution away from from a simple sports car. An attempt to keep the sports car lineage alive was the flashy "Boss" muscle car introduced in 1970, but the original spirit was quickly slipping away.

AU420	1964 1/2 convertible "D" code, 289 cid, April 1, 1964, restored	23850
AU421	1964 1/2 convertible, 1 of 5 "hi-po K"	42000
AU430	1965 fastback, restored, show winner	18500
AU431	1965 convertible, trophy winner	19500
AU432	1965 K convertible, restored	49000
AU433	1965 fastback, A-code, needs restor.	1900
AU434	1965 GT convertible, restored, show car	26000
AU435	1965 GT fastback, K engine	26000
AU436	1965 Shelby GT 350, #217	98500
AU437	1965 Shelby R-model, documented race history	155000
AU438	1965 Shelby 1/2 GT 350, #128	62500
AU440	1966 convertible, 289, show quality	19000
AU441	1966 coupe, restored, show winner	14950
AU442	1966 2+2 fastback, hi-po 289	24950
AU443	1966 GT hi perf. K convertible, 271 hp	32000
AU444	1966 GT coupe, K-model	15995
AU445	1966 GT 350H	37500
AU446	1966 GT convertible, show winner	24950
AU447	1966 Shelby GT 350H	59500
AU448	1966 Shelby GT 350 convertible	100000
AU450	1967 convertible, 289, 77000 original mi	15500
AU451	1967 GT convertible, 390 cid	18000
AU452	1967 GTA convertible	14900
AU453	1967 coupe, 87000 mi	14000-16000
AU454	1967 fastback, 289 V8, show car	13500-20000
AU455	1967 2+2 fastback GT	12500
AU456	1967 fastback, 390 GT 27000 mi	18500
AU457	1967 GT 500	45000
AU458	1967 Shelby GT 500 Dante restoration	56750
AU460	1968 GT-302 convertible, 0 mi, show car	20500
AU461	1968 fastback, 48000 mi	18000

AU462	1968 Shelby GT 500 convertible	39000
AU463	1968 Shelby GT 500 KR convert, restored	65000
AU464	1968 Shelby GT 350 convertible	43000
AU465	1968 Shelby GT 500, restored	30000
AU466	1968 Shelby fastback GT 350	35000
AU470	1969 GT convertible, 351 ci V8	12500
AU471	1969 Q-code coupe, 428	24500
AU472	1969 Boss 429 S, restored	58500
AU473	1969 Mach I, 428 CJ R code	24995-26500
AU474	1969 Shelby GT 350 convertible, 1 of 194	74500
AU475	1969 Shelby GT 500, 428 CJ	35500
AU480	1970 Boss 302	29500
AU481	1970 Boss 429, 5000 mi	75000
AU482	1970 Mach I 428, restored	15900
AU483	1970 Shelby GT 350 convertible	59000
AU484	1970 Shelby GT 500, 428, 42000 mi	55000
AU486	1971 Mach I, 429 SCJ, 39000 mi	27500

Ford Thunderbird

Ford's most enduring sports car entered production in September 1954. Beginning life as a two seat convertible (an optional removable hardtop was also available), the T-Bird was more of touring car than a true thrill machine. In 1958 the line was redesigned into a four-seater with both convertible and hardtop versions for wider appeal. Although the sports car crowd lamented the demise of the two-seater, the general public embraced the idea of sporty luxury.

AU490	1955, automatic, needs total restoration	9500
AU491	1955 90% restored	25000
AU492	1956, restored, award winner	48000
AU493	1957 E series, older restoration	38500
AU494	1957 partially disassembled, needs work	8200
AU495	1957 E series, rare combination of options	55000

Oldsmobile Cutlass 442

AU500	1966 coupe, restored, near mint	12000
AU501	1967 hardtop, restored, excellent	12500

Plymouth Road Runner

Taking advantage of the popularity of a Warner Brothers' animated character, this car proved Plymouth had a sense of humor. For years the Plymouth Belvedere had been evolving into a muscle car with the Belvedere GTX, the GTX, the GTX Road Runner, then simply the Road Runner. First introduced in 1968, the Road Runner came with either a 383 ci V8 or a 426 ci hemi. The model gained instant recognition and was voted 1968 "Car of the Year" by Motor Trend magazine. Addition of an aerodynamic nose and rear wing created the Superbird.

AU600	1968 426 ci hemi V8, near mint	35000
AU602	1969 440 6 pack convertible, near mint	19900
AU603	1969 61000 mi, good	7500
AU604	1970 convertible 383 ci V8, excellent	14000
AU605	1970 coupe 383 hp near mint engine, needs interior, overall good	8900
AU606	1970 Superbird 46000 mi, excellent	26500

Pontiac GTO

Designed by John DeLorean, GTO stood for Gran Turismo Omologato. The marketing strategy was copied from the Ferrari GTO. The line actually began by taking a V8 engine, increasing the horsepower, and putting it (as part of a high performance option package) into a compact Pontiac Tempest. Many consider this the original 1960s "muscle car" and its 1964 debut was the most successful in Pontiac's history. The series lasted through 1971.

AU700	1964 convertible, fully restored	21500
AU701	1964 convertible, needs restoration, good	16000
AU702	1964 2 post window, restored, loaded	17800
AU703	1965 convertible, excellent	21500
AU704	1965 hardtop, excellent	20000
AU705	1966 convertible, excellent	25000
AU706	1967 coupe, fair to good	790

Pontiac Firebird

Pontiac (under John DeLorean's leadership) was itching to produce a two seat sports car. But the GM brass wanted to meet the Mustang challenge in kind and Pontiac's best intentions ultimately led to a Camaro clone called the Firebird. Its job was to take on the Mercury Cougar (intended as an upscale Mustang) while the Camaro went head-to-head with the Mustang itself. Debuting as a 1967-1/2 model in February, 1967, the car was well received despite its late release. The popular Trans Am evolved from a 1969 option package to match the Camaro Z-28. It became a separate Firebird model in 1970. Trans Am sales took off in 1974; by 1978 half of all Firebird production was Trans Ams.

AU710	1967 coupe, 36000 mi, good	13000
AU711	1967 convertible, excellent	16800
AU712	1968 convertible, 71000 mi, good	8000
AU713	1968 coupe, poor but repairable	2000
AU716	1970 Trans Am, excellent	9300

Jaguar XKE

The E-type Jaguars (XKE in North America) were designed as follow-ons to the popular XK series built from 1949 through 1961. They were destined to become even more successful than the series they replaced. Originally designed in 1956 as a racing sports car, the first prototype appeared publicly as an entrant at Le Mans in 1960. The series is most famous for the monstrous V12 engine which first appeared in 1971. The last E-series were made in the winter of 1974/75, having themselves been replaced by the XJ-S.

AU910	1964 roadster, excellent	42000
AU912	1965 roadster, restored, excellent	45000
AU913	1965 coupe, needs total restoration	6000
AU914	1969 coupe, restored, show winner	33000
AU916	1971 2+2 series III, V12, 42000 mi, good	14900
AU918	1972 roadster, V12, needs work	20000

Mercedes-Benz 190SL

Product of Germany's Daimler-Benz corporation (Mercedes was the name of the daughter of one of the firm's directors), the 190SL first appeared in 1954. A comparatively modest two seat sports car, it's one of the more highly prized Mercedes models.

AU920	1955 190 SL, good	16400
AU922	1956 190 SL, good	12900
AU924	1957 190 SL convertible, restored, excellent	22500
AU926	1960 190 SL, excellent	19500

Mercedes-Benz 300SL

Mercedes-Benz re-entered racing in a big way in 1952 with an innovative multi-tubular frame chassis design, the 300SL (3 liter *Sport-Leicht* or light sports car). There was one problem - a door could not be cut through the tubing without structurally weakening the frame. The solution was roof hinged gull wing doors and a tilt steering wheel for easier driver access. The design was so successful, winning the 1952 Le Mans and several other prestigious events, that the company was persuaded to build a production version. Introduced in 1954, the gull wing design proved expensive and difficult to build and was replaced by a more conventional roadster in 1957. The roadster was produced through 1963. This combination of unique design and low production rates have made the 300SL a highly prized model series.

AU930	1954 gull wing, restored, near mint	335000
AU932	1955 gull wing, national prize winner	425000
AU934	1957 roadster, mint	229000
AU936	1963 roadster, excellent	310000

Porsche 356 Series

This was supposedly Porsche's 356th (although Dr. Porsche began with number seven so as not to appear inexperienced). It was also the first car to carry the Porsche name. Limited production began in 1948 and the model was officially launched in early 1949. Although the only major design change came in 1959 (larger windshield, slightly higher headlights and bumpers), the series saw many variations, both in the convertible and hard top. The most distinctive model was the austere Speedster convertible, produced from late 1954 until early 1959. The 356 line lasted until 1965, when it was superseded by the 911 series.

AU940	1955 speedster, being restored	29000
AU941	1956 356A cabriolet, needs restoration	13500
AU942	1957 speedster, excellent	45000
AU945	1960 356B sunroof coupe, 21000 mi, in storage 25 yrs.	18000
AU946	1963 356B restored	12500
AU947	1964 356C coupe, restored, excellent	16000
AU948	1965 356 SC coupe, restored, near mint	24000

Triumph TR Series

In the early 1950s, the Standard-Triumph Motor Co. (later British Leyland) was searching for a competitor to the MG and

Morgan. They improvised a fast, rugged sports car called the TR2 (Triumph Roadster 2) and rushed it into limited production in 1953. It was an unqualified success. The TR2 became the more powerful TR3 in 1955 and the still more powerful TR3A from 1958 through 1962. A 1961 redesign brought forth the TR4, followed by the TR4A in 1965. Nineteen sixty seven saw the introduction of the fuel-injected six cylinder TR5, then came the TR6 in 1969. Last of the series was the wedge shaped TR7, built from 1976 through 1981.

AU950	1954 TR2, fair, needs restoration	5000
AU952	1957 TR3 restored	12500
AU953	1957 TR3 small mouth, needs restoration	5900
AU954	1959 TR3A, good	6800
AU955	1963 TR4, 34000 mi, excellent	8000
AU956	1967 TR4, 65000 mi, fair	3500
AU957	1967 TR4A IRS, excellent	5000
AU958	1969 TR6, 51000 mi, good	8500

BANKS   by Lou Griswold

Banks have traditionally been popular gifts to encourage saving. Family and financial institutions have been major providers to help teach children the value of money. Manufacturers and advertisers have taken advantage of this fact to produce a wide variety of banks with collectible value.

The most highly prized are the cast iron mechanical banks of the late 19th and early 20th centuries. However, many valuable banks have appeared since 1950.

Virtually any material can be used to make a bank. Tin lithographed banks were popular in the middle of this century. Plastic has become the most popular material recently, although glass, vinyl, and aluminum are also common.

This section includes both mechanical and non-mechanical, or "still" banks. The prices range from excellent to near mint condition. Words in quotes appear on the banks.

BN670

BN110	"Elsie" tall full-dimensioned painted metal full color likeness of Elsie the Cow, 1950	75-100
BN120	"Esso" hard white plastic figure of Happy the Friendly Oil Drop w/logo on chest	75-100
BN140	"Speedy Alka-Seltzer" 6" tall flexible rubber figure bank.	100-200
BN230	"Roy Rogers & Trigger" 7-1/2" tall full color ceramic, slot on reverse	100-400
BN310	"Dracula's Bank" black plastic box, 1960s	50-100
BN330	"3 Stooges Bank" set of 3 ceramic banks, each in black jacket w/name on base.	400-700
BN410	"American League All-Stars" plastic baseball w/black base, bank premium	75-100
BN420	"Little League Bank" bobbing head, composition figure.	75-100

BN430	"New York Yankees" plastic baseball on black base. Bank premium, early '50s	100-200
BN440	Pittsburgh Pirates, plastic baseball on black base, 1962	50-75
BN510	Batman, ceramic	50-100
BN512	Batman, similar to BN510	100-200
BN518	Robin ceramic, matching bank to BN510	75-100
BN610	"The Addams Family/Thing" Small green hand comes grabs coin as bank makes screeching noise. Poynter, boxed	100-200
BN620	"Fred Loves Wilma" Flintstones, ceramic	100-400
BN630	Haunted House tin litho. Door opens to reveal plastic ghost which takes coin left on door step.	100-200
BN640	Howdy Doody ceramic bust	200-400
BN642	Howdy Doody head, ceramic	100-200
BN644	Howdy Doody riding on pig, ceramic	200-400
BN660	"Mr. Peabody Bank" 6" ceramic	100-200
BN670	"Prince Valiant" tin litho dime register bank	75-100
BN680	Sgt. Snorkel, 11" composition figure from Beetle Bailey comic strip.	75-100

See also: **Batman; Beatles; Peanuts; Star Trek; Star Wars; Western Heroes**

BARBIE   by Felicity Greenstreet

The first Barbie doll appeared in 1959. She represented an entirely new concept...a "big sister" fashion doll with a teenage figure and extensive wardrobe. Marketed by Mattel, Inc., she was the brainchild of one of Mattel's founders, Ruth Handler. She observed how her own daughter Barbara favored teenage paper dolls to dolls from her own age group.

Initial sales were slow. By the early 1960s, Mattel was selling in excess of six million Barbie dolls a year and could have been considered the world's largest manufacturer of women's clothing! Barbie's popularity spawned an entire line of dolls, clothes, and accessories.

The sheer volume of dolls, outfits, and accessories makes collecting Barbie a daunting task. Her friends, family, and celebrity friends number more than 60 dolls. The number of different Barbies is in the hundreds. This doesn't include miscellaneous items like toys, houses, cars, playsets, gift sets, carrying cases, books, magazines, etc.

Because millions of dolls and outfits have been produced, by far the most collectible are those that have never been removed from their original box. If the box is missing completely, the price drops substantially. For anything in less than near mint condition or missing parts the price will continue to drop accordingly. Some of the most highly prized collectibles are the accessories. Most collectors consider the main outfit to be the least valuable portion of an ensemble.

The following are for items in good to near-mint condition. Foreign items are not included.

Barbie - The first Barbie was 11-1/2" of flesh-toned vinyl plastic with movable head, arms, and legs. Her outfit was a black and white striped bathing suit, sunglasses, high heeled shoes, and gold colored hoop earrings. Two distinctive characteristics were pointed eyebrows and white irises for the eyes. Her rooted ponytail styled hair was either blonde or brunette. Metal cylinders in her legs opened in both feet to allow her to stand on a two pronged pedestal. The flesh color of these dolls has since faded, some all the way to white!

BA101	Barbie #1, 1959	2000-4000
BA102	Pedestal stand	150-400

A second Barbie model was produced in 1959. The cylinders in the legs were eliminated and a new stand was designed.

BA103	Barbie #2, 1959	1500-3200
BA104	Pedestal stand w/wire support	35-75

Barbie #3 had blue irises and curved eyebrows. Sometime during that year the vinyl plastic formula was changed to stabilize the flesh-tone color. Most collectors consider these non-fade

BA105

BA115

BA145

BA155

BA139

dolls to be Barbie #4. Barbie's identity was now established

BA105	Barbie #3, 1960	700-900
BA106	Pedestal stand w/wire support	20-50
BA107	Barbie #4 (non-fade), 1960	350-475
BA110	Bendable legs	500-900
BA111	Bendable legs w/side part hair	1500-3200
BA115	Bubble Cut Barbie	175-200
BA118	Color Magic Barbie (hair color could be changed w/special solution)	500-800
BA119	Talking Barbie	100-200
BA120	Complete in box, 1960-64	275-450
BA123	Fashion Queen Barbie	250-450
BA124	Hair Happenin's	450-575
BA126	"Miss Barbie" w/bendable knees, hard plastic head, and eyes that closed	500-650
BA128	Ponytail Barbie (1961-1964)	300-450
BA135	1967-1969 standard, straight legs	200-250
BA136	1970 standard, straight legs	175-225
BA137	1971 standard, straight legs	200-245
BA138	Swirl Ponytail Barbie	250-350
BA139	Twist 'N Turn	150-250
BA140	Ward's Anniversary (1972)	350-450

Ken - Barbie's boyfriend (named after Ruth Handler's son) first appeared in 1961. He was 12" tall with short flocked blonde, brunette, or brown hair. He had a red and white striped bathing suit and sandals. Most came with a yellow towel and black wire stand.

BA145	Straight leg w/flocked hair,	100-150
BA146	Painted hair, w/red and white beach jacket	75-125

In 1963 Ken was 1/4" shorter with legs loosely joined to the torso and shorter, thicker arms. Ken disappeared from the catalog in 1968, but reappeared in a talking version in 1969.

BA147	Bendable legs w/1962 face	300-425
BA148	Bendable legs w/painted cheeks	75-125
BA149	Ken doll in box	275-350
BA150	Talking Ken	75-100

Midge - Barbie's friend debuted in 1963. She came with a two piece bathing suit of assorted colors, high heeled shoes, and a black wire stand. Her hair was blonde, brunette, or titian.

BA155	Straight legs	100-125
BA156	Bendable legs	300-400
BA157	Complete in box	450-550

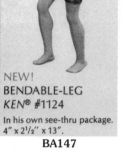

NEW!
BENDABLE-LEG
KEN® #1124
In his own see-thru package.
4" x 2½" x 13".

BA147

TWIST JULIA
#1127
© Savannah Productions, Inc.
ALL RIGHTS RESERVED.

BA187

Talking JULIA
#1128

BA188

BA195

Allan - Ken got a friend in 1964. Allan had molded red hair, brown eyes, a blue bathing suit, multi-colored striped jacket, and sandals. Allan was discontinued after 1966.

BA160	Straight legs	50-75
BA161	Bendable legs	200-300
BA162	Complete in box	300-425

Skipper - Barbie's little sister arrived in 1964. She had movable arms, legs, and head. She wore a brass colored headband in her long straight blonde, brunette, or titian hair. Her wardrobe was a one piece red and white bathing suit and red shoes, and came with a comb, brush, and black wire stand.

BA165	Straight legs	40-80
BA166	Bendable legs	175-275
BA167	Complete in box	200-450

Skooter - Friend of Skipper, debuted in 1965. She had straight legs and a double ponytail. She came with a two piece red and white bathing suit with blonde, brunette, or titian hair.

BA170	Skooter	75-120
BA171	Bendable legs	150-250
BA172	Complete in box	175-400

Francie's head.

BA190	Straight Legs	300-450
BA191	Talking, bendable legs	300-450
BA192	Either version, complete in box	500-900

Twiggy - Barbie's first licensed Celebrity Friend, Twiggy was based on the popular English fashion model. The same size as Francie, she was available in one model.

BA195	Twiggy	200-350
BA196	Twiggy in box	400-800

Clothing, Playsets, and Accessories (values are for complete boxed or packaged examples)

Clothing - Barbie

BA300	Beautiful Bride	300-425
BA304	Benefit Performance	500-600
BA308	Campus Sweetheart	300-425
BA320	Commuter Set	375-500
BA330	Debutante Ball	325-475
BA340	Easter Parade	1500-3500
BA348	Evening Enchantment	350-650

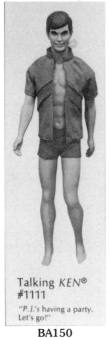

Talking KEN®
#1111
"P.J.'s having a party.
Let's go!"
BA150

MIDGE® KEN®
BA156   BA146

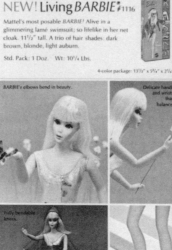

NEW! Living BARBIE #1116

BA110

TALKING BARBIE
BA119

Francie - Barbie's cousin Francie appeared in 1966. The first to have rooted eyelashes, she had bendable legs and old grayish tan tone skin. Later dolls had pink skin.

BA175	Bendable legs	125-200
BA176	Straight legs	125-200
BA177	Complete in box	175-400

Two new Francie models were introduced in 1967...twist waist and black.

BA178	Twist 'N Turn	200-300
BA179	Twist 'N Turn in box	400-500
BA180	Black Francie	400-600
BA181	Black Francie in box	800-1200
BA182	Busy, w/holdin' hands	175-250
BA183	Busy, w/holdin' hands, in box	300-600
BA184	Hair Happenin's, w/bendable legs	150-225
BA185	Hair Happenin's, w/bendable legs in box	350-650

Julia - a licensed Celebrity Friend from the TV series.

BA187	Twist 'n Turn Julia
BA188	Talking Julia

Truly Scrumptious - a licensed Celebrity Friend from the movie *Chitty Chitty Bang Bang*, made with Barbie's body and

BA351	Fashion Luncheon	475-700
BA356	Floating Gardens	475-750
BA358	Fraternity Dance	325-450
BA362	Garden Wedding	250-400
BA364	Gay Parisienne	800-1600
BA373	Here Comes The Bride	500-950
BA384	International Fair	200-450
BA386	Invitation to Tea	300-525
BA400	Miss Astronaut	475-800
BA404	Music Center Matinee	300-650
BA415	Outdoor Art Show	300-650
BA421	Pan American Airways Stewardess	1400-3500
BA427	Reception Line	350-450
BA429	Roman Holiday Separates	2200-3800
BA435	Shimmering Magic	625-1100
BA510	Underfashions	400-600

Gift Sets

BA850	Barbie, Ken, & Midge On Parade,	1200-2000
BA855	Barbie & Ken Little Theatre	1200-2000
BA860	Barbie & Ken (tennis outfits)	775-1200
BA865	Barbie's Wedding Party	1000-1700
BA870	Color Magic Barbie (Sears)	800-2000
BA875	Fashion Queen Barbie & Ken Trousseau	900-1400

TUTTI, IN "WALKING MY DOLLY" #3552
Pushing baby and buggy, TUTTI wears a polka dot broadcloth dress for her stroll through the park Tiny tot is removable and carriage has adjustable hood and wheels that turn.

TUTTI, IN "NIGHT-NIGHT, SLEEP TIGHT" #3553
Sweet dreams for a tired TUTTI! Her bedtime outfit is Cambric nightgown and floral patterned robe. Plastic bed, headboard and bedspread.

NEW! TUTTI
Gingham get-up for popular poseable miss. Only 6⅝" tall, Tutti's ribboned hair is groomed with included comb and brush. Blonde or brunette hair. Shoes included.
Std. Pack: 1 Doz. Wt: 4 Lbs.

TUTTI, IN "ME AND MY DOG" #3554
TUTTI pets friendly furry dog who's almost as tall as she! Her winter coat is felt with plush trim and bonnet. Shaggy dog is fully bendable and poseable.

TUTTI, IN "MELODY IN PINK" #3555
TUTTI loves a piano! Ready for recital, she sits on bench in lovely lace and nylon party dress. Plastic baby grand piano.

BA876	Party Set	BA993-6	1000-1200
BA877	Trousseau Set		1500-2000

Other Items

BA902	Barbie's Dream Kitchen & Dinette	150-300
BA906	Barbie Goes To College	135-250
BA915	Barbie's Sport Plane	350-450
BA950	Midge's Wig Wardrobe	75-200
BA970	Skipper's Dream Room	115-225

Playsets

BA990	Tutti & Todd Sundae Treat	200-400
BA991	Tutti Cookin' Goodies	160-340
BA992	Tutti Me and My Dog	150-325
BA993	Tutti Melody in Pink	100-275
BA994	Tutti Night-Night Sleep Tight	75-235
BA995	Tutti Swing-A-Ling,	180-350
BA996	Tutti Walkin' My Dolly	75-250
BA999	Store Display depicting a set of dolls and accessories	500-4000

BASEBALL CARDS   by Tim Turner & consultants
Photo assistance Hal Blevins

Once considered a cheap hobby for kids, today baseball cards are one of the fastest growing and most popular collectibles. Literally billions have been distributed since their first appearance over a hundred years ago to help advertise tobacco products. Associated with bubble gum from 1950 to the mid '80s, cards are now used to promote everything from cookies to shopping centers.

Since few people can ever hope to accumulate an example of every card produced, there are many collecting strategies. Some try to assemble a complete set for a specific year. Others prefer the cards of a particular team or favorite player. Another strategy is to collect special cards, such as rookie cards, or the occasional manufacturer's error, like name misspellings and picture mismatches.

As with any other collectible, a card's value is determined by several factors: age, scarcity, the player(s) pictured, the card set's overall popularity, and (probably most important) condition. Basically, older, scarcer cards in mint condition of Hall of Fame players will command the highest prices. Value can also vary significantly by region; a Carl Yastrzemski would be worth more in Boston than in Cincinnati.

In addition to general wear and aging, certain physical defects can also lower a card's value. If a card has been cut off-center, has rounded corners, or visible creases, the card will be worth substantially less.

The following listing is for cards currently deemed most valuable. Sets which were not distributed nationally were not considered for inclusion. Values are for fine to mint condition unless otherwise noted. Rookie cards are abbreviated R.

BB119   BB118   BB106   BB117

BB108   BB113

Bowman - 1948-1955
1950 - Two hundred fifty two card set. All mint, centered cards are worth at least $9.

BB100	1 Mel Parnell (R)	60-210
BB101	6 Bob Feller	120-160
BB102	8 George Kell	60-85
BB103	11 Phil Rizzuto	75-140
BB104	19 Warren Spahn	90-150
BB105	21 Pee Wee Reese	110-175
BB106	22 Jackie Robinson	250-600
BB107	23 Don Newcombe (R)	60-120
BB108	32 Robin Roberts	95-135
BB109	33 Ralph Kiner	55-100
BB110	35 Enos Slaughter	45-90
BB111	40 Bob Lemon	45-90
BB112	43 Bobby Doerr	45-90
BB113	46 Yogi Berra	250-350
BB114	75 Roy Campanella	160-275
BB115	77 Duke Snider	170-280
BB116	98 Ted Williams	450-700
BB117	112 Gil Hodges	60-90
BB118	217 Casey Stengel (manager)	60-100
BB119	252 Billy DeMars (R)	30-75

BB134   BB148   BB136   BB158

BB137

BB130   BB166   BB167

BB159

1951 - Three hundred twenty four card set. All mint, centered cards are worth at least $10.

BB130	1 Whitey Ford (R)	300-1200
BB131	2 Yogi Berra	200-450
BB134	26 Phil Rizzuto	50-75
BB135	30 Bob Feller	90-150
BB136	31 Roy Campanella	150-260
BB137	32 Duke Snider	125-200
BB140	80 Pee Wee Reese	60-100
BB144	122 Joe Garagiola (R)	75-120
BB145	134 Warren Spahn	50-90
BB148	165 Ted Williams	375-600
BB150	181 Casey Stengel (manager)	50-90

BB155	232	Nelson Fox (R)	50-90
BB157	253	Mickey Mantle (R)	3000-5000
BB158	254	Jackie Jensen (R)	50-100
BB159	259	Charlie Dressen (manager)	35-65
BB160	260	Carl Erskine (R)	70-110
BB162	275	Bucky Harris (manager)	30-70
BB164	282	Frank Frisch	65-100
BB166	290	Bill Dickey	90-150
BB167	291	Tommy Henrich	40-80
BB169	295	Al Lopez (manager)	50-100
BB171	305	Willie Mays (R)	1000-2000
BB172	306	Jim Piersall (R)	50-100
BB174	312	Gene Mauch (R)	35-75
BB175	314	Johnny Sain	30-60
BB176	317	Smokey Burgess (R)	35-65
BB179	323	Joe Adcock (R)	50-100
BB180	324	Johnny Pramesa (R)	50-120

1952 - Two hundred fifty two card set. All mint, centered cards are worth at least $8.

BB181	1	Yogi Berra	200-650
BB183	8	Pee Wee Reese	60-100
BB186	27	Joe Garagiola	35-70
BB188	43	Bob Feller	50-100
BB189	44	Roy Campanella	100-200
BB191	52	Phil Rizzuto	35-70
BB195	101	Mickey Mantle	800-1600
BB197	116	Duke Snider	100-200
BB199	156	Warren Spahn	50-100
BB200	196	Stan Musial	325-450
BB203	217	Casey Stengel	80-140
BB204	218	Willie Mays	500-800
BB206	232	Enos Slaughter	35-70
BB210	252	Frank Crosetti	50-125

BB225   BB233   BB240   BB242

1953 Color - One hundred sixty card set. All mint, centered cards are worth at least $15.

BB214	1	Dave Williams	50-125
BB215	9	Phil Rizzuto	50-100
BB217	21	Joe Garagiola	40-80
BB219	32	Stan Musial	300-450
BB220	33	Pee Wee Reese (horizontal pose)	200-350
BB222	44	Berra, Bauer, Mantle	250-400
BB223	46	Roy Campanella	175-275
BB225	59	Mickey Mantle	1000-1600
BB226	61	George Kell	40-80
BB228	65	Robin Roberts	40-80
BB230	80	Ralph Kiner	45-90
BB231	81	Enos Slaughter	45-90
BB233	92	Gil Hodges	70-125
BB234	93	Phil Rizzuto & Billy Martin	150-225
BB236	97	Ed Mathews	100-175
BB237	99	Warren Spahn	80-125
BB240	114	Bob Feller	185-275
BB241	117	Duke Snider	350-515
BB242	118	Billy Martin	200-325
BB244	121	Yogi Berra	300-500
BB245	124	Charlie Dressen (manager)	30-60
BB248	143	Al Lopez (manager)	40-75
BB249	146	Early Wynn	75-125
BB251	153	Whitey Ford	250-450
BB253	160	Cal Abrams	25-85

BB264   BB274   BB275   BB279

1953 Black & White - Sixty four card set. All mint, centered cards are worth at least $10.

BB255	1	Gus Bell	50-125
BB257	15	Johnny Mize	30-60
BB258	25	Johnny Sain	30-60
BB259	26	Preacher Roe	30-60
BB260	27	Bob Lemon	80-100
BB261	28	Hoyt Wilhelm	80-100
BB264	39	Casey Stengel	200-325
BB265	46	Bucky Harris	30-60

1954 - Two hundred twenty four card set. All mint, centered cards are worth at least $5.

BB270	1	Phil Rizzuto	75-150
BB274	65	Mickey Mantle	500-800
BB275	66	Ted Williams (deleted after first printing because of contract dispute)	1500-3000
BB276	66	Jim Piersall	60-120
BB278	89	Willie Mays	225-325
BB279	90	Roy Campanella	100-150
BB282	132	Bob Feller	50-80
BB283	161	Yogi Berra	100-150
BB285	170	Duke Snider	85-130

BB303   BB299

1955 - Three hundred twenty card set. All mint, centered cards are worth at least $4.

BB290	1	Hoyt Wilhelm	40-100
BB292	22	Roy Campanella	75-125
BB293	23	Al Kaline	75-125
BB298	168	Yogi Berra	50-100
BB299	179	Hank Aaron	100-200
BB303	184	Willie Mays	100-200
BB305	202	Mickey Mantle	225-450
BB308	242	Ernie Banks	175-300

Donruss - began producing cards in 1981. No cards of special value occurred until 1983.

1983 - Six hundred sixty card set.

BB310	507	Ryne Sandberg	20-35
BB315	586	Wade Boggs	10-25
BB317	598	Tony Gwynn	15-20
BB320	639	Ron Jackson (error - A's in glove)	5-15
BB321	639	Ron Jackson (corrected - Angels in glove, red border on photo)	.10-.20
BB322	639	Ron Jackson (corrected - Angels in glove, green border on photo)	.10-.20

1984 - Six hundred fifty-eight card set.

BB325	34	Kevin McReynolds (R)	7-14
BB326	41	Joe Carter (R)	10-18
BB328	68	Darryl Strawberry	35-70
BB329	248	Don Mattingly (R)	45-65

1985 - Six hundred sixty card set.

BB335	190	Dwight Gooden	8-14

BB338	273 Roger Clemens	15-28
BB340	295 Don Mattingly	5-10
BB342	325 Eric Davis	10-15
BB344	438 Kirby Puckett	15-25

1986 - Six hundred sixty card set.

BB350	39 Jose Canseco (Rated Rookie)	60-100

1987 Opening Day - included a card for each player in the lineup on opening day for all teams.

BB355	163 Barry Bonds (error: photo is Johnny Ray)	5-10

Fleer - produced cards in 1959-1961, 1963, 1970-1975, and 1981-present.

1959 - This 80 card set, labeled "Baseball's Greatest," honored Ted Williams. Card #68 is the only one of high value. It was withdrawn early in production because Ted was a contract holdout. This card has been counterfeited.

BB358	68 Ted Signs for 1959	150-500
BB359	Complete set	500-900

1960 - Baseball Greats - Set of seventy-nine. Because of a nostalgic printing style, some mistake these for a 1930s set.

BB360	3 George H. Ruth	30-60
BB363	28 Lou Gehrig	15-33
BB364	42 Tyrus Cobb	15-35
BB368	72 Theodore Williams	25-50

1961 - Baseball Greats - One hundred fifty-four cards in the set

BB375	1 Baker-Cobb-Wheat (checklist on back)	5-20
BB377	14 Ty Cobb	15-30
BB378	31 Lou Gehrig	15-30
BB380	75 Babe Ruth	30-60
BB383	150 Honus Wagner	15-30
BB384	152 Ted Williams	30-60

1963 - Contemporary Players - Sixty-seven cards featuring stand out players in set.

BB386	5 Willie Mays	25-70
BB387	8 Carl Yastrzemski	30-65
BB390	42 Sandy Koufax	35-75
BB392	43 Maury Wills (R)	25-45
BB393	45 Warren Spalin	15-28
BB394	46 Joe Adcock	55-110
BB396	56 Roberto Clemente	35-65
BB397	61 Bob Gibson	15-25
BB399	Checklist Card (unnumbered; apparently replaced Adcock)	75-300

1982 - Six hundred sixty card set.

BB410	438 "All" Hrabosky (error-1st name misspelled; height listed as 5'1")	10-20
BB411	438 Al Hrabosky (height listed as 5'1")	.35-1.25
BB412	438 Al Hrabosky (height listed as 5'11")	.05-.15
BB414	576 John Littlefield (error: left handed)	5-10
BB415	576 John Littlefield (corrected)	.05-.15

1983 - Six hundred sixty card set.

BB417	179 Wade Boggs (R)	17-24
BB419	507 Ryne Sandberg (R)	22-34

1984 - Six hundred sixty card set.

BB425	131 Don Mattingly (R)	32-45
BB429	599 Darryl Strawberry (R)	25-40

1984 Update - distributed through hobby channels only; short print run. One hundred thirty two card set.

BB430	U-27 Roger Clemens	125-175
BB432	U-43 Dwight Gooden	75-100
BB435	U-93 Kirby Puckett	130-180

BB437	U-103 Bret Saberhagen	20-35

1985 - Six hundred sixty card set.

BB440	82 Dwight Gooden	10-15
BB442	155 Roger Clemens	15-25
BB445	286 Kirby Puckett	15-20
BB447	533 Eric Davis	10-20
BB449	652 Glen Davis	10-15

1986 - Six hundred sixty card set.

BB458	649 Jose Canseco (R) & Eric Plunk	35-50

1989 - Six hundred sixty card set.

BB464	548 Ken Griffey, Jr. (R)	10-20
BB467	616 Bill Ripken (error: word on bat knob)	7-12
BB468	616 Bill Ripken (corrected)	.10-.25

BB518 BB565 BB555 BB570

Topps - Began producing cards in 1951. The first year they produced cards for a game which came with red or blue backs. These came in baseball candy. Topps' first gum card set appeared in 1952. The company dominated the production of cards until the early '80s, when baseball card collecting became a major hobby.

1951 Blue Backs - Fifty-two card set. All mint, centered cards are worth at least $20.

BB502	3 Richie Ashburn	60-120
BB503	6 Red Schoendienst	60-120
BB504	30 Enos Slaughter	70-120
BB505	37 Bobby Doerr	60-100
BB507	50 Johnny Mize	80-135

1951 Red Backs - Fifty-two card set. Design is identical to the Blue Backs. All mint, centered cards are worth at least $5.

BB510	1 Yogi Berra	75-140
BB511	5 Phill Rizzuto	15-35
BB513	22 Bob Feller	25-45
BB515	30 Warren Spahn	20-38
BB516	31 Gil Hodges	15-30
BB518	38 Duke Snider	40-80

1951 Team - Nine card set of unnunbered team cards. Some have "1950" printed in the name panel before the team name, but there is no difference in value for either version. All fine or better cards are worth at least $50

BB520	Boston Red Sox	75-150
BB521	St. Louis Cardinals	75-150

1951 Connie Mack All-Stars - eleven card set of fragile die-cut cards intended to be used as toy figures. All fine or better cards are worth at least $65

BB524	1 Grover C. Alexander	65-120
BB526	5 Lou Gehrig	400-900
BB527	6 Walter Johnson	150-300
BB529	9 Babe Ruth	500-750

1952 - Topps' first major gum card set, included four hundred seven cards. The first series (1-80) were issued with both black and red printing on the backs. All mint, centered cards are worth at least $20. Cards 311-407 were distributed in only the largest markets—less than 20 major cities in the U.S—and are worth at least $100-150. Extra valuable cards are noted below.

BB531	1 Andy Pafko	300-1800

BB534	11 Phil Rizzuto	90-180
BB536	33 Warren Spahn	120-240
BB537	36 Gil Hodges	85-160
BB538	37 Duke Snider	200-300
BB540	48 Joe Page (error-bio switched with Johnny Sain)	200-300
BB541	48 Joe Page (corrected)	35-70
BB542	49 Johnny Sain (error-bio switched with Joe Page)	200-300
BB543	49 Johnny Sain (corrected)	50-100
BB545	59 Robin Roberts	75-130
BB547	65 Enos Slaughter	75-130
BB550	88 Bob Feller	100-150
BB555	175 Billy Martin (R)	175-325
BB557	191 Yogi Berra	200-375
BB560	261 Willie Mays	700-1400
BB561	268 Bob Lemon	70-140
BB563	277 Early Wynn	70-140

Limited distribution high number series begins with 311

BB565	311 Mickey Mantle	5000-10000
BB566	312 Jackie Robinson	500-1000
BB567	313 Bobby Thomson	100-200
BB568	314 Roy Campanella	700-1400
BB569	315 Leo Durocher	170-300
BB570	320 John Rutherford	100-150
BB573	333 Pee Wee Reese	450-900
BB576	372 Gil McDougald	150-300
BB579	392 Hoyt Wilhelm (R)	300-550
BB582	400 Bill Dickey (coach)	300-525
BB584	406 Joe Nuxhall	150-275
BB585	407 Eddie Mathews (R)	800-1850

BB590	BB645	BB640	BB633

1953 - There are 274 cards in the set. Numbers go to 280, but some numbers were never issued. All mint, centered cards are worth at least $10.

BB590	1 Jackie Robinson	200-650
BB594	27 Roy Campanella	125-250
BB596	54 Bob Feller	50-100
BB598	76 Pee Wee Reese	75-150
BB599	82 Mickey Mantle	1000-2000
BB600	104 Yogi Berra	125-250
BB604	147 Warren Spahn	65-135
BB610	220 Satchel Paige (error-1st name misspelled on front)	200-425
BB613	228 Hal Newhouser	50-100
BB615	244 Willie Mays	800-1600
BB618	258 Jim Gilliam (R)	180-375
BB619	263 Johnny Podres (R)	150-275
BB620	265 Jackie Jensen	50-100
BB622	273 Harvey Haddix	50-95
BB624	280 Milt Bolling (R)	160-340

1954 - Two hundred fifty card set. All are worth at least $5.

BB625	1 Ted Williams	220-650
BB627	10 Jackie Robinson	150-280
BB630	32 Duke Snider	75-135
BB633	50 Yogi Berra	135-250
BB635	90 Willie Mays	200-400
BB636	94 Ernie Banks (R)	400-625
BB640	128 Hank Aaron (R)	850-1500
BB641	132 Tom Lasorda (R)	100-175
BB645	201 Al Kaline (R)	450-700

BB650	BB659	BB658

BB648	250 Ted Williams	350-750

1955 - Two hundred six card set. All mint, centered cards are worth at least $4.

BB650	2 Ted Williams	200-400
BB651	4 Al Kaline	100-175
BB654	47 Hank Aaron	150-300
BB655	50 Jackie Robinson	100-200
BB658	123 Sandy Koufax (R)	500-950
BB659	124 Harmon Killebrew	175-325
BB662	164 Roberto Clemente (R)	600-1200
BB664	187 Gil Hodges	75-140
BB665	189 Phil Rizzuto	75-140
BB667	194 Willie Mays	300-475
BB668	198 Yogi Berra	125-250
BB669	210 Duke Snider	200-500

1955 Double Header - Sixty-six card set of 132 players. Each card had a fold over section which used part of the legs of the player underneath to complete the photo of the player on top. All fine or better cards are worth at least $3.

BB675	25 Jackie Robinson & 26 Don Hoak	75-170
BB678	45 Al Kaline & 46 Harold Valentine	85-180
BB682	69 Ted Williams & 70 Mayo Smith	150-300
BB684	105 Hank Aaron & 106 Ray Herbert	175-350

BB690	BB693	BB698

1956 - Three hundred forty cards, worth at least $4 each.

BB690	5 Ted Williams	150-300
BB692	30 Jackie Robinson	80-150
BB693	31 Hank Aaron (small photo is Willie Mays)	125-225
BB694	33 Roberto Clemente	175-325
BB696	79 Sandy Koufax	175-325
BB698	101 Roy Campanella	75-125
BB700	110 Yogi Berra	75-135
BB703	130 Willie Mays	150-275
BB704	135 Mickey Mantle	500-950
BB706	150 Duke Snider	80-135
BB707	166 Brooklyn Dodgers team card	100-200
BB710	251 New York Yankees team card	120-210
BB711	260 Pee Wee Reese	70-140
BB713	292 Luis Aparicio	70-135
BB714	Checklist series 1 (unnumbered)	100-200
BB715	Checklist series 2 (unnumbered)	100-200

BB719	BB730	BB753

1957 - Four hundred seven card set. All mint, centered cards are worth at least $3.

BB716	1 Ted Williams	200-500
BB717	2 Yogi Berra	75-125

BB719	10 Willie Mays	100-200
BB721	18 Don Drysdale (R)	110-210
BB722	20 Hank Aaron (reverse negative photo on front)	100-200
BB724	35 Frank Robinson (R)	150-300
BB728	76 Roberto Clemente	125-250
BB730	95 Mickey Mantle	450-900
BB740	286 Bobby Richardson (R)	50-90
BB743	302 Sandy Koufax	200-335
BB745	312 Tony Kubek (R)	75-120
BB747	328 Brooks Robinson (R)	210-320
BB749	338 Jim Bunning (R)	65-110
BB752	400 Dodgers' Sluggers (Furillo, Hodges, Campanella, Snider)	100-200
BB753	407 Yankee Power Hitters (Mantle & Berra)	200-375
BB754	Checklist 1	75-150
BB755	Checklist 2	150-300
BB756	Checklist 3	200-400
BB757	Checklist 4	300-600

BB760   **BB766**

1958 - Four hundred ninety four card set. All mint, centered cards are worth at least $2.

BB758	1 Ted Williams	120-300
BB760	5 Willie Mays	90-175
BB762	30 Hank Aaron (yellow lettering)	165-325
BB763	30 Hank Aaron (white lettering)	100-175
BB766	47 Roger Maris (R)	175-310
BB767	52 Bob Clemente (yellow lettering)	125-200
BB768	52 Bob Clemente (white lettering)	75-150
BB775	150 Mickey Mantle	250-575
BB780	418 World Series Batting Foes (Mantle & Aaron)	75-150
BB783	485 Ted Williams (All Star)	35-75
BB784	487 Mickey Mantle (All Star)	50-100

1959 - Five hundred seventy two card set. All mint, centered cards are worth at least $1.50.

BB785	10 Mickey Mantle	175-350
BB790	514 Bob Gibson (R)	200-375
BB793	564 Mickey Mantle (All Star)	150-250

BB805   **BB807**
        BB816

1960 - Five hundred seventy two card set. All mint, centered cards are worth at least $1.

BB800	148 Carl Yastrzemski (R)	270-400
BB805	316 Willie McCovey (R)	100-235
BB807	350 Mickey Mantle	200-325
BB809	563 Mickey Mantle (All Star)	100-225

1961 - Five hundred eighty seven card set. All mint, centered cards are worth at least $1.

BB815	287 Carl Yastrzemski	75-175
BB816	300 Mickey Mantle	175-350
BB820	577 Hank Aaron (All Star)	75-150

BB830   **BB832**   **BB862**   **BB873**

BB821	578 Mickey Mantle (All Star)	190-350
BB822	579 Willie Mays (All Star)	75-160
BB824	589 Warren Spahn (All Star)	50-125

1962 - Five hundred ninety eight card set. All mint, centered cards are worth at least $.90.

BB825	1 Roger Maris	50-200
BB830	200 Mickey Mantle	225-400
BB832	387 Lou Brock	80-140
BB835	594 Rookie Catchers (Edwards, Retzer Uecker, Camilli, Pavletich)	75-115

1963 - Five hundred seventy six card set. All mint, centered cards are worth at least $.75.

BB840	200 Mickey Mantle	175-350
BB845	537 Rookie Stars (Pete Rose)	400-550
BB846	540 Bob Clemente	100-200
BB847	553 Rookie Stars (Davis, Stargell, Gosger, Herrnstein)	150-250

1964 - Five hundred eighty seven card set. All mint, centered cards are worth at least $.75.

BB850	50 Mickey Mantle	100-200
BB852	125 Pete Rose	100-150
BB854	541 Phil Niekro (R)	75-150

1965 - Five hundred ninety eight card set. All mint, centered cards are worth at least $.60.

BB859	170 Hank Aaron	40-60
BB860	207 Pete Rose	75-140
BB862	350 Mickey Mantle	225-400
BB864	477 Cards Rookies (Ackley, Carlton)	275-425
BB866	581 Tony Perez (R)	50-100

1966 - Five hundred ninety eight card set. All mint, centered cards are worth at least $.60.

BB870	1 Willie Mays	50-175
BB873	50 Mickey Mantle	125-200
BB874	126 Jim Palmer	40-85
BB876	550 Willie McCovey	50-100
BB878	598 Gaylord Perry	90-200

1967 - Six hundred nine card set. All mint, centered cards are worth at least $.50.

BB882	150 Mickey Mantle	125-250
BB885	569 Al Rookies (Rod Carew, Hank Allen)	300-500
BB886	581 Mets Rookies (Denehy, Seaver)	750-1075
BB888	600 Brooks Robinson	125-250

BB820   **BB859**   **BB870**

BB892	BB890	BB885

BB958	BB962	BB987

1968 - Five hundred ninety eight card set. All mint, centered cards are worth at least $.50.

BB890	177 Mets Rookies (Koosman, Ryan)	500-1000
BB892	247 Reds Rookies (Bench, Tompkins)	225-450
BB894	280 Mickey Mantle	100-200

1969 - Six hundred sixty four card set. All mint, centered cards are worth at least $.45.

BB897	260 Reggie Jackson (R)	225-400
BB898	500 Mickey Mantle	100-200
BB899	500 Mickey Mantle (Mantle in white)	300-600

BB897	BB926	BB920	BB928

1970 - Seven hundred twenty card set. All mint, centered cards are worth at least $.25.

BB920	189 Thurman Munson (R)	50-125
BB924	580 Pete Rose	40-65
BB926	660 Johnny Bench	100-175
BB928	712 Nolan Ryan	200-360

1971 - Seven hundred fifty two card set. All mint, centered cards are worth at least $.25.

BB930	341 Steve Garvey (R)	50-100
BB932	513 Nolan Ryan	80-175

1972

BB935	79 Carlton Fisk (R)	90-160
BB937	559 Pete Rose	25-50
BB938	686 Steve Garvey	50-75
BB939	695 Rod Carew	50-90

1973 - Six hundred sixty card set. All mint, centered cards are worth at least $.20.

BB940	130 Pete Rose	10-18
BB942	220 Nolan Ryan	25-50
BB944	614 Rookie Outfielders (Bumbry, Evans, Spikes)	35-75
BB945	615 Rookie 3rd Basemen (Ron Cey, Hilton, Mike Schmidt) (R)	250-450

1974 - Six hundred sixty card set. All mint, centered cards are worth at least $.15. All cards were issued at the same time rather than in series. Fifteen cards of the Padres were printed in a "Washington" version, anticipating a franchise move which never happened. These were reprinted as San Diego when the deal was concluded to keep the team in California. Most of these are worth $3 to $6.

BB950	1 Hank Aaron (complete ML record)	10-30
BB954	250 Willie McCovey (San Diego)	3-6
BB955	250 Willie McCovey (Washington)	15-30
BB956	252 Dave Parker (R)	25-50
BB958	283 Mike Schmidt	60-125
BB959	300 Pete Rose	10-20
BB962	456 Dave Winfield (R)	30-60

1975 - Six hundred sixty card set. Also issued as a test set

BB935	BB945

3/8" shorter than regular 2-1/2" x 3-1/2" cards. "Minis" are worth 50% to 75% more, depending on the player. All minis are worth at least $1.

BB965	70 Mike Schmidt	35-75
BB968	223 Robin Yount (R)	100-160
BB969	228 George Brett (R)	100-175
BB973	616 Rookie Outfielders (Augustine, Rice, Mangual, Scott)	20-35
BB974	620 Rookie Catcher/OF (Carter, Meyer, Hill, Roberts)	25-40
BB975	623 Rookie Infielders (Garner, Hernandez, Sheldon, Veryzer)	10-20
BB976	660 Hank Aaron	10-20

1977 - Six hundred sixty card set.

BB978	473 Rookie Outfielders (Dawson, Richards, Scott, Walling)	35-55
BB979	476 Rookie Catchers (Alexander, Cerone, Dale Murphy, Pasley)	35-60
BB980	488 Rookie Outfielders (Jack Clark, Ruppert Jones, Mazzilli, Dan Thomas)	10-18

1978 - Seven hundred twenty six card set.

BB982	36 Eddie Murray (R)	35-65
BB984	707 Rookie Shortstops (Klutts, Molitor, Trammell, U.L. Washington)	30-60
BB985	708 Rookie Catchers (Bo Diaz, Dale Murphy, Lance Parrish, Ernie Whitt)	15-30

1980 - Seven hundred twenty six card set.

BB987	482 Rickey Henderson	125-200

1982 - Seven hundred ninety two card set.

BB988	21 Cal Ripken (R)	20-35

BB965	BB968	BB969	BB974

BB982	BB984	BB985

BT300   BT501-2   BT315

| BB989 | 383 Pascual Perez (error-no position on front) | 15-30 |

1983 - Seven hundred ninety two card set.
| BB990 | 83 Ryne Sandberg | 25-50 |
| BB992 | 498 Wade Boggs | 20-40 |

1983 Traded - In some years Topps issued a supplemental set of rookies not in the regular set and players who had changed teams since that year's card was issued. This set was only available through hobby dealers.
| BB993 | 108T Darryl Strawberry | 65-115 |

1984 - Seven hundred ninety two card set.
| BB994 | 8 Don Mattingly | 15-30 |

1984 Traded
| BB995 | 42T Dwight Gooden | 30-50 |

1985 - Seven hundred ninety two card set.
BB996	181 Roger Clemens (R)	8-20
BB997	401 Mark McGwire (R)	10-25
BB999	627 Eric Davis (R)	10-20
See also: **Non-Sports Cards**

BATMAN   by Joe Desris

Batman first appeared in *Detective Comics* #27 (May 1939). Although popular, little licensing was done for the character until over a quarter century later. Excluding comic books, 99% of all Batman collectibles date from 1966 to the present.

The Batman TV series premiered January 12, 1966. The biggest flurry of publicity and licensing occurred during roughly the first eight months of the year, although Batman remained on ABC-TV until 1968. As with most unexpected successes, a significant amount of merchandise arrived too late to take advantage of the peak in popularity. The TV series went into syndication after its network run but licensing was almost nonexistent for the next six years.

It was not until 1972, when Mego introduced the first in a series of Batman-related figures, that more Caped Crusader collectibles became available. Batman remained popular during the balance of the 1970s because of the success of the movie Superman and licensing efforts by DC Comics.

The 1980s generally were a down period with few new Batman items available until late in the decade. The release of Warner Brothers' immensely successful movie *Batman* in June of 1989 resulted in worldwide licensing of the character.

Popularity reminiscent of the early months of 1966 caused another flood of merchandise and drove up both demand and prices for older Batman collectibles.

Rarity is the first factor to consider in determining the value of these items. The word "rare" can be subjective; many collectors frequently consider the rarest and most desirable items to be those which they do not yet own, regardless of genuine scarceness. Several items in this list are easy to locate, yet very rare in complete, unused, perfect condition.

Age is not necessarily a major factor when defining rare Batman merchandise. All 1940s items could be considered rare due to age and availability, but some are not particularly pricey. Although of comparatively recent vintage, a number of items from the 1960s are mystifyingly impossible to find at any price.

The lowest price guideline is about what one might typically expect to pay for an unboxed but complete piece while the higher price is for a boxed, complete and perfect example. Prices for items without boxes (e.g. movie posters) indicate a range from good, complete condition up to near mint. Outstanding examples in exceptional condition can command a higher price if one finds the right dealer or collector.

BT200-5

1950s
Movie material

Full-color one-sheets (27" x 41") were originally released for the 1943 and 1949 Batman movie serials. The 1943 serial was re-released in 1954 and the 1949 serial returned to theatres in 1958. These reissues are printed in duotone, not full-color. The 1958 version is rarest of all, probably due to low distribution, although it is printed with a garish green ink.

| BT110 | One-sheet poster, 1954 | 100-400 |
| BT111 | One-sheet poster, 1958 | 100-500 |

Several other serial-related items have surfaced over the years. They are extremely rare with only one or two examples apparently having survived.

BT120	Silkolene valance (a large silk banner for theatres)	600-2000
BT123	3-sheet (with artwork similar to the one-sheets, but three times the size)	500-1500
BT125	6-sheet	600-2000

1966
Model kits

These plastic model kits were released by Aurora during the 1960s. Empty display boxes and built-up kits frequently are found while unopened kits with the original shrinkwrapping intact are significantly more difficult to find. Batcycle and Penguin are the rarest.

BT200	Batman	75-225
BT201	Robin	10-90
BT202	Batmobile	75-300
BT203	Batboat	75-300
BT204	Batplane	50-150
BT205	Penguin	150-600

Captain Action

BT210	Batman uniform, boxed	300-600
BT211	Batman uniform, boxed, with flasher ring	400-800
BT215	Captain Action figure with Batman uniform	200-300
BT216	Captain Action figure, boxed	150-250
BT218	Robin uniform, boxed	500-900

Bend A Bitty figures (Diener Industries)

BT230	Batman	15-200
BT231	Robin	15-200
BT232	Joker	15-250
BT233	Riddler	15-250

Soaky figures

These are easy to come by with the typical paint chips and scratches, yet are extremely rare in perfect condition.

BT240-1

| BT240 | Batman | 25-75 |
| BT241 | Robin | 25-75 |

Ideal Playset

This 23-piece playset was made by Ideal in 1966. The M-shaped carrying case was sold separately.

| BT250 | Playset | 600-1400 |
| BT251 | Carrying case | 150-350 |

Topps Batman bubble gum card items

Manufactured in quantity, the cards and display boxes can be easily located. The rare items from this popular 1966 series are:

BT260	vending display box	75-300
BT261	complete, unopened boxes for any of the five series	800-2000
BT262	uncut sheets for any of the five series	200-900
BT263	original art (depending on condition and subject matter)	200-400

Batman Equipment

Other smaller utility belts were manufactured in the 1970s and 1980s, but this 1966 version from Ideal is the most elusive. The belt is usually found missing most of the loose pieces, making for a rare item when complete.

BT335

BT250-1

BT270

BT430

BT270	Utility belt	300-1000
BT271	Batman Equipment Set	300-800

A large boxed set which includes the above utility belt plus a Batman cape and cowl.

Cereal Boxes

Kellogg's Sugar Frosted Flakes, Stars, Froot Loops and Raisin Bran had Batman premiums and special offers. The two premiums (periscope, printing set) are not considered rare.

BT280	Kellogg's cereal boxes	40-150

Other Most Valuable Batman Items from the 60s

BT300	Switch 'N Go Batmobile Set (Mattel)	400-2000
BT305	Batman telephones (Remco)	300-600
BT308	Trace-a-graph (Emenee)	100-400
BT310	Batplane (Irwin)	100-300
BT312	Ice cream container lids (All-Star Dairy)	25-50
BT315	Magnetic Gotham City (Remco)	200-1000
BT318	Working Batmobile dashboard (Remco)	200-700
BT320	The Joker's Practical Jokes comic book premium from Prell shampoo	25-100
BT325	Tin battery-operated robot (Japan)	700-2000
BT327	Bat Brush (toothbrush, by Butler)	75-125
BT330	6-sheet movie poster from movie Batman	75-300
BT333	Pillow	30-100
BT335	Bat-watch (Amsco)	100-300
BT338	Bank (Transogram)	40-150
BT140	Sheet music (Viva Music Inc.)	25-200
BT342	Joker hand puppet (Ideal)	75-250

BT400   BT402   BT401

1970s

Fist Fighting figures (Mego)

BT400	Batman	250-500
BT401	Joker	300-600
BT402	Riddler	300-600
BT403	Robin	250-500

Secret identity figures (Mego)

BT410	Bruce Wayne	200-700
BT411	Dick Grayson	200-700

Wristwatches (Dabs Inc.)

BT421	Batman	75-200
BT422	Joker	100-300

Other 1970s items

BT430	Super Streak (AHI, 1974)	125-150
BT431	Lantern (AHI, 1977)	100-125

BT433	Elastic Batman (Mego)	150-200
BT434	Super Friends Car (AHI)	50-300
BT435	Batman's Wayne Foundation (Mego)	150-1000
BT436	Talking Batman (24" doll by Mego, 1974)	400-800

1980s

Joker and Batman statues

This limited edition of 50 pair was sold exclusively through a 1989 Warner Bros. merchandise catalog. Each 9" tall statue was signed and numbered by the artist.

BT501	Batman	250-1000
BT502	Joker	250-1000

Batman Rarities

All collectibles in this list are American releases. Some foreign products that are common in their countries of origin are uncommon in the U.S. and are not discussed here.

BT510	Batman (Sears version, shipped in plain brown box)	65
BT515	Batman Playset (in display box)	400-1600
BT520	Batman/Justice League Playset (in display box)	500-1800

See also: **Comic Books; Model Kits; Non-Sports Trading Cards**

BT434

Medium Yellow Submarine Puzzle (BE802), Yellow Submarine 3-ring Binder (BE204) and spiral Notepads (BE642-4), Small Yellow Submarine Puzzle (BE804), Licorice Record (BE560), Wallet (BE964), Yellow Submarine Photo Book (BE725), Guitar String (BE429), Bust of Ringo (BE280), "Twig" (BE955), and Record Box (BE810).

BE440   BT441

ABOVE—Large Yellow Submarine Puzzle (BE800), Ball (BE121), Apple (BE105), Yellow Submarine Costume (BE465), Yellow Submarine Glass Candle (BE300), Cellophane Tape (BE320), and Record Carrier (BE812).
AT RIGHT—Shoulder Bag (BE882), Beatle-ist Guitar (BE439), Thermos and Lunch Box (BE948-49).

THE BEATLES   by Bob & Joan Gottuso (BOJO)

John Lennon, Paul McCartney, George Harrison, and Ringo Starr (born Richard Starkey) grew up in Liverpool, England. Lennon and McCartney had been part of a group named The Quarrymen. They organized their own group with Harrison in 1959 called The Silver Beatles; Ringo became their drummer in 1962. As The Beatles, they swiftly became Great Britain's top rock group with such hits as "Love Me Do" (1962) and "Please Please Me" (1963). By the end of 1964 they were an international phenomenon.

Writing their own music, they developed new styles, experimented with sounds, produced social commentary, and appeared in several movies. Many consider the album "Sergeant Pepper's Lonely Hearts Club Band" (1967) to be their greatest achievement.

The group broke up in 1970. There were many attempts to get them back together, but all chances were ended when John Lennon was murdered by a 25 year old former mental patient in Manhattan on Dec 8, 1980.

Whether their popularity was fueled by the social upheaval of the decade or whether they were the catalyst for the massive movements of social and cultural change is a matter of historical interpretation. In any event, their impact on music, art, fashion, and even hair styles, was profound. It is impossible to consider the sixties without including the Beatles. Indeed, they have become a symbol for the entire decade.

Beatles memorabilia has been a prized collectible since the early 1970s and annual gatherings of dedicated fans since the mid 70s has created a marketplace for buying, selling, and trading an astonishing array of merchandise which today remains unequalled for a musical group.

Most licensed merchandise was marked NEMS (manager Brian Epstein's company) or Seltaeb, which is Beatles spelled backwards. But be forewarned: reproductions abound, and most bear a counterfeit NEMS mark.

The prices in the following listing are a general guide for memorabilia in fine to near mint condition (unless otherwise noted). Words in quotes actually appear on the item.

BE100	Alarm clock, Yellow Submarine, Sheffield, England	250-500
BE105	Apple, foam, Merry Christmas	300-600

BE670

BE545

BE224

ABOVE—Yellow Submarine Model (BE625), Clutch Purse (BE792), Pencil By Numbers (BE705), Lampshade (BE552), Shoulder Bag (BE880), Candy Dish (BE305), and Play Ball (BE750).

BE711   BE710

BE590

BE460

ABOVE—Hangers (BE490-91), Glass (BE420), Blowup Doll (BE210), Clutch Purse (BE790), and New Beat Guitar (BE441).

BE110	Apron, black & white, w/stars, pictures, song titles	130-260
BE111	Apron, red, white & black mop tops	100-200
BE120	Ball, 9", black rubber, inflatable	170-340
BE121	Ball, 8" Pearlescent, UK	190-375
BE130	Balloon, packaged, various colors, United Industries	30-65
BE140	Bamboo plate, China, 11" & 12", each	50-100

BE390

BE141	Bamboo plate, China, 7"	40-80	BE230	Bongos, Mastro, 2 different sizes, each	300-600
BE150	Banjo, Mastro Industries	325-650	BE240	Book covers, set of 7, sealed	35-65
BE160	Banks, paper mache figures of each Beatle		BE250	Booty bag, w/printed insert	75-125
	in Yellow Submarine costume, stopper		BE260	Brief cover, Select-O-Pak, w/	
	on bottom, Pride Creations, each	125-250		ID & photo cards	100-200
BE170	Beach hat, red or blue, blocked	50-100	BE265	Brunch Bag	180-360
BE175	Beach towel, "The Beatles"	85-160	BE270	Bubble bath soaky, Colgate, w/original	
BE180	Bed sheets, small squares of cloth, set			packaging	100-200
	of 4, w/photos, Riviera, NY	50-100	BE271	Bubble bath soaky, Colgate, Paul	
BE190	Belt, blue or red w/silver half-faces	40-75		or Ringo only	45-90
BE200	Binder, 3 ring, New York Looseleaf		BE280	Bust, Ringo, gold colored rubber	60-120
	or SPP, white	40-75	BE290	Calendar, "Make A Date With..."	130-250
BE201	Binder, same as above, colors	50-100	BE300	Candle, inside Yellow Submarine glass	200-400
BE202	Binder, star burst patterns inside	60-125	BE305	Candy dishes, 4 diff, UK, ea	70-140
BE204	Binder, 3 ring, Yellow Submarine	125-225	BE310	Candy cigarette box, single cartoon	
BE210	Blow up dolls, vinyl, set of four	50-80		Beatle on front	35-70
BE220	Bobbin' heads, 4" plastic "swingers"		BE320	Cellophane tape, single roll, sealed	50-100
	in pkg.	45-75	BE330	Cartoon Kit, Colorforms, complete w/	
BE222	Bobbin' heads, without pkg. (beware			instruction book	180-365
	reproductions)	15-30	BE340	Coloring book, Saalfield	30-60
BE224	Bobbin' head dolls, 8" papier mache	150-300	BE350	Comb, Lido Toys, oversize novelty, different	
BE226	Bobbin' head dolls, 14" store			colors (beware reproductions)	65-125
	displays, each	250-650	BE360	Compact, brass, girl's makeup case	100-200

Remco Mascot Doll (BE393), Ceramic Tile (BE947), Yellow Submarine Thermos and Lunch Box (BE948-49), Lamp, UK (BE549), Pencil Case (BE702), Purse (BE790), Overnight Bag (BE660), and Pillow (BE730).

Glass (BE424), Flip Your Wig Game (BE415), Flasher Buttons (BE411), and Flasher Rings (BE413).

Puzzle, UK (BE806), Pillow, photo w/instruments (BE731), Mug, Canada (BE628), Guitar, "Four-Pop" (BE434), Harmonica, on display card (BE500), and Drum (BE400).

Cartoon Kit (BE330), Yellow Submarine Photo Album (BE720), Ringo Cap (BE820), and Hair Pomade (BE452).

BE170

BE626-7

BE980

Handbag (BE482), Tennis Shoes (BE940-44), Guitar, UK (BE442), Bubble Bath Soakies (BE270-71), and LP Record Box (BE811).

Snack Plate, UK (BE895), Cup, UK (BE381), Jr. Guitar (BE432), Hummer (BE530), Red Jet Guitar (BE443), Gum Card Box (BE448), and Bongos (BE230).

Headphones (BE520), Handbag (BE480), Purses, figural (BE793), Wallet (BE962), and New Sound Guitar (BE437).

BE370	Cork stopper, one of each Beatle's head	100-190
BE380	Cup, plastic, w/photo insert	35-65
BE381	Cup, UK	55-110
BE385	Drinking Glasses, 4 diff, ea	60-110
BE390	Dolls, complete set w/instruments, Remco	150-300
BE391	Doll box only, w/cellophane & insert, Remco	35-75
BE392	Doll, Paul or Ringo w/instruments, Remco, each	30-60
BE393	Doll, John or George w/instruments, Remco, each	45-90
BE400	Drum, Selcol, Ringo Starr w/stand, tuning key, drumsticks, instruction booklet	300-600
BE410	Figure, 2" of each Beatle w/plastic fan shaped back, Subbuteo, set of four	50-100
BE411	Flasher Buttons, on display card	60-120
BE412	Flasher Buttons, ea	3-5
BE413	Flasher Rings, on display card	60-120
BE414	Flasher Rings, ea	3-5
BE415	Flip Your Wig Game	55-110
BE420	Glass, Dairy Queen, Canada, white star burst	65-130
BE422	Glass, jelly, one of each Beatle, each	60-120
BE423	Glass, w/colored decal, UK	65-130
BE424	Glass, w/insulating coating, group picture	65-130
BE429	Guitar String	65-130
BE430	Guitar, 5", Mastro plastic	50-100
BE432	Guitar, 14", Mastro, "Jr. Guitar"	150-300
BE434	Guitar, 21", Mastro, "Four Pop," red	170-325

BE435	Guitar, 21", Mastro, "Yeh, Yeh"	250-500
BE436	Guitar, 21", Selcol, "Big Beat"	250-500
BE437	Guitar, 23", Selcol, "New Sound"	150-300
BE439	Guitar, 30", Mastro, "Beatle-ist"	240-480
BE440	Guitar, 32", Big 6	250-500
BE441	Guitar, 32", New Beat	200-400
BE442	Guitar, 30", Selcol, UK	250-500
BE443	Guitar, 31" Red Jet Electric	350-700
BE445	Gumball figures, 3" tall, soft rubber, black, blue, or red, on gum ball machine insert card	35-65
BE446	Gumball figures, without card	3-5
BE448	Gum Card Box (no cards)	50-100
BE450	Hair bow, Burlington, on original card	125-250
BE452	Hair pomade packets, ea	40-80
BE455	Hair spray, Bronson Products	300-600
BE460	Halloween costume, Ben Cooper, w/mask, costume, & box	180-360
BE461	Mask & costume only	110-220
BE462	Mask only (was also sold separately)	40-80
BE465	Halloween costume, Yellow Submarine, w/mask and box	125-250
BE470	Hand puppet, Ringo, plastic, came in case of Beatles cigarette candy	150-300
BE480	Handbag, brass handle, zipper, decorated w/black & white heads & signatures	160-320
BE482	Handbag, w/brass handles	120-225
BE490	Hangers, black & white photo of head & shoulders, Famous Faces, set of 4, ea	40-80

BE491	Hangers, cardvoard, UK, set of 4, ea	40-80
BE500	Harmonica & box on original display card	90-175
BE501	Harmonica & box without card	40-75
BE510	Head band, Better Wear, in pkg.	25-50
BE512	Head band, Burlington	90-180
BE520	Head phones, Koss, in original box w/ flyer & warranty	500-1000
BE521	Head phones only	250-500
BE530	"Hummer," 11" cardboard tube, plastic ends	60-115
BE540	Irish linen, Ulster	60-120
BE545	Kaboodle Kit	300-600
BE549	Lamp, UK	325-650
BE550	Lamp, table, 14", oval	200-400
BE552	Lamp shade, 14", wall	200-400
BE560	Licorice record candy wrapper, paper sleeve w/photo insert, photo of each Beatle plus group photo, ea.	65-125
BE561	same as above without licorice	50-100
BE570	Loot Tray, smoked glass dish, rectangular	125-250
BE575	Lunch Bag, Air Flite	240-480
BE580	Lux Soap Box package, w/ad for blow-up dolls, w/soap & insert	100-200
BE585	Magnetic Hair Game	200-400
BE590	Marionettes, one of each Beatle, w/collarless suits & cardboard guitars, each	150-300
BE600	Mascot doll, Remco, cloth doll w/ cardboard guitar & picture tag	225-450
BE610	Mask, thin plastic, no flocking on hair, one of each Beatle, each	30-55
BE612	Mask, hard plastic, "strange mask," set of 4 w/header	125-200
BE620	Megaphone, Yell-a-Phone (beware reproductions)	150-300
BE625	Model Kit, Yellow Submarine	125-250
BE626	Model Kits, Paul or Ringo, Revell, ea	100-200
BE627	Model Kits, John or George, Revell, ea	150-250
BE628	Mug, Canada	75-150
BE630	Nestle Quick Can, w/ad for inflatable dolls	100-200
BE640	Notebook, writing paper, Westab, one of each Beatle, each	45-90
BE642	Notepad, spiral, Yellow Submarine, 9" X 12"	60-120
BE644	Notepad, spiral, Yellow Submarine, 5" X 7-1/2"	30-60
BE650	Nylons, Ballito, faces & guitars in mesh	65-125
BE660	Overnight bag, round w/group photo & signatures, Air Flite, black or red	200-385

BE670	Paint by Numbers, Artistic Creations, oil paint set	250-500
BE680	Party Coasters, Yellow Submarine, in original package	60-120
BE690	Pen, Press Initial Co., Beatles' heads on clip, on card, each	55-110
BE691	same as above, without card	35-65
BE700	Pencil case, black vinyl	60-120
BE702	Pencil case, zippered, w/group photo & signatures, SPP, multi-colors	50-100
BE705	Pencil By Numbers, UK	300-600
BE710	Phonograph, 4 speed, picture of group on top & inside, mint	550-1100
BE711	same as above w/original box	1000-2100
BE720	Photo album, Yellow Submarine, 3 ring, 7-1/2" X 10"	75-150
BE725	Photo book, Yellow Submarine	70-140
BE730	Pillow, Nordic House, w/tags, group photo from chest up	60-115
BE731	same as above, photo w/instruments	80-155
BE732	same as above, full figure	110-210
BE740	Platter Sack record holder, flat vinyl w/paper insert	40-80
BE750	Play Ball, 14" inflatable ball	150-300
BE760	Playing cards, photo of group in doorway	100-200
BE762	Playing cards, double deck	150-300
BE770	Pouch, Select-O-Pak, clear vinyl, w/paper insert, zipper	65-125
BE780	Punch Out Portraits, Whitman, perforated	40-75
BE790	Purse, clutch, black & white photos, signatures, vinyl or cloth	125-250
BE792	Purse, clutch w/zipper & leather strap	90-180
BE793	Purses, figural, ea	15-25
BE800	Puzzle, Yellow Submarine, 19" X 19", complete	45-90
BE802	Puzzle, Yellow Submarine, medium size, over 100 pieces, complete	40-80
BE804	Puzzle, Yellow Submarine, 5" X 7", over 100 pieces, complete	35-70
BE806	Puzzle, UK	100-200
BE810	Record box for 45's, Air Flite, group photo & signatures on front, red or green, cardboard	100-200
BE811	same as above for LPs, cardboard	150-300
BE812	Record carrier, Seagull, UK	70-140
BE815	Record holder, Disk-Go-Case, various colors	45-90
BE820	Ringo Cap, leather, corduroy, or denim, gold stamp inside	60-115

BE585

BE265

BE575

BE990

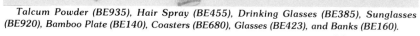

Talcum Powder (BE935), Hair Spray (BE455), Drinking Glasses (BE385), Sunglasses (BE920), Bamboo Plate (BE140), Coasters (BE680), Glasses (BE423), and Banks (BE160).

BE830	Scarf, square w/autographs over large records	45-90
BE832	Scarf, triangular, w/faces & signatures, leather tie string	30-55
BE834	Scarf, triangular, w/larger faces & signatures	40-75
BE836	Scarf, triangular, w/faces & signatures similar to SPP pencil case	45-90
BE838	Scarf, w/faces, records, instruments, on white w/fringe	20-40
BE840	School bag, Canadian	250-450
BE850	School report covers, by Select-O-Pak, thin cardboard	45-90
BE860	Scrapbook, Whitman, plain paper inside	25-50
BE870	Shirt, white, 3 button w/black trim, w/original tag	75-150
BE871	same as above without original tag	40-75
BE880	Shoulder bag, Canadian, oversized, w/ extra snap pouch, rare	225-450
BE882	Shoulder bag, vinyl w/rope or cord strap, attached thru eyelets, various colors	120-225
BE890	Skateboard, Surfskater Co., w/original box	320-640
BE891	same as above without original box	200-400
BE895	Snack Plate, UK	55-110
BE900	Socks, white crew w/square patch on ankle, pair	125-250
BE910	Spatter toy, Spatter Toy Co., "Twirl w/the Beatles"	90-175
BE920	Sunglasses, Solarex, w/paper stickers	60-120
BE930	Sweatshirt, white cotton, long sleeve	40-75
BE935	Talcum Powder, Margo of Mayfair, UK, tin	200-375

Tennis shoes, Wingdings

BE940	blue, low cut	150-300
BE942	white, low cut	120-225
BE944	white or blue high tops	200-400
BE946	shoe box only	50-100
BE947	Tile, ceramic, 4 diff, ea	75-150
BE948	Thermos	50-85
BE949	Lunch Box	100-250
BE950	Tumbler, Burrite, "Lips Tumbler," paper insert under plastic	35-65
BE955	"Twig" in original package	140-260
BE960	Wallet, checkbook size, photo under plastic	75-150

BE962	Wallet, color pictures under plastic vinyl	55-110
BE964	Wallet, SPP, pictures on one side, autographs on other, coin holder, 2 photos, comb, mirror, nail file, photo sleeves	45-90
BE966	Wallet, vinyl, pictures under plastic, brass edging	65-120
BE970	Wallpaper, 21" wide, 21" pattern	15-25
BE972	16', 24', 30' roll	100-300
BE980	Wig, Lowell Toy, hair in pkg w/ cardboard header	30-60
BE990	Yellow Submarine diecast toy, Corgi, w/box, England	165-330

See also: **Animation Art; Autographs; Character & Promotional Glasses; Games, Character and TV Show, Model Kits; Lunch Boxes; Records;**

BICYCLES
by Michael Kaplan

Bicycles can be worth a lot of money They're also fun to search for, find, polish, restore, admire, and ride.

Condition is all-important. Missing or bent parts, twisting, corrosion, or fading seriously reduce value. Depending on the bike, components can usually be located, replaced, or restored with original or reproduction parts. This can become costly. Some collectors will buy as many bikes as they can just to strip them for pedals, seats, handlebars, lights, and other components to create an inventory so when that special bike turns up, even if it is missing a pedal or fender, it can be made complete again.

Desirability of girls' bicycles depends upon the individual collector. Generally speaking, there are far more girls' bikes around in good to excellent condition than boys'. Girls took care of their bikes, or at least didn't ride them as hard as the boys who practiced "crash and burn" dismounts. The laws of supply and demand make boys' bikes (especially deluxe models) considerably more valuable than girls'. But girls' bikes can be a valuable source of such parts as knee action or springer front ends, carrier racks, and chain guards that are often interchangeable with boys' models.

Age is not the determining factor in evaluating a bike's worth. Some bikes from the 1920s are only worth $100, while one of the most valuable was made in 1960: the Bowden Spacelander. Made of fiberglass, it's as futuristic as the name suggests. A model in near mint condition is worth well over $5000!

BI201

Schwinn Black Phantom, restored.

BI310

BI310

Schwinn Green Phantom.

There are many unusual specialty bikes sought by collectors. The Shelby Donald Duck bike, complete with quack-quack horn and illuminated eyes on Donald's head is one example; a restored specimen recently sold for $3000. The Huffy Radiobike, as the name implies, had a transistor radio built into the horn tank. Today, it brings up to $2500.

The last four decades have seen some clear trends in bicycle manufacturing and marketing. Bikes with 26" or 24" X 2-1/4" tires, called full balloon tire bikes, were common up until the 1950s. In the late 1950s and early 1960s, the "British Invasion" went beyond the Beatles and Rolling Stones to include a lightweight type of bicycle which proved very popular. American manufacturers scurried to keep a share of the market the British bikes were expropriating; they were forced to lighten their heavy bikes and switch to a 26" or 24" X 1-3/4" tire size. These are referred to as middleweights. Around this time a mechanical bell built into the tank started replacing the battery operated horn on some models, and single or twin headlights protruding off the tank in front became the predominant style. Also in the early 1960s, bikes began mimicking America's preoccupation with space exploration. Names such as Spaceliner, Spacelander, Flying Star, and Flightliner popped up on sleek new models.

With the exception of the Bowden, which had very limited production, the bikes listed show up frequently and can usually

be bought inexpensively. Since tens of millions were produced, there are still plenty to be found. The more unusual ones, particularly those with rocket ship styling and graphics, have proven desirable.

The values are based on boys' models in good to near mint condition.

Bowden

BI201	Spacelander, 1960	5000-9000

DPH Rollfast

BI205	Hopalong Cassidy, western design	1000-3500

Huffy

BI210	Radiobike, transistor radio in horn tank	500-2500

Monark

BI220	Gene Autry, western design	1000-3500
BI222	Holiday (single springer)	450-1600
BI224	Super Deluxe (double springer)	500-2000

Raleigh

BI230	Chopper, 1960s (very similar to Schwinn Stingray) high-rise handlebars, small front wheel, 5 speed stick-shifter	100-500

Schwinn - Bike model is designated on the chain guard.

BI240	Applecrate, 1968, red	100-500
BI242	Corvette, 1960s	250-450

BI264

BI205

BI264

BI244	Corvette II, 1960s	175-300		integrated into fender	1000-3500
BI246	Cottenpicker, 1968, white	100-500	BI315	Racer, 1960s	100-200
BI248	Cycletruck, 1950s	400-1300	BI318	Spitfire, 1960s	100-300
BI250	Deluxe Hornet, 1950s	300-800	BI320	Starlet, 1950s	150-250
BI255	Flying Star, 1960s	100-300	BI325	Stingray, 1960s (very similar to Raleigh	
BI260	Grey Ghost, 1968, gray	100-500		Chopper) high rise handle-bars, small	
BI262	Hollywood, 1950s	75-175		front wheel, 5 speed stick-shifter	100-500
BI264	Hornet, 1950s	200-500	BI330	Streamliner, 1960s	300-550
BI270	Jaguar Mark II, 1960s	400-1000	BI335	Tiger, 1960s	100-275
BI272	Jaguar Mark III, 1960s	200-600	BI340	Travelor, 1960s	100-300
BI274	Jaguar Mark IV, 1960s	200-575	BI345	Wasp, 1960s	100-275
BI276	Jaguar Mark V, 1960s	175-500	**Sears**		
BI278	Jaguar Mark VI, 1960s	150-300	BI350	J.C. Higgins, various models, 1950s	400-2000
BI280	Lemonpeeler, 1968, yellow	100-500	BI355	Spaceliner	100-350
BI282	Orangecrate, 1968, orange	100-500	**Shelby - motorcycle appearance commands highest values**		
BI290	Panther, similar to Phantom, but with		BI370	Donald Duck, quack-quack horn, Donald's	
	larger tank & headlight on fender, 1950s	600-2000		head with illuminated eyes	800-3000
BI292	Panther II, with front carrier rack, 1960s	200-575	BI375	Model 52A ,1950s	600-1500
BI294	Panther III, 1960s	150-375	**Wards**		
BI301	Paramount, 1960s	400-900	BI380	Hawthorne, 1950s	300-1200
BI305	Peapicker, 1968, green	100-500	**Westfield Columbia - marked on downtube from steering**		
BI310	Phantom, red, green, & black, 1949-1959,		**head to pedal assembly.**		
	teardrop tank, heavily chromed, headlight		BI390	3-Star, 1950s	100-500

BI392	5-Star, 1950s	650-2000
BI394	Thunderbolt 1960s	50-150

Westfield Manufacturing

BI401	Western Flyers, sold in Western Auto Stores, various models	100-2000

BOOKS   by John Wade

A book doesn't have to be an exquisitely bound 18th century volume to be collectible. A 25 cent paperback or a ten year old plain cover cloth bound book without illustrations may also be valuable.

What makes a book expensive and desirable? One prevalent factor is rarity of an early edition by an author who later becomes famous. It's not uncommon for rare first editions to be worth many times their cover price. Stephen King's first novel *Carrie* is worth $600-800 in fine condition. Books 30 or 40 years old have had even more dramatic price increases. Ian Fleming's first "James Bond" novel *Casino Royale*, published in 1953 (London 1953) and sold for less than $10, is now worth $2000-3000. Even paperbacks published in the 1950s-60s with cover prices of 15-35 cents are potentially worth a lot. The first edition of Dell #11, New York (NY) 1953, entitled *Marihuana* by William Irish is now worth $150-200.

Of the hundreds of thousands of titles published after World War II, most are not worth their cover price...but many have astounding value. Science fiction and fantasy enjoy strong collectors' interest. Art books published in limited numbers on high quality paper, finely bound, and richly illustrated are desirable. Teriade, a French book publisher, created Verve, a fine art periodical with special issues by artists like Picasso, Bonnard, Chagall and Matisse. He published 38 issues between 1937 and 1960. The last double issue 37/38, *Designs For The Bible*, illustrated by Marc Chagall, is worth $4000-6000. Books about movies and movie stars (Marilyn Monroe and James Dean) and sports stars (Willie Mays and Muhammad Ali), TV shows ("Star Trek"), and music stars (Elvis Presley and the Beatles) are collectible. Space exploration and aeronautics have a strong following, as well as the Vietnam War, "Beatnik" poetry, and jazz books.

Book publishers also have their share of unique terms. A first edition is the first time an original manuscript appears in printed book form. The term applied to all the copies in the first printing. As an example, a publisher decides to initially print 5,000 copies. If he later prints more, these copies are not firsts even though they may be identical to the original print run. In later printings, there is usually some indication as to which edition, printing, or impression (these terms are synonymous) the book is from. Issues or states are simply variations in printing or binding within an edition. A first edition second issue may vary from the first issue in minute ways...spelling corrections or a change in cover color. The number of copies of a limited edition is always fixed, normally to 1200 copies or less. A limited edition can be a first edition, but often it's a later specially illustrated and bound edition, maybe even signed and numbered by the author or artist. Trade editions are books made available to the public in bookstores after a limited edition. They are usually of lesser quality.

A stumbling block for collecting recently published books is the reprint. Publishers don't make clear when their books are not first editions. A good example is the Book of the Month Club (BOMC). Very often these reprints are almost identical to the first editions including the statement on the verso of the title page indicating it to be a first. The binding and printing may be virtually identical. Some detective work is required: usually the top edge of BOMC's editions are unstained with no headband. There is usually a small indented dot or mark on the lower corner of the back cover, but many times this dot has disappeared. The dust jacket flap should state BOMC and there should be no price. Other problem reprints are Science Fiction Book Club and Book Club editions. Without a dust jack-

et, sometimes the only way to tell is to look for variant or cheaper cloth covers, slightly thinner paper or a smaller volume.

It also helps to become familiar with publishers. Among the many publishers of the most collectible post-1950 first editions are: Abrams, Ace, Arkham House, Avalon, Avon, Bantam, Crown, Dell, Doubleday, Dutton, Fantasy Press, Garden City, Gnome Press, Harper and Row, New Era, Prentice Hall, Putnam, Random House, Scribners, and Simon & Schuster. Doubleday was the major hardback publisher of first editions during the 1950s and 60s, and Ace was the major paperback first edition publisher.

Features adding value over the price for a first edition are signed & inscribed copies and review & advance copies. *The Old Man and the Sea* by Ernest Hemingway, New York 1952 is worth about $200 in fine condition in dust jacket. But Mr. Hemingway's autograph is valuable. If he signed the book and added an interesting anecdote on the flyleaf, the book might be worth more like $2000. An unsigned copy reprinted by BOMC might be worth about $10.

Review and advance copies are special books given to book reviewers, editors, and distributors before the actual first edition is sent to bookstores. The science fiction novel, *Alas Babylon* by Pat Frank, New York 1959 is worth $200-250 as a first edition; a more scarce advance copy in plain paper wrappers without a dust jacket is $600-800.

Condition is critical. A book in fine condition in its dust jacket may be worth ten times one in good condition without the jacket. Very often, especially in the case of fictional works, the dust jacket is worth more than the book. A first edition of the science fiction novel *A Maze of Death* by Philip K. Dick, NY 1970 may be worth $500 in fine condition in the dust jacket, but an ex-library copy (formerly property of a public library) in good condition with no dust jacket may be worth less than $50. The first edition of the science fiction novel *Green Odyssey* by Philip Jose Farmer, NY 1957 is worth $1200 in fine condition with dust jacket. Without the jacket, it may be worth $500, and an ex library copy without jacket may be worth only $100.

Books are usually graded as mint, fine, very good, good, fair, or poor. A book in mint condition is totally unused, never opened, right off the store shelf or from the box. Fine refers to a book that appears very close to mint but has been opened and may have slight shelf wear such as slightly bumped corners or a crinkled backstrip. Very good is somewhere between fine and good. Good is a book that has obviously been opened and handled with light soiling, creasing of some pages, a faded spine, and very minor defects. A book in fair condition is faded and frayed with soiling, possible stains and small tears. The spine may be loose or shaken with some pages ready to pull out. A book in poor condition is so bad it's not only uncollectible but hardly readable.

Art and Fiction are the leading value categories for post-1950 books.

Check for the availibility of *Tomart's Price Guide to 20th Century Books* by John Wade for more extensive listings.

Abbreviations: vol—volume; ed—editor

ART
Audubon, John James

BO001	Davidson, M. (ed) *The Original Watercolor Paintings By John James Audubon For The Birds of America* New York: 1966, 2 vols, folio in slipcase	300-400

Blake, William

BO010	*All Religions Are One* London: Trianon Press, 1970 (36 deluxe copies)	400-600
BO012	Same a BO010, London: Trianon Press, 1970 (600 copies)	150-200
BO014	*America A Prophecy* London: Trianon Press, 1963 (20 copies, colored plates)	1500-2000

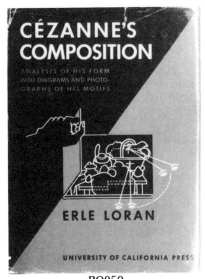
BO050

BO070

BO016 Same a BO014, London: Trianon
Press, 1963 (trade edition)   400-600

Braque, Georges
BO020 *Braque Lithographie* Monte Carlo:
Fernand Mourlet, 1963 (folio)   1000-1200
BO022 *Carnets Intimes* Paris: Verve 31/32,
1955   300-400
BO024 Coqwiat, Raymond *Braque* New York:
Abrams, 1980   100
BO026 *Georges Braque, His Graphic Works*
New York: Abrams, 1961 (folio)   150-200
BO028 Grohmann, Will *The Intimate Sketchbooks
of Georges Braque* New York: 1955 250-300
BO030 *Hommage De Georges Braque* Paris:
Derriere De Miroir, 1964 (folio, 350 copies)   500

Buffet, Bernard
BO045 *Lithographies de Bernard Buffet 1952-
1966* Paris: Fernand Mourlet, 1967   250-300
BO047 *Oeuvre Grave* Paris: Fernand Mourlet, '67   250-300

Cezanne, Paul
BO050 *Cezanne's Composition* Los Angeles: 1959   30-40

Chagall, Marc
BO055 Bonnefoy, Ives *Chagall* Paris: 1962 (folio)   150-200
BO057 *Ceramics And Sculptures of Chagall*
Monte Carlo: 1972   400-500
BO059 *Chagall Lithographie* Monte Carlo:
Fernand Mourlet, 1960-74, 4 vols.   10000-12000
BO061 Chagall, Marc *Designs For the Bible*
New York: Verve 37/38, 1960   4000-6000
BO063 Same as BO061, Paris: 1960   4000-6000
BO065 Chagall, Marc *My Life* New York: 1960   50
BO066 same as BO065, signed copy   150-200
BO068 Chagall, Marc *The Bible* New York &
Paris: Verve 33/34   4000-6000
BO070 *Daphnis & Chloe* New York:
Braziller, 1977   75-100
BO072 Leymarie, Jean *Jerusalem Windows*
New York: 1962 (folio)   1000-1200
BO074 San Lazzaro, G. *Homage to Marc Chagall*
New York: 1969   150-200

Dali, Salvador
BO080 *Hidden Faces* London: 1973 (100 copies,
signed & boxed)   250-350

Degas, Edgar
BO085 Dunlop, Ian *Degas* New York: 1979   25-35
BO087 Rich, Daniel *Degas* New York: Abrams, '70s   30-40

Disney, Walt (the artists of)
BO090 Finch, Christopher *The Art of Walt Disney*
New York: Abrams , 1973 (folio with

plastic dust jacket and high relief figure
of Mickey Mouse mounted on front cover   100-150

Duerer, Albrecht
BO095 *The Little Passion* Vienna:
1971 (140 copies)   400-500

Dufy, Raoul
BO100 *Ten Colour Collotypes After Watercolours*
London: 1961 (200 copies)   200-300

Homer, Winslow
BO105 Gardner, Albert *Winslow Homer*
New York: 1961   40-50

Icart, Louis
BO110 Schessel, Michael *Icart* New York: 1976   30-40

Kane, Paul
BO115 *Paul Kane's Frontier, Including Wanderings
of an Artist Among the Indians*
Toronto: 1971 (300 copies)   400-500
BO117 Same as BO115 Austin, TX: 1971
(300 copies)   400-500

Mariani, Marino
BO120 Waldberg, Patrick *The Complete Works of...*
New York: 1970   30-40

Matisse, Henri
BO125 Jacobus, John *Henri Matisse*
New York: 1972   50-75
BO127 *Jazz* New York: Braziller, 1983   150-200
BO129 *The Last Works of Matisse 1950-54*
Paris & New York: Verve 35/36, 1958   300-400
BO131 *Portraits* Monte Carlo: 1954   200-300
BO133 Same as BO133 Monte Carlo: 1955
(500 copies)   400-500

Miro, Joan
BO140 Balthazar, A. & Jacques Dupin *Scriptures*
Paris: Galerie Maeght, 1970 (150 copies,
signed, folio)   800-1000
BO142 Dupin, Jacques *Peintures Sur Cartons*
Paris: Galerie Maeght, 1965
(150 copies, signed, folio)   1000-1200
BO144 Leiris, Michel & Fernand Mourlet
Lithographs New York: 1972
(4 vols., folio)   800-1000
BO146 Waldberg, Patrick *Loseal Solaire, Loiseal
Lunaire Enticelles* Paris: Galerie Maeght,
1967 (150 copies, signed)   800-1000

Moore, Henry
BO150 Hall, Donald *As The Eye Moves...A
Sculpture by Henry Moore*
New York: Abrams, 1970s   100-125
BO152 Mitchinson, David *Henry Moore:*

BO090

Unpublished Drawings New York:
Abrams, 1970s   40-50

BO154 Moore, Henry Catalog of Graphic Works
1931-79 Geneva: 1973-80 (3 vols.)   400-500

BO156 Moore, Henry Heads, Figures and Ideas
Greenwich: 1958 (folio)   200-300

BO158 Sketchbook 1926 London: 1976 (100
copies with original etching, 2 vols.)   800-1000

O'Keefe, Georgia

BO160 Georgia O'Keefe New York: 1976 (folio,
200 copies, signed)   1500-2000

BO162 Same as BO160 New York: 1976 (folio,
trade edition)   150-200

Picasso, Pablo

BO170 Boeck, William & Jaime Sabartes Pablo
Picasso New York: 1955   75-100

BO172 Benoit, Pierre Autre Chose Paris: 1956
(35 copies)   4000-5000

BO174 Buchlein, L. G. Picasso, a Pictorial
Biography New York: 1959   30-40

BO176 Daix, Pierre & Georges Boudaille Picasso:
The Blue and Rose Period 1900-1906
New York: 1967   200-300

BO178 Duncan, David Goodbye Picasso London:
1975 (folio)   150-200

BO180 Foster, Joseph Posters of Picasso
New York: 1957   50-75

BO182 Foy, Helen Picasso's World of Children
New York: 1960s   40-50

BO184 Mourlet, Fernand Picasso Lithographs,
Boston: 1970   150-200

BO186 Penrose, Roland The Sculpture of Picasso
New York: Museum of Modern Art, 1967   40-50

BO188 Picasso: His Recent Drawings, 1966-1968
New York: Abrams, 1969   75-100

BO190 Picasso in Antibes New York:
Pantheon Books, 1960 (boxed)   150-200

BO192 Picasso 347 New York: 1970
(folio, 2 vols.)   200-300

BO194 Suite of 180 Drawings New York:
Verve 29/30, 1954 (folio)   250-300

Rembrandt

BO200 Benesch, Otto The Drawings of
Rembrandt London: 1954-57 (6 vols.)   400-500

BO202 Same as BO200 London: 1973 (6 vols.)   200-300

BO204 Boon, K.G. Rembrandt: The Complete
Etchings Abrams, 1970s   40-50

BO206 Gerson, Horst Rembrandt Paintings
New York: Artabas, 1968   50-75

BO208 Rembrandt: Paintings From the Soviet
Museums Leningrad: 1975 (folio, slipcase)   40-60

Remington, Frederic

BO210 McCracken, Harold Remington's Own
West New York: 1960 (167 copies,
cowhide bound, boxed)   600-800

BO212 Same as BO210 New York: 1960
(1st trade edition)   50-75

Rockwell, Norman

BO215 Buechner, Thomas S. Norman Rockwell:
Artist and Illustrator New York: 1970   150-200

Russell, Charles M.

BO220 McCracken, Harold The Charles M. Russell
Book New York: 1957   40-50

Van Gogh, Vincent

BO225 Bernard, Bruce Vincent by Himself
New York: New York Graphic Society, 1985   40-60

BO227 Complete Letters of Vincent Van Gogh
Greenwich: New York Graphic Society,
1955 (3 vols.)   200-300

BO228 BO227, later editions   150-200

BO230 Same as BO227, New York: 1958
(leather bound, 100 copies)   400-600

BO232 La Faille, J.B. The Works of Vincent Van
Gogh New York: 1970 (folio)   75-100

BO178

BO188

BO240

BO234 Pickvance, Ronald, *Van Gogh in Arles*
New York: Abrams, 1984   30-40
Vasarely, Victor
BO240 *Vasarely* Paris: 1965   50-75
Wyeth, Andrew
BO245 *Four Seasons* New York: Art in America,
1962 (with separate portfolio of prints)   150-200

FICTION (NOVELS, POETRY, PLAYS; LISTED ALPHABETICALLY BY AUTHOR, THEN BY YEAR)

Anderson, Poul
BO250 *Star Ways* New York: 1956   100-150
BO252 *Three Hearts and Three Lions*
New York: 1961   250-300

BO325 *Killer in the Rain* London: 1964   150-200
BO327 Same as BO325, Boston 1964   75-100
BO329 *The Smell of Fear* London: 1965   150-200
Christie, Agatha
BO335 *Hickory Dickory Dock* London: 1955   50-75
BO337 *The Adventure of the Christmas Pudding
and a Selection of Entrees* London: 1960   75-100
BO339 *A Caribbean Mystery* London: 1964   25-50
BO341 *At Bertram's Hotel* London: 1965   25-50
BO343 *Nemesis* London: 1971   30-40
BO345 Same as BO343, New York: 1971   20-30
BO347 *Elephants Can Remember* New York: 1972   25-35
BO348 Same as BO347, London: 1972   35-50
BO350 *An Autobiography* London: 1977   30-40

BO250

BO252

BO255

BO357

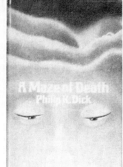
BO359

BO361

Asimov, Isaac
BO255 *Pebble in the Sky* New York: 1950 (author's
1st book)   200-300
BO257 *I, Robot* New York: 1950   400-600
BO260 *Foundation* New York: 1951   200-300
BO261 *Foundation and Empire* New York: 1952   200-300
BO263 *The Currents of Space* New York: 1952   75-100
BO265 *Second Foundation* New York: 1953   200-300
BO267 *The End of Eternity* New York: 1955   150-200
BO269 *The Death Dealers* New York:
Avon, 1958 (paperback)   25-50
BO271 *Fantastic Voyage* Boston: 1966   100-150
BO273 *Opus 100* Boston: 1969   25-50
BO275 *More Tales of the Black Widowers*
New York: 1976   25-50
BO277 *Murder at the ABA* New York: 1976   25-50
BO279 *The Robots of Dawn* Huntington
Woods: 1983   150-200

Bradbury, Ray
BO290 *The Silver Locusts* London: 200-300
BO292 *The Illustrated Man* New York: 1951   200-300
BO294 *Fahrenheit 451* New York: 1953   300-400
BO295 Same as BO294, New York:
Ballantine, 1953 (paperback)   50-75
BO296 Same as BO294, London: 1954
(200 signed copies in asbestos covers)   800-1200
BO298 *The October Country* London: 1956   125-175
BO300 *Dandelion Wine* London: 1957   150-200
BO302 *Something Wicked This Way Comes*
London: 1963   200-300
BO304 *The Anthem Sprinters and Other Antics*
New York: 1963   150-200
BO306 *I Sing the Body Electric!* New York: 1969   75-100
BO308 *When Elephants Last in the Dooryard
Bloomed* London: 1975   35-50
BO310 *Long After Midnight* New York: 1976   35-50

Chandler, Raymond
BO315 *The Simple Art of Murder* Boston: 1950   300-400
BO317 *The Long Goodbye* London: 1953   250-350
BO319 Same as BO317, Boston: 1954   150-200
BO321 *Playback* Boston: 1958   75-125
BO323 Same as BO321, London: 1958   150-250

Dick, Philip K.
BO355 *A Handful of Darkness* London: 1955   600-800
BO357 *Now Wait For Last Year* New York: 1966   200-300
BO359 *Ubik* New York: 1969   500-750
BO361 *A Maze of Death* New York: 1970   400-600
BO363 *Flow My Tears, The Policeman Said*
New York: 1974   75-100
Dickey, James
BO365 *Drowning With Others* Middletown, CT:
1962, cloth   200-300
BO366 Same as BO365, paper wraps   100-150
BO368 *Spinning the Crystal Ball* Washington: 1967   30-40
BO370 *Babel to Byzantium* New York: 1968   25-50
BO372 *Deliverance* New York: 1970   25-50
BO374 *Sorties* New York: 1971   30-40
BO376 *Tucky the Hunter* New York: 1978   30-40
Farmer, Philip Jose
BO380 *Green Odyssey* New York: 1957
(author's 1st book)   1200-1500
BO382 *Flesh* New York: 1968   300-400
BO384 *Doc Savage* New York: 1973   30-40
BO386 *The Adventures of the Peerless Peer*
Boulder, CO: 1974   75-100
BO388 *The Fabulous Riverboat* London: 1974   75-100
BO390 *The Dark Design* Berkley, CA: 1977   25-50
Faulkner, William
BO395 *Notes on a Horse Thief* Greenville, MS:
1950 (975 copies, signed)   400-600

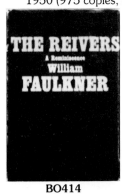
BO414

BO470

BO397	*Collected Stories of...* New York: 1950	75-100
BO399	*Requiem For A Nun* New York: 1951	75-100
BO401	*A Fable* New York: 1954	75-100
BO402	BO401, (1000 copy signed limited edition)	300-400
BO404	*Big Woods* New York: 1955	100-125
BO406	*The Town* New York: 1957	75-100
BO408	*New Orleans Sketches* New Brunswick: 1958	50-75
BO410	Same as BO408, Tokyo 1955	200-300
BO412	*The Mansion* New York: 1959	75-100
BO414	*The Reivers* New York: 1962	30-50
BO416	*The Wishing Tree* New York: 1964 (500 copies, boxed, with dust jacket)	150-200

BO457

BO458

BO454

Fleming, Ian

BO420	*Casino Royale* London: 1953 (author's 1st book)	2000-3000
	(An inscribed copy brought £5500 in 1988)	
BO422	Same as BO420, New York: 1954	300-500
BO424	*Live and Let Die* London: 1955	400-600
BO425	Same as BO425, New York: 1955	200-300
BO427	*Diamonds are Forever* London: 1956	600-800
BO428	Same as BO425, New York: 1956	75-100
BO430	*From Russia, With Love* London: 1957	250-350
BO432	*The Diamond Smugglers* London: 1957	300-400
BO433	Same as BO432, New York: 1957	25-50
BO435	*Doctor No* London: 1958 (1st state without silhouette on cover)	200-300
BO436	Same as BO435, London: 1958 (2nd state)	100-125
BO437	Same as BO435, New York: 1958	25-50
BO439	*For Your Eyes Only* London: 1960	200-250
BO441	*Thunderball* London: 1961	150-200
BO443	*The Spy Who Loved Me* London: 1962	75-100
BO444	Same as BO443, New York 1962	25-50
BO446	*On Her Majesty's Secret Service* London: 1963 (250 copies, signed)	2000-3000
BO449	*Thrilling Cities* London: 1963	100-150
BO451	*You Only Live Twice* London: 1964	75-100
BO452	Same as BO451, New York: 1964	20-30
BO454	*The Man With the Golden Gun* London: 1965	75-100
BO457	*Octopussy and The Living Daylights* London: 1966	50-75
BO458	*Octopussy* New York: 1966	30-40
BO460	*Chitty Chitty Bang Bang* London: 1971	50-75
BO461	Same as BO460, New York: 1971	25-50

Frank, Pat

BO470	*Alas, Babylon* New York: 1959	200-250

Gardner, Erle Stanley

BO475	*The Case of The Sun Bather's Diary* New York: 1955	35-50
BO478	*The Case of The Calendar Girl* New York: 1958	35-50
BO481	*The Case of The Beautiful Beggar* New York: 1965	20-30

Ginsberg, Allen

BO485	*Howl For Carl Solomon* San Francisco: 1955 (50 mimeographed copies)	5000-7000

BO487	*Howl and Other Poems* San Francisco: 1956 (1st printing, paper wraps)	250-350
BO488	Same as BO487, signed copy	400-600
BO489	Same as BO487, San Francisco: 1971 (275 signed copies)	150-200
BO491	*Kaddish and Other Poems* San Francisco: 1961	50-75
BO493	*Notes After an Evening With William Carlos Williams* Brooklyn: 1960s? (300 copies)	50-75
BO495	*Ankor Wat* London: 1969 (100 copies)	100-150
BO497	*The Moments Return* San Francisco: 1970 (200 copies)	100-150
BO499	*The Gates of Wrath* Bolinas: 1972 (100 copies)	100-150
BO501	*Allen Verbatim* New York: 1974	20-40
BO503	*First Blues* New York: 1975	20-40

BO487

BO558

BO562

Heinlein, Robert (wrote over 30 Sci-Fi novels 1950s-80s)

BO550	*Waldo & Magic Inc.* New York: 1950	150-200
BO552	*Tomorrow the Stars* New York: 1952	200-300
BO554	*Revolt in 2100* Chicago: 1953	250-350
BO556	*Assignment in Eternity* Reading: 1953	150-200
BO558	*Starman Jones* New York: 1953	200-250
BO560	*Double Star* London: 1958	150-250
BO562	*Glory Road* New York: 1963 (book club reprints are almost identical and difficult to identify without dust jacket)	400-500
BO564	*I Will Fear No Evil* New York: 1970	75-100
BO566	*Friday* New York: 1982 (500 copies, signed, with slipcase)	200-300
BO568	*Job, A Comedy of Justice* New York: 1984 (750 copies, signed, with slipcase)	150-200

Hemingway, Ernest

BO580	*The Old Man And The Sea* New York: 1952 (30 presentation copies, signed)	2000-3000
BO581	Same as BO580, New York: 1952 (1st trade edition)	150-250
BO582	Same as BO580, London: 1952	75-100
BO585	*Across The River And Into The Trees* New York: 1950	100-125
BO587	Same as BO585, London: 1950	75-100
BO590	*The Wild Years* New York: 1962	35-50
BO592	*A Moveable Feast* New York: 1964	40-60
BO594	*The Fifth Column And Four Unpublished Stories Of The Spanish Civil War* New York: 1969	35-50
BO600	*Islands In The Stream* New York: 1970	40-60

Howard, Robert

BO602	*Conan The Conqueror* New York: 1950	200-300
BO604	*The Sword of Conan* New York: 1952	200-300
BO606	*King Conan* New York: 1953	200-300
BO608	*The Coming of Conan* New York: 1953	200-300
BO610	*Conan The Barbarian* New York: 1954	200-300
BO612	*Tales of Conan* New York: 1955	150-200
BO614	*Always Comes Evening* Sauk City: 1957	300-400
BO616	*Great Iron Trail* New York: 1962	50-75
BO618	*The Dark Man And Others* Sauk City:	

	1963	200-300
BO622	*Almuric* West Kingston: 1975	35-50

Kerouac, Jack

BO625	*The Town & The City* New York: 1950 (author's 1st book)	250-350
BO627	*On The Road* New York: 1957	250-350
BO629	*The Dharma Bums* New York: 1958	100-125
BO631	*Lonesome Traveler* New York: 1960	75-100
BO633	*Big Sur* New York: 1962	40-60
BO635	*Vanity of Duluoz* New York: 1968	75-100
BO637	*Not Long Ago Joy Abounded At Christmas* New York: 1972 (195 copies)	75-100
BO639	*Home At Christmas* New York: 1973 (195 copies)	75-100
BO641	*Two Early Stories* New York: 1973 (175 copies)	75-100

BO664

BO686

BO705

BO688	New York: 1959	50-75
BO688	*Deaths For The Ladies* New York: 1962	50-75
BO690	*An American Dream* New York: 1964	35-50
BO692	*Cannonballs And Christians* New York: 1966	30-40
BO694	*Marilyn* New York: 1973 (limited edition, signed, boxed)	200-300
BO695	Same as BO694, New York: 1973 (1st trade edition)	40-60
BO697	Same as BO694, Grosset & Dunlap reprint, 1973	20-30
BO699	*Genius And Lust* New York: 1976	20-30

Michener, James

BO705	*Tales of the South Pacific* New York: 1950 (1500 copies, signed)	100-150
BO707	Same as BO705, New York: 1951 (first trade edition)	25-50
BO709	*Return To Paradise* New York: 1951	50-75
BO711	*The Bridges At Toko-Ri* New York: 1953	75-100
BO713	*The Floating World* New York: 1954	125-150
BO715	*The Bridge At Andau* New York: 1957	25-50
BO716	Same as BO715 London: 1957	50-75
BO718	*Report of the Country Chairman* New York: 1961	35-50
BO720	*The Source* New York: 1965 (500 copies, signed, boxed)	100-150
BO722	*Iberia* New York: 1968 (500 copies, signed, boxed)	100-150
BO724	*The Quality of Life* London: 1971	30-40
BO726	*Centennial* New York: 1974 (500 copies, signed, with slipcase)	100-150

Queen, Ellery (Frederic Danay & Manfred Lee)

BO730	*The Literature of Crime* Boston: 1950	25-50
BO732	*The Origin of Evil* Boston: 1951	50-75
BO734	*The King Is Dead* Boston: 1952	50-75
BO736	*The Calendar of Crime* Boston: 1952	50-75
BO738	*The Glass Village* Boston: 1954	50-75
BO740	*Finishing Stroke* New York: 1958	40-60
BO742	*Inspector Queen's Own Case: November Song* New York: 1956	40-60

BO651

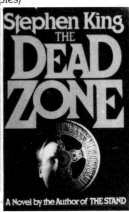

BO653

BO660

King, Stephen

BO643	*Carrie* London: 1974 (author's 1st book) (1000 copies, signed)	600-800
BO645	Same as BO643, New York: 1974	200-300
BO647	*Salem's Lot* London: 1975	400-600
BO649	*The Shining* London: 1977	200-300
BO651	*The Stand* New York: 1978	150-200
BO653	*The Dead Zone* London: 1979	150-200
BO655	*Firestarter* Huntington: 1980 (750 copies, signed)	700-1000
BO657	*Danse Macabre* New York: 1981	35-50
BO658	without dust jacket	10-15
BO660	*The Dark Tower: The Gunslinger* West Kingston: 1982 (500 copies)	700-1000
BO662	*Christine* West Kingston: 1983 (1000 copies, signed)	400-600
BO664	*Pet Sematary* New York: 1983	30-50
BO666	Same as BO664, advance copy 1983, pictorial wraps	100-150
BO668	Same as BO664, advance copy (photo offset from typescript) 50 copies	300-400
BO670	*The Talisman* West Kingston: 1984 (1200 copies, signed, 2 vols. in slipcase)	600-800
BO672	*Skeleton Crew* Santa Cruz: 1985 (1000 copies)	300-400
BO674	*The Dark Tower II: The Drawing of the Three* West Kingston: 1987 (850 copies, signed)	500-700
BO676	*My Pretty Pony* New York: 1988 (250 copies, signed by author & artist)	2000-3000
BO678	*Dolan's Cadillac* Northridge: 1989 (1000 copies, signed)	200-300

Mailer, Norman

BO680	*Barbary Shore* New York: 1951 (circled "R" on copyright page)	75-100
BO682	*The Deer Park* New York: 1955	50-75
BO684	*The White Negro* San Francisco: 1957	50-75
BO686	*Advertisements For Myself*	

BO745

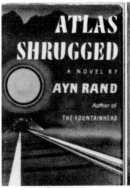

BO754

BO770

Rand, Ayn
BO745 *Atlas Shrugged* New York: 1957   50-75
Steinbeck, John
BO750 *Burning Bright* New York: 1950   100-150
BO752 *The Log From the Sea of Cortez*
          New York: 1951   150-200
BO754 *East of Eden* New York: 1952   100-150
BO756 *Sweet Thursday* New York: 1954   75-100
BO758 *The Short Reign of Pippin IV, A*
          Fabrication New York: 1957   50-75
BO760 *Once There Was a War* New York: 1958   50-75
BO762 *The Winter of Our Discontent*
          New York: 1961   50-75
BO764 *Steinbeck: A Life In Letters* New York:
          1975 (1000 copies, with slipcase)   100-150

BO772   **BO776**   **BO779**

Tolkien, John R. R.
BO770 *Farmer Giles of Ham* New York: 1950   100-150
BO772 **Lord of The Rings Trilogy** (*The*
          Fellowship of The Ring/The Two Towers/
          The Return of The King), London:
          1954-55 (3 vols. published separately
          w/dust jackets)   5000-7000
BO774 Same as BO774, New York: 1954-56
          (3 vols. published separately w/dust
          jackets)   600-800
BO776 *The Adventures of Tom Bombadil*
          London: 1962   100-150
BO777 Same as BO776, New York: 1962   75-100
BO779 *Tree and Leaf* London: 1964   200-300
BO781 Same as BO779, New York: 1965   50-75
BO783 *The Road Goes Ever On* Boston: 1967   75-100
BO785 *Smith of Wootton Major* London: 1967   100-150
BO786 Same as BO785, Boston: 1967   50-75

BO785   **BO786**

Thurber, James
BO790 *Thurber Country* New York: 1953   25-50
BO792 *Further Fables For Our Time*
          New York: 1956   50-75
BO794 *The Wonderful O* New York: 1957   25-50
BO796 *Alarms & Diversions* New York: 1957   50-75
Williams, Tennessee
BO800 *The Rose Tattoo* New York: 1951   50-75
BO802 *Baby Doll* New York: 1956   50-75
BO804 *In The Winter of Cities Poems*

          New York: 1956   50-75
BO806 *Suddenly Last Summer* New York: 1958   75-125
BO808 *Sweet Bird of Youth* New York: 1959   75-100
BO810 *Period of Adjustment* New York: 1960   50-75
BO812 *The Night of the Iguana* New York: 1963 50-75
BO814 *The Milk Train Doesn't Stop Here*
          Anymore Norfolk: 1964   50-75
Williams, William Carlos
BO820 *The Collected Later Poems*
          Norfolk: 1950 (100 copies, signed)   300-400
BO822   New York: 1952   35-50
BO823- *Paterson* (Books 1-5), New York:
27   1946-58 (separately published volumes) 100-150 ea
BO828 *The Collected Earlier Poems*
          New York: 1951   35-50
BO830 *The Build-Up* New York: 1952   75-100
BO832 *The Desert Music and Other Poems*
          New York: 1954   100-150
BO834 *Many Loves and Other Plays*
          New York: 1961   35-50
BO836 *Farmer's Daughter* New York: 1961   25-50

BO888

Wolf, Gary
BO888 *Who Censored Roger Rabbit?*
          New York: 1980   125-200
See also: **Golden Books; James Bond; Disney; Marilyn Monroe**

BUTTONS, PIN-BACK   by Ted Hake

Pin-back buttons are nearly one hundred years old. Introduced in 1896, they consisted of a round paper bearing the printed design covered by a thin celluloid sheet. Both layers were wrapped around a metal backing and held together by a metal ring, known as the collet, pressed into the reverse. Current printing technology could produce beautiful milticolored designs and the celluloid provided a glossy and durable covering. The button found immediate acceptance among plitical parties, advertisers, and the general public. New technology developed during World War I produced buttons with the colors printed directly on the metal. These lithographed tin buttons reduced costs by eliminating the celluloid covering, the paper with the design, and the collet. Celluloid buttons remained popular, but to stay competitive the expensive printing processes used to produce designs with an immense range of colors were most often avoided. By the early 1920s, the production of beautifully colored celluloid buttons plummeted.

But the basic concept survived. The 1960s produced a revival of sorts with many colorful "cause" buttons, followed by a flood of eye-catching "rock group" buttons in the 1970s.

Today buttons have largely become the province of greeting card manufacturers and retail gift shops. Modern political buttons, although frequently using color, are usually candidate photo or text-only pieces with few references to campaign issues. The number of giveaway buttons has also diminished greatly over the years. But recently button creativity appears to be in a mild resurgence and buttons continue to enjoy a loyal following as a collectible.

A button's value is determined by many factors: (1) the number of collectors looking for a particular category, (2) scarcity, (3) design and/or color quality, (4) whether the button is picture or text-only, (5) age, (6) size, and (7) condition. Due to the immense variety of buttons, this section is divided into three parts. Values are for items in excellent condition with no stain, scratches, dents, or other damage.

Entertainment Pin-Back Buttons

Beginning in the 1930s, many different buttons were issued to promote cowboy stars, movies, cartoon characters, singers, and other entertainment personalities. This tradition was carried on after World War II with the notable addition of television-related buttons. After presidential campaign buttons, entertainment is the most widely-collected category. Numerous examples of common buttons are in the $1 to $10 value ranges but a significant number are more scarce with values of $15 to $50. Only a few select post-1950 buttons have values exceeding $50.

BU105   BU141   BU160   BU171

BU100	Alfred E. Neuman for President/What - Me Worry/I'm Voting Mad, 2-1/4", 1960	75-100
BU105	Bill Haley and his Comets, 1-1/2", 1950s	75
BU110	Bugs Bunny leaning against tree, 1-3/4", 1950s	45
BU115	Dale Evans Fan Club Member, 1-3/4", 1950s	40
BU120	Davy Crockett Fan Club/Pfeiffers, 1-1/4", 1950s	30
BU125	Dick Clark of "Bandstand" WFIL-TV Channel 6, 1-1/4", 1950s	25
BU135	Dustin Hoffman/Mia Farrow - John and Mary, 2-1/4", 1970s	15
BU140	Elvis Presley Best Wishes, 3", 1956	50
BU141	Elvis Presley National Fan Club/R.C.A. Records, 1-1/2", 1956	125
BU145	Everly Brothers Fan Club, 1-3/8", 1950s	30
BU150	Gene Autry & Champion with gold or sliver star design, 1-3/4", 1950s	30
BU155	Happy Anniversary [King] Kong 1933-1983, 2-1/4", 1983	15
BU160	Have You Voted For Lassie? 1-3/4", 1950s	15
BU170	Hopalong Cassidy Club/Filene's and Loew's State, 2-1/4", 1950s	150
BU171	Hopalong Cassidy Daily in the Chicago Tribune, 1-5/8", 1950s	20
BU172	Hopalong Cassidy in the Daily News, 2-1/4", 1950s	25
BU180	Howdy Doody For President, 1-1/2", 1952	40
BU185	I'm An Official Beatles Fan, 4", 1960s	15
BU190	J. R. Ewing For President, 2-1/4", 1980	10
BU195	Jackie Gleason/Reggie Van Gleason The III, 1-3/4", 1950s	30

BU196   BU205   BU220

BU196	Jackie Gleason/The Loud-Mouth, 1-3/4", 1950s	15
BU200	James Dean color photo, 2-1/2", 1950s	50
BU205	Matt Dillon's Favorite/All Star Dairies, 1-3/8", 1960s	20
BU210	Mary Hartline Super Circus Club, 1-5/8", 1950s	15

BU215	Maurice Sendak/In The Night Kitchen, 4", 1970s	35
BU220	Mickey Mouse Club/KVOS-TV 12, 1-1/4", 1950s	30
BU221	Mickey Mouse Club Member, 7/8", 1960s	20
BU222	Mickey Mouse Seed Shop/Let's Grow America, 3", 1970s	60

BU230   BU240   BU251   BU275

BU230	Pogo Possum or other Walt Kelly Characters, 1-3/4", 1968	25-75
BU235	Popeye/Cap'n Jim Channel 11, 1-1/2", 1950s	25
BU240	Ramar Safari Scout/Jon Hall, 1-1/4", 1950s	25
BU245	Rocky Jones Space Ranger, 1-3/8", 1950s	15
BU250	Roy Rogers & Trigger, 1-3/4", 1950s	20
BU251	Roy Rogers/My Pal, marked Ideal Novelty & Toy Co., 1-3/4", 1950s	75
BU260	6 Million Dollar Man Club/Official Member, 2-1/4", 1970s	15-50
BU265	Shmoo Club/Shmoo Member, 1", 1950s	30
BU270	Sincerely, Fats Domino, 2-1/2", 1950s	20
BU275	Sky King/Safety Is No Accident, 1-1/8", 1950s	50
BU280	Soupy [Sales] Sez Do The "Mouse," 1", 1960s	15

BU285   BU290   BU315   BU325

BU285	Superman Muscle Building Club, 1-3/8", 1950s	50
BU290	The Lone Ranger, 1-1/4", 1950s	15
BU300	The Man From U.N.C.L.E./Illya Kuryakin, 3-1/2", 1960s	15
BU301	The Man From U.N.C.L.E./Napoleon Solo, 3-1/2", 1960s	15
BU310	The Rolling Stones, 3-1/2", 1960s	35
BU315	Tom & Jerry/Go For Stroehmann's Bread, 1-1/8", 1950s	15
BU320	Walt Disney's Davy Crockett Frontiersman, 1-3/8", 1950s	25
BU325	Wild Bill Hickok and Jingles/We're Partners, 1-3/8", 1950s	30
BU330	Winky Dink, 1-1/8", 1950s	20

Presidential Campaign Buttons

Each election year sees hundreds of button designs produced for the major party candidates. Many of these designs are produced in large quantities and the vast majority of buttons from 1952 through the 1980s are valued between 50¢ and $5.00. However, as the following selections show, for each candidate there are certain specific buttons whose value can reach hundreds of dollars. The most popular post-war candidate among presidential item collectors is John F. Kennedy.

BU400   BU401   BU403   BU420   BU421

Dwight Eisenhower 1952-1956

BU400	Let's Back Ike & Dick (blue photos of both) 1-3/8"	15
BU401	They're For You/Ike-Dick (color photos of both) 1-3/8"	20
BU402	I Like Ike For President (red & white with	

blue photo) 1-1/4"   15

BU403   My Friend Ike (white & brown shaking hands) 1-1/8"   60

BU404   Get Right With Ike (photo shows military uniform) 5/8"   20

BU405   Womanpower for Eisenhower (shows lady elephant) 1-1/2"   175

BU406   Richard M. Nixon For Vice-President (with photo) 7/8"   100

BU422   BU423   BU440   BU441   BU406

Adlai Stevenson 1952-1956

BU420   I Like Stevenson (drawing of GI by Bill Mauldin) 1-3/8"   20

BU421   Go Forward With Stevenson/Sparkman (color photo) 1-3/8"   35

BU422   Dollars For Democrats (photo in TV screen design) 1-3/8"   100-200

BU423   Stevenson Clothing Button (photo with red/white fabric rim) 1-1/8"   40

BU424   Vote Democratic And Don't Let Them Take It Away (photo of Stevenson) 2-1/4"   280

BU425   Adlai And Estes Are Best For You (clover design with photos of both) 2-1/4"   350

John F. Kennedy 1960

BU440   Kennedy - Johnson/New Leadership (photos of both) 1-5/8"   20

BU441   Kennedy - Johnson/44th Inauguration/1961 The New Frontier (photos of both) 1-3/4"   30

BU442   Elect Kennedy President (young photo) 2-1/4"   350

BU443   Youth For Kennedy (red letters/blue photo) 2-1/4"   250

BU444   Our Next President (blue photo over flag design) 1-3/4"   250

BU445   Jack Once More In '64 (red letters/blue photo) 4"   500

Richard Nixon 1960

BU460   Man Of Steel/Richard Nixon (with photo) 3-1/2"   125

BU461   Not For Sale/Elect Nixon (shows White House) 4"   200

BU463   Goldwater Says/Don't Dodge/Vote Nixon And Lodge (slogan) 1-3/4"   70

BU464   Don't Be A "Jack" Ass/Vote Republican (slogan) 1-3/4"   20

BU465   The Winning Team/Nixon and Lodge (photos of both) 1-5/8"   8

BU465   BU480   BU500   BU501

Lyndon B. Johnson 1964

BU480   Johnson - Humphrey/Responsible Leadership (photos of both) 1-3/4"   5

BU481   In Your Guts You Know He's Nuts (shows Goldwater) 3-1/2"   110

BU482   Welcome Ladybird/Flying Whistlestop (shows bi-wing plane) 3"   50

BU483   Let Us Continue (shows Kennedy & Johnson) 3-1/2"   40

BU484   Dr. Strangewater (Anti-Goldwater showing atomic symbol & skull) 1-1/4"   45

BU485   Prosper More/Vote LBJ In '64 (with photo) 6"   60

Barry Goldwater 1964

BU500   Turn Out Light Bulb Johnson (Anti-LBJ with cartoon design) 2"   15

BU501   Goldwater in '64 (photo with six stars on rim) 1-3/4"   50

BU502   Stop Socialism/Vote For Goldwater And Miller (slogan) 1-3/4"   20

BU503   Look Ahead With Goldwater (illustrated portrait) 2-1/4"   100

BU504   Coloradans For Goldwater (with photo) 1-3/4"   200

BU505   Indiana's Favorite Family (Goldwater & wife) 3"   375

BU502   BU540   BU580   BU600

Richard Nixon 1968

BU520   Nixon in '68 (Nixon with Lincoln, Washington & T. Roosevelt) 3"   20

BU521   Nixon - He's Good Enough For Me in '68 (Nixon with Uncle Sam pointing finger) 3"   20

BU522   Nixon - Victory '68' (photo with eagle below) 1-1/2"   25-50

BU523   This Is No Yoke! (cartoon of Humphrey as Humpty Dumpty on a wall) 2-1/2"   20

BU524   Dick For President/Pat For First Lady (photos of both) 3"   15

BU525   Now Is The Time! For Nixon (slogan) 3-1/2"   10

Hubert Humphrey 1968

BU540   HHH Fills The Prescription (cartoon with photo portrait) 1-1/2"   20

BU541   Now Power/Humphrey - Muskie (shows both) 3-1/2"   35

BU542   We're For Him/HHH (shows children with plastic flasher eyes) 3-1/2"   65

BU543   Behind All Great Men (Mrs. Humphrey/Mrs. Muskie) 3-1/2"   25

BU544   America Needs Humphrey - Muskie (shows both with "Minnesota" credit on edge) 3-1/2"   150

BU545   My Man Humphrey (cartoon portrait with plastic flasher eyes) 3-1/2"   60

Richard Nixon 1972

BU560   Nixon Free Hoffa/Teamsters Convention 1971 (slogan) 4"   35

BU561   Puerto Rican - Hispanic Young Republicans (cartoon elephant) 4"   30

BU562   Nixon For Peace (shows dove) 2-1/4"   15

BU563   Bergen Young Voters For The President (shows photo) 2-1/8"   60

BU564   Mississippians For Nixon! (slogan) 2-1/4"   35

BU565   Youth For Nixon (shows photo) 1"   10

George McGovern 1972

BU580   McGovern/Eagleton (white & light blue name button) 1-1/8"   8

BU581   Robin McGovern (McGovern in Robin Hood costume) 4"   60

BU582   Come Home America (trees form shape of U.S.) 3"   25

BU583   Make America Happen Again (pine trees & mountains with serial number) 2-1/4"   15

BU584   McGovern (slogan with photos of Carole King, Barbra Streisand, James Taylor) 3-1/2"   250

BU585   George McGovern/A President For The People/Oklahoma (slogan) 3"   20

Jimmy Carter 1976

BU600	The Grin Will Win/Jimmy in '76 (smiling peanut cartoon) 1-3/4"	5
BU601	Dairyland Democrats For Carter - Mondale (photos over outline of Wisconsin) 3"	15
BU602	Inauguration January 20, 1977 (photo of Carter, wife & child with White House in background) 6"	20
BU603	The Tennessean Inaugural Special 1977 (illustrated portrait) 2-1/2"	20
BU604	Vote With Love For Carter Mondale (slogan) 4"	30
BU605	Texans For Carter (photo with state outline) 2-1/4"	35

Gerald Ford 1976

BU620	Ford - Dole/Prosperity, Peace And Public Trust (shows both) 2-1/4"	12
BU621	New Jersey/Ford Country (slogan with state outline) 2-3/8"	12
BU622	Committed To President Ford (slogan) 2-1/2" oval	12
BU623	Vote Conservative/Keep A Dependable President (illustrated portrait & U.S. flag) 3"	8
BU624	Friends Of The White House/Indiana '76 (slogan & state outline) 2-1/2"	8
BU625	Ford - Dole in '76 (full color photos of both) 4"	6

Miscellaneous

Buttons provide a fascinating documentary record of American history, life-styles, and popular culture. Their small size, attractive colors and designs, and relative affordability appeal to many collectors. The most popular categories include advertising, sports, social causes, famous people, transportation and space exploration. While most buttons in these categories are under $5.00 in value during the 1950-1989 time period, a number of scarcer examples can achieve values of $10-$50.

BU810   BU813   BU815   BU825

BU805	America Salutes First Men On The Moon, 1-3/4", 1969	10
BU810	America's First Astronaut/Navy Lt. Comdr. Alan B. Shepard, 1-3/4", 1961	20
BU813	Detroit says: "Watch Ford in '48"/Car of the Year, 1-1/8", 1948	40
BU815	Ducks Unlimited, 1951, (members' button) 1-1/4"	40
BU820	Enough (anti-Vietnam War button designed by Jules Feiffer), 2-1/4", 1960s	15
BU825	Ernie Banks Day/Aug. 15, 1964 (photo on baseball design), 2"	30
BU830	First Men On The Moon Sunday - July 20, 1969, 1-3/4", 1969	15

BU835   BU840   BU860   BU895

BU835	I've Seen The 1953 Chevrolet, 1-5/8", 1953	20
BU840	Jackie Robinson (photo on yellow background), 1-3/4", 1950s	40
BU845	Joe DiMaggio/New York Yankees, 1-3/4", 1950s	35
BU850	March On Washington For Jobs & Freedom, August 28, 1963, 2-1/4"	20
BU855	Member Coca-Cola Bottler Hi-Fi Club,	

	1-3/8", 1950s	25
BU860	Mickey Mantle, 1-3/4", 1960s	35
BU865	New York Yankees 1953 (team photo), 3-1/2",	200
BU870	Ray Robinson, 1-1/4", 1950s	25
BU875	Reddy Kilowatt/25th Anniversary Public Service, 1-1/4", 1951	25
BU880	Retire J. Edgar Hoover (anti-FBI director with caricature), 1-1/2", 1960s	30
BU885	Ted Williams/Boston Red Sox, 1-1/4", 1950s	10
BU890	The New Frontier/Man Of The Year/Astronaut John Glenn, 3-1/2", 1962	20
BU895	Queen Elizabeth II, 1-3/4", 1953	10

BU900   BU905   BU910   BU915

BU900	Vote For Buster Brown, 1-1/4", 1950s	25
BU905	Welcome Fidel Castro, 1-3/4", 1950s	15
BU910	Welcome "Yogi" (Berra) Day - Yankee Stadium, 1-3/8", 1964	15
BU915	Well Done, Col. Glenn/First American In Orbit, 1-3/4", 1962	15

See also: **Disney**

CAPTAIN ACTION   by Carol Markowski

Finding 12" Captain Action figures boxed is rare. Finding the 13 costume sets is nearly impossible. Even more difficult to find are Dr. Evil, Captain Action's enemy, and his accessories.

Second series and re-issued costumes included a flasher ring which showed Captain Action in his original costume and dressed as the character when the ring was flashed.

Since several of the super heroes had youthful counterparts, Action Boy was created. Four costumes were availible for this 8" figure. The series was loaded with numerous accessories which are essential when determining values, so a detailed listing of contents has been provided for each product.

Prices are for "Complete No Package" (CNP), "Mint in Package" (MIP), and "Mint in Mint Package" (MMP). Complete definitions are in the Action Figures section.

Tomart's Price Guide to Action Figure Collectibles includes a complete listing of Captain Action items, plus a detailed listing of each item's contents. See page 150 for ordering information.

CA322, CA347, and CA301

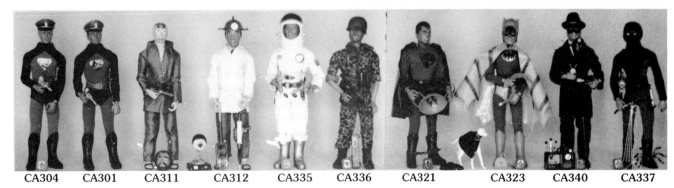

| CA304 | CA301 | CA311 | CA312 | CA335 | CA336 | CA321 | CA323 | CA340 | CA337 |

12' poseable doll	CNP	MIP	MMP
CA301 Captain Action	200	250	375
CA302 CA301, 1966	200	260	400
CA303 CA301 in re-issue box	200	300	400
CA304 CA301 w/Parachute	235	335	750
CA305 CA301 in 1967 photo box	200	425	800

DR. Evil the Sinister Invader of Earth 1967

CA311 Dr. Evil, 1967	225	400	700
CA312 Dr. Evil Gift Set, 1968,	600	950	1200
CA313 Dr. Evil Sanctuary (carry case)	150	200	275

SUPERHERO COSTUMES FOR CAPTAIN ACTION

CA320 Superman Costume, 1966	200	325	500
CA321 CA320 w/flasher ring	210	375	550
CA322 Batman Costume, 1966	300	325	600
CA323 CA322 w/flasher ring	210	375	550
CA324 Aquaman Costume, 1966	160	300	425
CA325 CA324 w/flasher ring	170	350	475
CA326 Captain America, 1966	190	325	550
CA327 CA326 w/flasher ring	200	350	575

CA328 Phantom, 1966	160	300	425
CA329 CA328 w/flasher ring	170	300	425
CA330 Lone Ranger, 1966	170	375	500
CA331 CA330 w/blue outfit and ring	300	660	875
CA332 Steve Canyon, 1966	150	225	350
CA333 CA332 w/flasher ring	160	250	375
CA334 Flash Gordon, 1966	180	350	450
CA335 CA334 w/flasher ring	190	350	450
CA336 Sergeant Fury, 1966	100	360	450
CA337 Spider-Man, 1967	425	750	1200
CA338 Tonto, 1967	325	655	1000
CA339 Buck Rogers, 1967	350	600	900
CA340 Green Hornet, 1967	1200	2500	3500

ACTION BOY

CA343 Action Boy, 1967	325	500	900
CA344 Action Boy w/space suit	400	575	800
CA345 Aqualad costume, 1967	275	425	800
CA346 Superboy costume, 1967	300	525	850
CA347 Robin costume, 1967	300	500	800

| CA339 | CA330 | CA338 | CA331 | CA329 | CA327 | CA325 |

CA321

CA340

CA339

CA343	CA344	CA346	CA347	CA345

CAPTAIN ACTION ACCESSORIES

CA351	Directional Communicator Set	125	225	325
CA352	Power Pack	125	225	325
CA353	Weapons Arsenal	125	225	325
CA354	Jet Mortar	125	225	325
CA355	Parachute Pack	110	225	325
CA356	Survival Kit	150	225	325
CA357	Silver Streak Amphibian	550	1000	1400
CA358	Captain Action's Action Cave	400	475	600
CA359	Vinyl Headquarters	360	675	900

SEARS EXCLUSIVES

CA361	Cardboard Garage	800	1200	1500
CA362	Captain Action w/Batman costume and Secret Chamber	700	850	1000
CA363	Caption Action w/Quick-Change Chamber	700	850	1000

CEREAL BOXES   by Jerry Cook & Duane Dimock

Packaged, ready-to-eat cereal became a popular breakfast food around the turn of the century. Hot, cooked oatmeal and wheat cereal were available long before and are still sold in relative plain packaging. For over 30 years the marketing of ready-to-eat cereals was aimed at mothers.

Then in the early '30s General Mills, Quaker, Post, and Ralston started to appeal to the kids who had to eat the stuff by using premiums they could get free for boxtops. General Mills successfully introduced Kix and Cheerioats (later Cheerios) by the early '40s. Kids were the prime target for all cereal makers by the time sugar-coated brands began to proliferate in the mid-50s. It took 10 to 12 years for the makers to run out of flavors, colors, and different dehydrated marshmallow ideas ... and turn to licensed promotional brands in the late '60s and early '70s. Initially there were attempts at making these permanent brands, but sales proved to be tied to the popularity of the character. Thus was born the age of changing the box rather than the cereal inside.

The number of promotional cereals has increased dramatically since 1980. Ralston has been the leader in disposable brands.

With the increased availability of here-today, gone-tomorrow cereals associated with movies, cartoon characters, and other licensed properties, it was predictable the colorful graphics designed to capture immediate consumer attention wouldn't pass collectors unnoticed.

The value of used cereal boxes is determined by one of two factors: 1) the desirability of the character or offer illustrated on the box or 2) errors, withdrawn box or discontinued brands. Values are for complete cereal boxes with all six sides intact in fine or better condition.

CB001	All-Stars (Kellogg)	10-35
CB002	Miscellaneous offers and prizes	15-50
CB003	Alpha Bits (Post), vintage	20-30
CB004	Archies Cut-Out Yellow Record on back	30-70
CB005	Baseball or Football cards on back	50-120
CB010	Apple Jacks (Kellogg)	1-15
CB011	Banana Splits Flashlight Offer	75-100
CB012	Banana Splits Poster Offer	75-100
CB013	Camel Train	20-50
CB014	Daffy Dogs	20-50
CB015	Tooly Birds	20-50
CB020	Banana Frosted Flakes (Kellogg)	15-40
CB030	Banana Wackies (General Mills)	15-40
CB040	Baron Von Redberry (General Mills)	40-65
CB050	Betty Crocker Cereal Tray (General Mills)	60-150
CB060	Boo Berry (General Mills), vintage	20-30
CB070	Bozo's Little O's	10-35
CB080	C-3PO's (Kellogg)	20-30
CB081	Set of 6 boxes w/different masks	120-180
CB090	Cabbage Patch Kids (Ralston)	15-25
CB100	Cheerios (General Mills), vintage	30-50
CB101	Bionic Man/Bionic Woman	15-32
CB102	Bullwinkle or Jay Ward characters on back & front	25-100
CB103	Disneyland Park Light-Up	50-75
CB104	Glass Pals	15-30
CB105	Legend of the Lone Ranger (1980)	10-25
CB106	Lone Ranger Fun Kit	100-150
CB107	Lone Ranger Movie Film Ring/ Badge/Flashlight Ring, 3 diff, ea	200-300
CB108	Lone Ranger Movie Ranch	100-150
CB109	Lone Ranger Picture to Color	75-100
CB110	Lone Ranger Shirt/Tie/Gun & Holster Set	200-250
CB111	Mickey Mouse Circus Wiggle Picture Badge offer	75-100
CB112	Snoopy Joe Cool	10-25
CB113	Star Trek offers	15-25
CB114	Star Wars offers	20-45
CB115	Super Hero Magnetic Dart game	50-75
CB116	Wyatt Earp Western Hero Cut-out Guns	35-100
CB117	Annette Paper Dolls (Mickey Mouse Club)	50-100
CB120	Choco Crunch (Quaker)	25-75
	Cocoa Krispies (Kellogg)	
CB131	Snagglepuss big on front	75-100

CB005	CB005	CB010	CB060	CB070

	CB080		CB110		CB117		CB115		CB131

	Count Chocula (General Mills)			CB265	Roy Rogers & Trigger Pop-Out Card	250-400
CB141	Bela Lugosi Star of David	10-20		CB266	Roy Rogers Button (16 different)	200-350
CB142	Star Wars Stickers	30-40		CB267	Roy Rogers offers on front & back	150-400
CB143	Wacky Races	15-25		CB270	Grape-Nuts (Post)	
CB150	Cracker Jack (Ralston)	10-25		CB271	Baseball cards on back	50-100
	Crispy Critters (Post)			CB280	Gremlins (Ralston)	30-45
CB161	Bugs Bunny	25-100		CB290	Grins & Smiles & Giggles & Laughs (Ralston)	35-60
CB162	Sealed box w/Golden Book attached	30-40		CB291	Character magnets	35-60
CB170	Donkey Kong (Ralston)	15-30		CB292	Character walkers	50-75
CB180	Donkey Kong Jr. (Ralston)	15-30			Honey Comb (Post)	
CB190	E.T. (General Mills)	40-50		CB301	Archies Cut-Out Brown Record on back	25-100
	Franken Berry (General Mills)			CB302	Superman Action Poster in-pack	10-20
CB201	Star Wars Stickers	30-40		CB310	Huskies (Post)	20-30
CB202	Wacky Races	15-25		CB320	Ice Cream Cones Chocolate (General Mills)	15-25
CB210	Freakies (Ralston), 1981	20-60		CB325	Ice Cream Cones Vanilla (General Mills)	15-25
CB211	PVC Freakies characters in-pack	30-75		CB330	Instant Ralston (Ralston)	30-50
	Freakies (Ralston), 2nd introduction 1989			CB331	Commander Corey Space Patrol fronts	600-800
CB216	Hologram boxes	10-20		CB332	Cadet Happy Space Patrol fronts	400-600
	Froot Loops (Kellogg)			CB333	Space Patrol premium offers	300-500
CB221	Banana Splits Flashlight Offer	45-110		CB334	Tom Mix Trading Post backs	300-400
CB222	Banana Splits Poster Offer	50-125		CB340	Jean La Foote's Cinnamon Crunch	15-20
CB223	Banana Splits Ring in-pack (4 different)	50-125		CB350	Kellogg's Corn Flakes, vintage	20-50
CB224	Hanna Barbera offers on front & back	20-100		CB351	Atomic Submarine offer	50-75
CB225	Hologram boxes	10-20		CB352	Baseball Sun Visors	75-100
CB230	Frosty O's (General Mills)	10-25		CB353	Bullwinkle or Jay Ward characters	60-75
CB231	Dudley Do-Right on front	40-75		CB354	Chiquita Banana Cloth Doll	60-75
CB240	Fruit Brute (General Mills)	20-25		CB355	Eisenhower/Stevenson Vote	100-125
CB250	G.I. Joe Action Stars	20-35		CB356	Flying Superman	150-200
	Grape-Nut Flakes (Post)			CB357	Hanna-Barbera character offers	25-150
CB261	Bugs Bunny or Warner Bros. characters on front & back	25-100		CB358	Norman Rockwell kids painting fronts	25-65
CB262	Fury Neckerchief Set	75-100		CB359	Space Cadet Equipment (cut-out package backs)	100-150
CB263	Hopalong Cassidy offers on front & back	100-275		CB360	Superman Action Poster	75-100
				CB361	Superman Belt/Buckle	300-400
CB264	Mighty Mouse offers on front & back	50-150		CB362	Superman Krypton Rocket Launcher	200-250

	CB142		CB141		CB150		CB170		CB171

CB201

CB211

CB250

CB270

CB280

CB363	Superman Records	50-100
CB364	Superman Space Satellite	250-300
CB365	Sweetheart Doll	60-75
CB366	Tom Corbett membership kit	150-300
CB367	Yogi Bear Birthday Box	150-200
CB370	Kellogg's Raisin Bran, vintage	20-60
CB371	Batman Rubber Ring in-pack	75-100
CB372	Disney joinies	50-200
CB373	Monkees offers on front & back	75-150
CB380	Kix (General Mills), vintage	10-50
CB381	Railroad	50-75
CB390	Krinkles (Post)	175-400
CB400	Life (Quaker) w/Mikie's picture	5-30
	Lucky Charms (General Mills)	
CB411	Star Wars	10-40
CB412	Star Wars stickers	30-40
CB420	Mighty Mouse Cereal	10-75
CB430	Moonstones (Ralston)	20-40
CB440	Mr. T (Quaker)	25-60
CB450	Mr. Wonderful Surprise (General Mills)	25-50
CB460	Nerds Grape 'n Strawberry (Ralston)	10-20
CB470	Nerds Orange 'n Cherry (Ralston)	10-20
CB480	O.J.'s (Kellogg)	15-20
CB490	OK's (Kellogg)	30-50
CB491	Yogi Bear on front	100-400
CB500	PEP Wheat Flakes (Kellogg), vintage	20-60
CB501	Donald Duck Living Toy Ring	150-200
CB502	Freedom Train	50-75
CB503	Game backs	20-60
CB504	Magno-Power '50 Ford	100-125
CB505	Quick Draw McGraw Flicker Picture Ring	50-75
CB506	Tom Corbett package backs	100-200
CB507	Tom Corbett package fronts	100-300
CB510	Pink Panther Flakes (Post)	75-150
	Post Toasties Corn Flakes	
CB521	Baseball Cards (200 different cards)	75-100

CB522	Bugs Bunny or Warner Bros. characters	
	on front & back	200-400
CB523	Football Trading Cards	60-75
CB524	Hopalong Cassidy offer on front & back	100-400
CB525	Mighty Mouse offers on front & back	50-150
CB526	Monkees Doll offer	75-100
CB527	Monkees Finger Doll Offer	100-500
CB528	Roy Rogers Ranch Set	200-250
CB529	Roy Rogers & Trigger Pop-Out Card	200-600
CB530	Roy Rogers offers on front & back	100-600
	Post's 40% Bran Flakes	
CB541	Baseball cards on back	60-75
CB542	Roy Rogers & Trigger Pop-Out Card	200-600
	Post's Raisin Bran	
CB551	Captain Video Spaceman	150-200
CB552	Hopalong Cassidy offers	100-400
CB553	Monkees Mobile Car offer	75-100
CB554	Roy & Dale record offer	250-400
CB555	Roy Rogers pop-up cards	200-600
CB560	Puffa Puffa Rice (Kellogg)	15-60
CB561	Banana Splits Flashlight Offer	75-100
CB570	Punch Crunch (Quaker)	25-75
CB580	Puppets (Nabisco)	15-50
CB581	Donald	15-25
CB582	Mickey	15-25
CB583	Winnie the Pooh	25-50
CB590	Quake (Quaker)	15-100
	Quaker Oats	
CB601	Gabby Hayes Comics	50-75
CB602	Roy Rogers Branding Iron Ring	75-100
CB603	Roy Rogers Cup	50-75
CB604	Roy Rogers Deputy Sheriff's Badge	75-100
CB605	Roy Rogers Microscope Ring	75-100
	Quaker Puffed Rice	
CB611	Distance finder	75-125
CB612	Dog cards	75-125

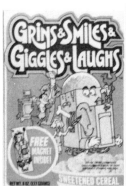
CB291

CB325

CB333

CB333

CB350

CB356

CB362

CB361

CB359

CB370

CB613	Gabby Hayes Clipper Ship	100-150
CB614	Gabby Hayes Western Wagons	100-150
CB615	Model Farm	35-50
CB616	Sgt. Preston Pedometer	150-200
CB617	Sgt. Preston Police Whistle	200-300
CB618	Sgt. Preston Records	150-175
CB619	Sgt. Preston Yukon Trail	100-150
CB620	Space Flight to Moon	60-75
CB621	Square inch of land	150-200
CB622	Trail Goggles	100-150
CB630	Quaker Puffed Wheat (same offers as Quaker Puffed Rice)	
CB650	Quangaroos (Quaker)	50-100
CB660	Quisp (Quaker)	15-100
	Rice Chex (Ralston)	
CB671	Space Patrol offers	150-450
	Rice Honeys (Nabisco)	
CB681	Beatles Rub-ons	150-550

CB682	Beatles Yellow Submarine w/stickers	200-550
CB683	Disney characters offers & prizes	25-100
CB684	Prehistoric Mammals or Dinosaurs and prizes on front & back	25-75
CB685	Rin Tin Tin Hero Medal	75-100
CB686	Rin Tin Tin Mask	100-125
CB687	Rin Tin Tin Masks	50-100
CB689	Rin Tin Tin Signal Flashlight	60-75
CB690	Rin Tin Tin Telegraph Key	75-100
CB691	Winnie the Pooh character spoon riders	15-75
CB700	Rice Krinkles (Post)	10-75
CB701	1966 Mustangs Free Inside	50-75
CB702	Bugs Bunny or Warner Bros. characters on front & back	25-100
	Rice Krispies (Kellogg)	
CB711	Hanna Barbera character offers	15-75
CB712	Howdy Doody	100-200
CB713	Smokey the Bear Cut-Out Mask	25-50

CB381

CB412

CB412

CB430

CB440

CB480

CB490

CB504

CB510

CB521

CB521	CB581-3	CB630

CB621

CB714	Monkees offers and prizes	75-150	CB772	Treasure Map offer	125-175
CB715	Snap, Krackle, Pop ring offer	125-200	CB773	Wild Bill Hickok Rifles	150-200
CB716	Woody Woodpecker Door Knocker	25-50	CB774	Wild Bill Hickok Marshal Badge/	
CB717	Woody Woodpecker offers	15-75		Indian Pictures	150-200
CB718	Yogi Bear Iron-On in-pack (6 different)	15-50	CB775	Wild Bill Hickok on front	125-175
	Shredded Wheat (Nabisco)		CB776	Wild Bill Hickok w/Superman	
CB721	Lionel Train offers on front & back	50-150		Rocket Launcher	200-300
CB722	Lionel Train pop-up cards	100-175	CB777	Wild Bill Hickok Western Wagons	150-200
CB723	Promotion for Straight Arrow show	75-125		Sugar Crisp (Post)	
CB724	Rin Tin Tin Rifle Pen	100-150	CB781	Baseball Cards	50-150
CB725	Rin Tin Tin Televiewer	100-150	CB782	Bugs Bunny or Waner Bros. characters	25-100
CB726	Rin Tin Tin Walkie Talkie	100-125	CB783	Dick Tracy Magic Decoder	75-100
CB727	Straight Arrow premium offers	150-200	CB784	Mighty Mouse box on front	150-200
CB728	Straight Arrow TV Theatre	75-100	CB785	Mighty Mouse offers	75-150
CB730	Shredded Wheat Juniors (Nabisco)	30-75	CB786	Railroad Emblems	75-100
CB731	Rin Tin Tin & Runny offers and prizes	75-150	CB787	Roy Rogers Record offer	150-200
CB732	Spoonmen offers and prizes	15-50	CB788	Roy Rogers & Trigger Pop-out cards	150-200
CB740	Sir Grapefellow (General Mills)	50-75	CB789	Spy-Master Command Belt	100-150
CB750	Strawberry Shortcake (General Mills)	10-30		Sugar Frosted Flakes (Kellogg)	
	Street Kids		CB791	Superman offers	100-450
CB761	Heathcliff	10-30	CB800	Sugar Jets (General Mills)	10-60
CB762	Raisin People	10-30	CB801	Disneyland Park Light-Up	50-150
	Sugar Corn Pops (Kellogg)		CB810	Sugar Krinkles (Post)	30-60
CB771	Jingles on front	100-150			

CB671

CB686

CB681

CB717

CB717

CB789

CB787

CB822

CB821

CB801

CB811

CB841

CB850

CB930

CB963

CB956

CB964

CB980

CB990

CB910	Twinkles (General Mills)	25-75
CB911	Bullwinkle or Jay Ward characters	25-100
CB920	Wackies (General Mills)	15-50
CB930	Waffelos (Ralston)	15-30
CB935	Waffelos Blueberry	15-50
	Wheat Chex (Ralston) (same as Rice Chex)	
	Wheat Honeys (Nabisco) (same as Rice Honeys)	
	Wheaties (General Mills)	
CB951	6-Power Microscope	60-75
CB952	Disney comic masks (8 different), ea	50-75
CB953	Disneyland Light-Up boxes (18 diff), ea	100-200
CB954	Esther Williams Pool	75-100
CB955	Foreign License Plates	60-75
CB956	Hopalong Cassidy picture back	400-500
CB957	License Plate offers	75-100
CB958	Lone Ranger Hike-O-Meter offer	150-250
CB959	Lone Ranger life-size poster offer	150-300
CB960	Lone Ranger Masks (8 different), each	125-175
CB961	Lone Ranger offers	100-400
CB962	Mickey Mouse Club record	100-250
CB963	Other record fronts	60-100
CB964	Walt Disney miniature comic books (4 set offer)	100-200
CB970	Wheaties Excel (General Mills)	15-25
CB980	Winnie the Pooh Great Honey Crunchers (Nabisco)	50-75
CB990	Wishing Stars (Post)	50-125

CHARACTER & PROMOTIONAL GLASSES
by Carol Markowski

Decorating glasses with brand names or characters dates back to the Coca-Cola fountain glasses with syrup line produced before the turn of the century. Around 1930 glasses featuring comic and radio characters were offered as premiums. Character and promotional glassware really took off in the 1950s as companies began looking for ways to make their products stand out in the supermarket crowd. Their success inspired oil companies to begin offering collectible glasses as gas station premiums.

The popularity of collectible glassware waned in the 1960s. The few glasses issued were usually mail-in premiums produced by cereal and drink mix manufacturers.

The early 1970s, however, saw the rise of what would be the biggest distributor of premium glasses - the "fast food chain." The Pepsi Cola Company was first to recognize the promotional possibilities in 1973 when they issued 18 glasses bearing the images of different Warner Brothers cartoon characters. These glasses were made available to any fast food restaurant which offered Pepsi Cola as a selection. The idea was so successful other soft drink companies followed suit to remain competitive. Glasses have continued to be issued sp radically throughout the 1980s, but began to be displaced by the cheaper, larger plastic cup.

CB811	Roy Rogers Western Medals	100-150
CB820	Sugar Pops (Kellogg)	2-50
CB821	Jingles on front	100-150
CB822	Wild Bill Hickok on front	125-175
CB830	Sugar Rice Krinkles (Post)	30-60
CB840	Sugar Smacks (Kellogg)	10-50
CB841	Quick Draw McGraw on front	100-200
CB850	Sugar Stars (Kellogg)	30-50
	Super Sugar Crisps (Post)	
CB861	Famous Monsters Glow In Dark Posters	25-50
CB862	Sabrina's Super Bounce Crystal Ball (75th Anni)	25-50
CB863	The Three Stooges Poster Offer	25-50
CB870	Swiss Mixed Cereal Love (Peter Max)	25-100
CB880	Top 3 (Post)	20-30
CB881	Bugs Bunny	75-150
CB890	Triple Snack (Kellogg)	15-50
CB891	Boo Boo on front	25-100
CB900	Trix (General Mills) Star Wars sticker set	30-40

Glass collecting is a hobby almost anyone can afford. The average collectible glass is still under $10, and valuable glasses can be found at yard and garage sales for 25¢-50¢.

Many isolated or test character glass issues, such as Sneaky Pete Li'l Abner, Popeye's Famous Fried Chicken Popeye character, and certain Disney sets are in strong demand at $30-$50 per glass.

The prices in this section are for Fine to Mint condition. In this case "Fine" means the item is complete with absolutely no chips or paint missing. Slightly faded graphics, minor scratches, out-of-register or bad silk screen jobs and similar shortcomings are factors that depreciate value and lower an item below Fine. The upper price is "Mint" - like-new condition, no scratches, never repaired, free of any defects whatsoever. Mint items were probably never used and especially never washed in a dishwasher.

Tomart's Price Guide to Character and Promotional Glasses offers a complete collector's price guide to collectible glasses from 1930 to 1990, with more than 3,000 color and b&w photos in 152 pages. See page 150 for ordering information.

A&W Family Restaurant
CH100	A&W Bear, "The Great Root Bear"	8-10
CH101	A&W Bear, "The Great Root Bear" (pitcher)	20-30

Actors
CH102	Marilyn Monroe	20-40
	All others	20-30

Al Capp
CH103	Daisy Mae	40-60
CH104	Joe Btsptflk	40-60
CH105	Li'l Abner	40-60
CH106	Mammy Yokum	40-60
CH107	Pappy Yokum	40-60
CH108	Sadie Hawkins	40-60
CH109	Kickapoo Joy Juice Glass	15-20

CH110 CH111 CH112

CH113 CH114 CH115

Al Capp Sneaky Pete's Hot Dogs 1975
CH110	Daisy Mae	30-60
CH111	Joe Btsptflk	30-60
CH112	Li'l Abner	30-60

CH113	Mammy Yokum	30-60
CH114	Pappy Yokum	30-60
CH115	Sadie Hawkins	30-60

Beatles
CH116	John	50-100
CH117	George	50-100
CH118	Paul	50-100
CH119	Ringo	50-100

CH120 CH121 CH128

Beatles Single Glasses
CH120	Mop Heads (not the Beatles)	25-45
CH121	Yellow Submarine graphics on this glass are not the same as the movie, looks like the record album cover, perhaps unofficial	100-150
CH122	Group (all four)	25-50

Coca-Cola
CH123	1976, reproduction gift pack of 4 flare glasses & a pewter holder	20-40

The Coca-Cola Company issued glasses to commemorate 25th and 50th anniversaries, grand openings of new plants, new contracts and officer presentations.

CH124	50th Anniversary, bell shape (dipped in gold)	150-250
CH125	Pewter, bell shape (only 1000 made)	150-250
CH126	Dura-Cast "Enjoy Coke" Pewter Mug (only 1000 made)	20-40
CH127	100th Anniversary, cocktail crystal/cut glass	10-20

Tiffany Style Glasses (stained glass) Promoting Coca-Cola
ENJOY COKE - The following is a tiffany style glass that says "Enjoy Coke."
CH128	Stained glass & filigree (w/sports figure Terry Bradshaw) (There is also a smilar glass w/the image of George Brett)	25-40

Dick Tracy (Domino's Pizza)
CH129	Dick Tracy	100-200

DISNEY
Alice in Wonderland
CH130	#1 Alice	20-25
CH131	#2 Alice & Eaglet	20-25
CH132	#3 Alice & Tweedledee & Tweedledum	20-25
CH133	#4 Alice & Walrus & Carpenter	20-25
CH134	#5 Alice & Caterpillar	20-25
CH135	#6 Alice & Cheshire Cat	20-25
CH136	#7 Mad Hatter & March Hare	20-25
CH137	#8 Queen of Hearts & Rabbit	20-25

Disneyland Juice Set 1955
Has logos for each land on the reverse.
CH138	Mickey Frontierland	20-30
CH139	Tinker Bell Fantasyland	20-30
CH140	Donald Adventureland	20-30
CH141	Goofy Tommorrowland	20-30

Lady & the Tramp Series
Lady and Tramp's images appear on the front of all of the glasses in this set with the supporting characters in silhouette or two color drawings on the reverse. There are two sizes, 5-1/4" & 6-1/4"
CH142	Jock (the Scotty)	60-100

CH130-7

CH142-9   CH142

CH129

CH138-41

CH160	Flunkey	60-100
CH161	King Louie	60-100
CH162	Mowgli	60-100
CH163	Shere Khan	60-100

Disneyland Edition (Coke)

CH164	Mickey	20-50
CH165	Minnie	20-50
CH166	Donald	20-50
CH167	Pluto	20-50
CH168	Goofy	20-50
CH169	Dumbo	20-50

Harvey Cartoons Collector Series (Pepsi)

CH170	Hot Stuff (no sponsor, white letters)	15-25
CH171	Casper (no sponsor, white letters)	15-25
CH172	Wendy (no sponsor, white letters)	15-25
CH173	Big Baby Huey (no sponsor, white letters)	15-25

McDonald's Characters (no date, no McDonald's logo)

These glasses were found with the word "Rejected" on them in red crayon. They could be prototypes.

CH174	Ronald	50-100
CH175	Captain Crook	50-100
CH176	Major McCheese	50-100

PEPSI COLA

Pepsi Stain Glass Look (Tiffany)

CH177	Pepsi Cola 75th Anniversary Commemorative Set, in presentation box. Box contains shaker and 12 glasses. Six 8 oz glasses and six 12 oz glasses, dated 1898, 1905, 1906, 1950, 1962 & 1973. Set	150-200
CH178	Individual Glasses	5-8
CH179	Shaker	15-25

Pepsi, through its local bottling compaines, distributed many glasses with the PEPSI trademark celebrating local events.

CH180	Hot Sam's	20-30
CH181	Food Service	20-30

Popeye's Pals

CH184	Popeye	8-12
CH185	Olive Oyl	8-12
CH186	Brutus	8-12
CH187	Swee'Pea	8-12

Popeye's Fried Chicken, 10th Anniversary (Pepsi)

CH191	Popeye	12-15
CH192	Olive Oyl	12-15
CH193	Brutus	12-15
CH194	Swee'Pea	12-15

Robin Hood, Canadian

CH202	#1 Robin Hood	15-40
CH203	#2 King Richard	15-40
CH204	#3 Friar Tuck	15-40
CH205	#4 Little John	15-40
CH206	#5 Maid Marian	15-40
CH207	#6 Will Scarlett	15-40
CH208	#7 Prince John	15-40
CH209	#8 Sheriff of Nottingham	15-40

Sparkie GPG Company, Cincinnati, Ohio

CH210	Sparkie with drum	15-30
CH211	Sparkie with trombone	15-30
CH212	Sparkie with trumpet	15-30

CH143	Trusty (the Hound)	60-100
CH144	Bull (the Bulldog)	60-100
CH145	Pedro (the Chihuahua)	60-100
CH146	Peg (the Pomeranian)	60-100
CH147	Si & Am (the Cats)	60-100
CH148	Toughy (the Mutt)	60-100
CH149	Dachsie (the Dachshund)	60-100

Jungle Book (Pepsi)

Nowhere on these glasses does the name "Jungle Book" appear, nor is there a date on the glass. You would have to be familiar with the characters of this Disney version of the Richard Kipling story.

CH150	Bagheera (the panther)	60-100
CH151	Baloo (the bear)	40-60
CH152	Colonel Hathi (the elephant)	40-60
CH153	Kaa (the snake)	60-100
CH154	King Louie (the monkey)	40-60
CH155	Mowgli (the boy)	40-60
CH156	Rama (the wolf)	40-60
CH157	Shere Khan (the tiger)	60-100

Jungle Book (Pepsi) Canadian

CH158	Bagheera	60-100
CH159	Baloo	60-100

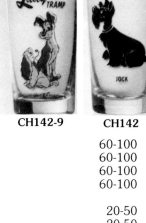

CH151   CH150   CH152   CH153

CH154   CH156   CH157   CH156

CH164-9

CH184-7

CH191-4

CH174-6

CH213	Sparkie with xylophone		15-30
CH214	Sparkie with ukelele		15-30
CH215	Sparkie with piano		15-30
CH216	Sparkie with saxophone		15-30
CH217	Sparkie playing glasses		15-30

SPORTS
Baseball
Super Action Series (baseball) Pepsi 1982

The baseball set was issued in Kansas and Missouri. George Brett is a little more difficult to find in circulation because he's a native of Kansas and most Kansas dwellers hold on to him.

CH301	George Brett	25-40
CH302	Jim Rice	25-40
CH303	Reggie Jackson	25-40
CH304	Tom Seaver	25-40
CH305	Mike Schmidt	25-40

CH306	Dave Parker	25-40

Horse Racing

There are several series of glasses based on horse racing events: Preakness, Jim Beam Stakes and, of course, the Kentucky Derby. Derby glasses are the most collectible & command the highest prices. These official Derby glasses are sold at the concession stands at Chruchill Downs. There are other nonofficial glasses sold at local bars in the Churchill Downs area.

CH307	1950 reg. frosted - Middleground	50-100
CH308	1951 reg. frosted - Count Turf	100-200
CH309	1952 reg. frosted - Hillgail	50-100
CH310	1953 reg. frosted - Dark Star	25-50
CH311	1954 reg. frosted - Determined	25-50
CH312	1955 reg. frosted - Swaps	25-50
CH313	1956 reg. frosted - Needles	20-40
CH314	1957 reg. frosted - Iron Liege	20-40
CH315	1958 frosted gold - Tim Tam	20-40
CH316	1958 - Iron Liege	50-75
CH317	1959 reg. frosted - Tommy Lee	10-25
CH318	1960 reg. frosted - Venetian Way	10-25
CH319	1961 reg. frosted - Carry Back	10-25
CH320	1962 reg. frosted - Decidedly	10-25
CH321	1963 reg. frosted - Chateaugay	10-25
CH322	1964 reg. frosted - Northern Dancer	10-25
CH323	1965 reg. frosted - Lucky Debonair	10-25

From 1966 through 1989 they range from $2.00 to $10.00. There are some errors & color variations that may alter this price range.

Star Trek, Dr. Pepper 1976
From the animated TV series

CH325	Kirk (cartoon)	20-30
CH326	Spock (cartoon)	20-30
CH327	McCoy (cartoon)	20-30
CH328	Enterprise	20-30

Star Trek, Dr. Pepper 1978

CH329	Kirk	35-50
CH330	Spock	35-50
CH331	McCoy	35-50
CH332	Enterprise	35-50

Star Trek: The Motion Picture Coke 1980

CH333	Kirk/McCoy/Spock	15-30
CH334	Ilia/Decker	15-30
CH335	Enterprise	15-30

Sunday Funnies, no sponsor 1976 open distribution

CH336	Broom Hilda	80-150

Super Heroes

CH337	Batman, 1960s, "Crack Whack Zok"	10-20
CH338	Robin, 1960s, "The Boy Wonder"	10-20

Superman, National Periodical Publications, M. Polaner and Son Inc., Newark, NJ 1964 5-3/4" or 4-1/4"

The label on this glass said "Polaner's TV Treat Pure Concord Grape Jam."

CH339	Superman Uses X-ray Vision	50-80
CH340	Superman in Action	50-80
CH341	Superman Finds the Spaceship	50-80
CH342	Superman to the Rescue	50-80
CH343	Superman Fighting a Dragon	50-80

CH301   CH302   CH303   CH304   CH305   CH306

CH353   CH336

CH313   CH315   CH317   CH320   CH321   CH322

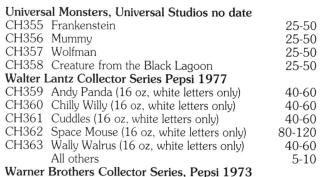

CH180   CH337   CH338

CH344	Superman	50-80

Super Series (Super Heroes) Pepsi 1976

This set of 14 comes with both the DC & NPP logos (Detective Comics & National Periodical Publications).

CH345	Batgirl	8-12
CH346	Batman	12-20
CH347	Green Arrow	25-50
CH348	Green Lantern	25-50
CH349	Joker	30-60
CH350	Penguin	30-60
CH351	Riddler	30-60
CH352	All others	5-8

Terry Toons

CH353	Mighty Mouse	350-400

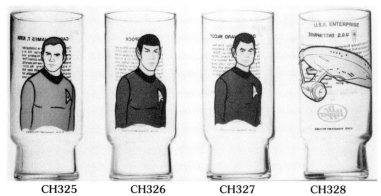

CH325   CH326   CH327   CH328

CH329   CH330   CH331   CH332

Universal Monsters, Universal Studios no date

CH355	Frankenstein	25-50
CH356	Mummy	25-50
CH357	Wolfman	25-50
CH358	Creature from the Black Lagoon	25-50

Walter Lantz Collector Series Pepsi 1977

CH359	Andy Panda (16 oz, white letters only)	40-60
CH360	Chilly Willy (16 oz, white letters only)	40-60
CH361	Cuddles (16 oz, white letters only)	40-60
CH362	Space Mouse (16 oz, white letters only)	80-120
CH363	Wally Walrus (16 oz, white letters only)	40-60
	All others	5-10

Warner Brothers Collector Series, Pepsi 1973

This 1973 Warner Brothers cartoon set comes in both black letters & white letters and thick glass (Brockway Glass Company) & thin glass (Federal Glass Company). The same 18 images appear on a 15 oz thin (Federal) set of glasses. All come in a 16 oz size. These are the most valuable:

CH375	Cool Cat	
	Black & white, thick	4-6
	Black, thin	5-8
	White, thin	25-40
CH380	Foghorn Leghorn	
	Black & white, thick	4-6
	Black, thin	8-10
	White, thin	25-40
CH385	Henry Hawk	
	Black & white, thick	5-8
	Black, thin	8-10
	White, thin	25-40
CH390	Slow Poke Rodrigues	
	Black & white, thick	5-8
	Black, thin	8-10
	White, thin	25-40

See also: **Batman; Beatles; Disney; Elvis; Marilyn Monroe; Star Trek; Star Wars**

COINS   consultant Jim Hargett

A coin's value is determined by a complex combination of rarity, age, condition, and demand. Collectors also look for the infrequent mistake or anomaly. As in any manufacturing process, many things can go wrong during minting. A blank, or planchet, can be flawed to begin with. A planchet can slip by

CH348	CH349	CH350	CH351	CH355	CH356	CH357	CH358

to remain blank through the entire process, or it can be clipped during punching, resulting in a coin with a "bite" out of it. Coins can be struck off-center or can be double struck if not promptly ejected from the press. However, the anomalies which elude a mint's many inspections are few and far between.

Coin grading has always been highly subjective. To make the process more precise, the American Numismatic Association introduced a grading scale from 1-70 in 1977. The scale also matches the numeric values to more traditional descriptive terms, from About Good (AG-3) to Mint State (MS-60 to 70). Although these measures have been a big help, subjectivity inevitably remains.

Mint Mark refers to the letter associated with the date to indicate the producing mint; D - Denver, S - San Francisco, no letter - Philadelphia.

This section will be limited to U.S. coins in general circulation. Values listed are from fine to uncirculated. Proof set values are for sealed sets in original mint packaging.

Penny - Lincoln

CN103	1951S	1-2
CN107	1952S	1-2
CN110	1953	2-5
CN145	1960 small date	1-2
CN188	1970S	2-5

Nickel - Jefferson

CN201	1950	1-2
CN202	1950D	5-10
CN205	1951	1-2
CN206	1951D	1-2
CN207	1951S	1-3
CN211	1952D	1-2

Dime - Roosevelt

CN300	1950	1-4
CN301	1950D	1-4
CN303	1950S	8-20
CN305	1951	1-3
CN306	1951D	1-3
CN307	1951S	4-12
CN310	1952	1-3
CN311	1952D	1-2
CN312	1952S	1-4
CN315	1953	1-2
CN320	1955	1-3
CN331	1957D	1-2

Quarter - Washington

CN400	1950	2-6
CN401	1950D	2-6
CN402	1950S	3-10
CN405	1951	2-6
CN406	1951D	2-5
CN407	1951S	3-12
CN412	1952S	2-10
CN417	1953S	2-5
CN426	1955D	3-6

Half Dollar - Franklin

CN600	1950	5-50
CN601	1950D	3-30
CN605	1951	2-18
CN606	1951D	4-40
CN607	1951S	4-38
CN612	1952S	4-40
CN615	1953	3-32
CN617	1953S	3-25
CN622	1954S	2-18
CN625	1955	2-17

Half Dollar - Kennedy

CN781	1970D	4-20

Proof Sets

CN801	1950	385
CN802	1951	260
CN803	1952	150
CN804	1953	105
CN805	1954	50
CN806	1955	50
CN807	1956	28
CN808	1957	15
CN809	1958	20
CN810	1959	15
CN811	1986	25

Prestige Sets

CN820	1983	75
CN821	1984	40
CN822	1985	30
CN823	1986	30
CN824	1987	22
CN825	1988	50
CN826	1989	58

COMIC BOOKS   by Howard Lowery

Nostalgia undoubtably plays a major part in the recent interest in, and subsequent increase in value of, collectible comic books. Almost everyone has fond memories of comics from their youth, yet few people, for one reason or another, still possess their original collections. So they set about to recapture the magic (at a substantially greater cost) and, hopefully, make a solid financial investment, too.

Comic book collecting is one of the more organized fields among those areas of popular culture to undergo spectacular growth in collector interest in the past few decades. Comic book shops offering new titles and back issues now number in the thousands. Specialized price guides are published quarterly, even monthly, to keep collectors abreast of changing prices and new trends.

The market can be volatile, especially in regards to issues published in the 70s. Prices can fluctuate dramatically as interest in a character, story line, or artist waxes and wanes. It isn't surprising to see a comic book go from ignored to red hot in the space of a few months or years, and the inverse can be true as well. A few guidelines may help the buyer to choose wisely:

CO141   CO070

CO083   CO092

1) Condition is all important. Collectors seek comics as close to mint condition as possible; the fewer defects there are, the more desirable the comic. And age is *not* a factor. Grading rules are identical for all comics, whether they be from the 50s or the 90s.

2) Certain issues within a title are more valuable than others. First issues are always desirable, as are first appearances of popular characters. Issues which feature the work of a popular artist or writer are sought after, as are ones in which an established character dies or gets a new costume. Even an appearance by a favorite villain (i.e., The Joker) can affect an issue's value.

3) Keep abreast of what is happening in the field. Like any market, the comic field is constantly changing. One way to learn of these changes is to read periodicals devoted to the field; The Comic Buyers Guide, a trade newspaper, is published weekly and is available at many comic shops.

4) Use common sense and stick to mainstream titles, publishers, and characters that have proven their staying power and popularity over the decades. Comic book collectors have been subjected at times to the unremitting hyperbole of publishers and dealers — *hot* titles, *hot* artists, *rare* variant editions, etc. Most of the samples cited in this section are comic books that have stood the test of time and held the attention of serious collectors almost from the day they were published.

5) Keep looking. Thought it is a much rarer occurrence now than, say, ten years ago, valuable comics can still be found in unlikely places at extremely low prices. And garage sales are good places to hunt; you'll never know when you'll stumble across something really valuable.

The comics listed in this section are all in fine to very fine condition. Abbreviations: app—appearance; EC—E. C. Comics. All values listed are actual sales at auction in the year preceeding publication.

CO050   Adventure #210, 1955, 1st app Krypto
        the Super Dog   430

CO081   CO082

CO055   Adventure #247, Apr 1958, 1st app
        Legion of Super Heroes   720
CO060   All Star Comics #56, Dec-Jan 1950-51,
        Justice Society app   220
CO070   Amazing Fantasy #15, Aug 1962,
        1st Spider-Man app   1400
CO081   Amazing Spider-Man #1, Mar 1963,
        retells origin   1360
CO082   Amazing Spider-Man #2, 1963,
        1st app Vulture   430
CO083   Amazing Spider-Man #3, 1963,
        1st app Dr. Octopus   300
CO088   Amazing Spider-Man #14, 1964,
        1st app Green Goblin   267
CO092   Amazing Spider-Man #50, 1966,
        1st app Kingpin   63
CO094   Amazing Spider-Man #129, Feb 1974,
        1st app Punisher   117
CO098   Amazing Spider-Man Annual #1, 1963,
        1st app Sinister Six   72
CO111   Aquaman #1, Jan-Feb 1962   78
CO121   Archie Comics Annual #1, 1950 (rare)   257
CO131   Atom #1, Jun-Jul 1962   171
CO141   Avengers #1, Sep 1963, 1st app Avengers   375
CO144   Avengers #4, Mar 1964, 1st Silver Age
        app Captain America   192
CO150   Batman, Son of the Demon, 1987, hardcover
        graphic novel signed by Mike Barr
        & Jerry Bingham   99

CO151   CO154

CO151   Batman: The Dark Knight Returns #1,
        Mar 1986, 1st printing   25
CO154   Batman: The Killing Joke, 1988, 1st printing 15
CO161   Blue Beetle #1, Jun 1967, Ditko art & story   21
CO171   Brave & the Bold #1, Aug-Sep 1955,
        Viking Prince by Kubert   270
CO174   Brave & the Bold #14, Oct-Nov 1957,

CO341   CO361

CO201   CO261

CO373   CO404

CO471	Star Wars #1, Jul 1977, rare version w/35¢ cover price	140
CO489	Strange Adventures #9, Jun 1951, 1st app Captain Comet	280
CO495	Strange Adventures #180, 1964, 1st app Animal Man	77
CO498	Strange Adventures #190, 1965, 1st Animal Man in costume	51
CO511	Strange Tales #1, Jun 1951, pre-superhero Atlas horror	270
CO517	Strange Tales #101, Oct 1962, 1st Kirby Human Torch	140
CO520	Strange Tales #110, Jul 1963, 1st app Dr. Strange	120
CO525	Strange Tales #115, Dec 1963, origin Dr. Strange	60

CO410   CO531

CO531	Sub-Mariner #1, May 1968, origin Sub-Mariner	40
CO547	Superboy #7, Mar-Apr 1950, (rare)	209
CO555	Superboy #68, Oct-Nov 1958, 1st app Bizarro	64
CO558	Superman #76, 1951, Batman & Superman discover each other's secret ID's	235
CO566	Tales From the Crypt #20, Oct-Nov 1950, famous EC horror	205
CO569	Tales of Suspense #39, Mar 1963, 1st app Iron Man	460
CO570	Tales of Suspense #40, Apr 1963, new armor for Iron Man	235
CO575	Tales of Suspense #59, Nov 1964, Iron Man/ Captain America double feature begins	48
CO587	Tales to Astonish #27, Jan 1962, 1st app Antman	385
CO595	Tales to Astonish #35, Sep 1962,	

2201   2203

DA341   DA342

DA520   DA501   DA504   DA502   DA503

	2nd Antman app (1st in costume)	270
CO601	Teenage Mutant Ninja Turtles #1, 1984, 1st printing	163
CO616	Uncle Scrooge 4-Color #386, Mar 1952, Carl Barks' art	180
CO622	Vault of Horror #12, Apr-May 1950, EC horror	450
CO632	Weird Science #12, May-Jun 1950, EC science fiction	290
CO641	X-Men #1, Sep 1963, 1st app X-Men & Magneto	530
CO653	X-Men #93, Aug 1975, 2nd app new X-Men	60

DAKIN & SIMILAR
CHARACTER FIGURES   by Susan Hufferd

"Dakin" refers to a brand of hollow vinyl figure pioneered by the R. Dakin Co. There are several variations... articulated and non-articulated, cloth clothing and molded costumes.

During the 1970s I.A. Sutton & Sons, Inc. of New York made several jointed characters which are highly collectible. In 1970 they sold four Hanna Barbera characters: The Banana Splits - Fleagle Beagle the Dog; Snorky the Elephant; Drooper the Lion; and Bingo the Bear. In 1972, Sutton put out a favorite character from Harvey Famous Cartoons, Casper the Friendly Ghost, and added another Hanna Barbera Character, Scooby Doo.

Not to be confused with I.A. Sutton & Sons is A.D. Sutton & Sons, Inc. Probably in the 1970s, A.D. Sutton made a series called Walt Disney Golden Fantasy. These characters are about 7" tall with cloth clothing and are jointed at the head and arms. They include standing poses of Donald, Mickey, and Pluto, and sitting poses of Peter Pan, Tinker Bell, and Captain Hook. The last three are the most desirable of the group.

In 1980 several different Hanna Barbera characters appeared. Although articulated and Dakin-like in appearance, the manufacturer has not been identified. Serious collectors refer to these as the "CW's" because the numbers on the back of the characters start with CW. These characters are about 6-1/2" tall, and include Fred Flintstone with the older style squared-off nose, Barney Rubble, Dino, Yogi Bear,

2207   2214

DA345   DA346

Huckleberry Hound, Scooby Doo, and his son Scrapper. These have become a must for the jointed character collector. Both the Dakin and CW's Hanna Barbera characters are strikingly similar. Also like Dakin, CW put out the same characters in a hard rubber 3-4" version and a squeeze figure jointed at the head.

Over the years The Knickerbocker Toy Company also produced, in bags and boxes, Snoopy and Belle in cloth costumes. Different outfits could be purchased separately. These are about 7" tall and fit in nicely with the Dakins and Suttons.

All these figures were produced between 1968 and 1984. Most cost less than $2 new but have captured the imagination of collectors.

The following values are for items in excellent condition without package to mint condition in mint package.

DAKIN

DA211	Big Boy	20-50
DA221	Bozo the Clown	15-30

Dakin Fun Farm DA231-34

DA231	Tasmanian Devil	10-35
DA232	Elmer Fudd	10-30
DA233	Mighty Mouse	35-70
DA234	Deputy Dawg	30-55

Dakin T.V. Cartoon Theater DA241-56

DA241	Bugs Bunny	8-20
DA242	Daffy Duck	8-20
DA243	Wile E. Coyote	8-20
DA244	Road Runner	8-20
DA245	Yosemite Sam	10-25
DA246	Speedy Gonzales	8-20
DA247	Tweety Bird	8-20
DA248	Sylvester	8-20
DA249	Porky Pig	10-25
DA251	Dudley Do-Right	10-25
DA252	Rocky the Flying Squirrel	15-45
DA253	Bullwinkle	15-45
DA254	Underdog	15-40
DA255	Popeye	15-40
DA256	Olive Oyl	15-38

Disney DA261-72

DA261	Mickey Mouse	10-20
DA262	Minnie Mouse	10-20
DA263	Donald Duck, bent legs	20-35
DA264	Donald Duck, straight legs	10-25
DA265	Goofy	10-20
DA266	Pluto	10-20
DA267	Huey	15-25
DA268	Louie	15-25
DA269	Dewey	15-25
DA270	Pinocchio	15-25
DA271	Dumbo	8-15
DA272	Bambi	15-25
DA275	Freddy Fast Gas	15-35

Hanna-Barbera DA281-92

DA281	Fred Flintstone	12-30
DA282	Barney Rubble	12-30
DA283	Dino	12-30
DA284	Pebbles	12-30
DA285	Bamm-Bamm	12-30
DA286	Baby Puss	30-65
DA287	Hoppy	30-65
DA289	Yogi Bear	20-45
DA290	Huckleberry Hound	20-45
DA291	Snagglepuss	30-65
DA292	Hokey Wolf	30-65
DA295	Stan Laurel	20-35
DA296	Oliver Hardy	20-35
DA308	Miss Liberty Bell	10-30
DA309	Mister Magoo	30-50
DA310	Pink Panther	10-20
DA315	Smokey Bear (Aim toothpate premium)	20-35

Warner Brothers DA330-49

DA330	Bugs Bunny	10-20
DA331	Bugs Bunny Happy Birthday	10-20
DA332	Bugs Bunny in stars and stripes	10-20
DA333	Daffy Duck	10-20

2208   2205

DA339   DA340   DA349

2261   2262   2258   2259   2254

DA285   DA287   DA283   DA291   DA284   DA290   DA289

DA261   DA262

DA334	Porky Pig w/black jacket	10-20
DA335	Porky Pig w/pink jacket	10-20
DA336	Sylvester the Cat	10-20
DA337	Tweety Bird, jointed arms	10-20
DA338	Tweety Bird, non-jointed arms	10-20
DA339	Wile E. Coyote	10-20
DA340	Road Runner	10-20
DA341	Yosemite Sam	10-25
DA342	Speedy Gonzales	10-20
DA343	Elmer Fudd w/black jacket	15-25
DA344	Elmer Fudd w/hunting outfit	20-45
DA345	Merlin the Magical Mouse	20-35
DA346	Second Banana, Merlin's nephew	20-35
DA347	Cool Cat	20-35
DA348	Pépé LePew	30-60
DA349	Foghorn Leghorn	30-60
DA350	Woodsy Owl	20-45
DA351	Woody Woodpecker	30-65

DURHAM

Mickey Mouse DA402-07

DA402	Chef	10-20
DA403	Cowboy	10-20
DA404	Drum Major	10-20
DA405	Ring Master	10-20
DA406	Sailor	10-20
DA407	Super Mickey	10-20

Walt Disney Characters on Safari DA410-12

DA410	Mickey Mouse	15-35
DA411	Donald Duck	15-35
DA412	Goofy	15-35

A.D. SUTTON & SONS

Walt Disney Golden Fantasy DA420-27

DA420	Mickey Mouse	15-35
DA421	Donald Duck	15-35
DA422	Pluto	15-35
DA423	Peter Pan	15-35
DA424	Tinkerbell	20-45
DA425	Captain Hook	15-35
DA426	Alice in Wonderland	15-35
DA427	Pinocchio	15-35

I.A. SUTTON & SONS, INC.

Bannana Splits, the DA501-04

DA501	Fleagle Beagle the Dog	15-35
DA502	Snorky the Elephant	15-35
DA503	Drooper the Lion	15-35
DA504	Bingo the Bear	15-35
DA510	Casper the Friendly Ghost	20-40
DA520	Scooby-Doo	20-40

DISNEYANA   by Tom Tumbusch

Any item associated with The Walt Disney Company or its affiliated operations, past or present, is considered to be Disneyana. What is utilitarian today will become collectible tomorrow. Certainly some segments of the total Disneyana spectrum are more popular than others. Disneyana is art. In most cases, it is good art which often reflects the popular culture of the era in which it was produced. Older pieces are recognized as art and are exhibited in some of the world's most famous museums. Yet, Disneyana is art anyone can own.

Disneyana has been produced in large quantities since the 1920s. There are millions of Disneyana items floating around out there to keep intriguing the collecting interest. Disneyana is found worldwide.

Disneyana is associated with Walt Disney, one of the world's best known and respected individuals. Even though a minute portion of Disneyana was created by him, Walt Disney continues to be a major driving force behind his company's characters long after his death in 1966.

Disneyana is still being produced. Some items are being manufactured as limited editions. Many are marketed by mail, thus creating a larger market for Disney collectibles with each passing day. With such an intense interest in Disney many items achieve substantial value increases within months after they are produced. *The Little Mermaid*, for example, is one of Disney's most merchandised and widely collected characters. The prices in this section are based on items sold at leading antique shows and flea markets, as well as toy and antique advertising shows. The range is from fine to mint condition.

Tomart's *Illustrated DISNEYANA Catalog and Price Guide* series is the complete guide to Disney collecting. The four volume series pictures more than 20,000 items, with 80 pages in full color, providing value estimates for more than 40,000 Disney items. See page 150 for ordering information.

America on Parade

America on Parade was a bicentennial historical pageant presented over 1200 times in parade form at Disneyland and Walt Disney World from June 1975 to September 1976. It employed a logo that was first designed for the July 1939 *Mickey Mouse Magazine* cover. The logo appeared on a large

DA741

DA750

DA711

DB407

DB451

DB255

DC618

DC650

DC940

DC636

DB156

DC955

variety of merchandise sold at the Disney theme parks. A few America on Parade items were sold nationwide.

DA711	Press giveaway mirror	50-250
DA740	Collector's plate, Walt Disney World (logo)	25-100
DA741	Plate, Disneyland (logo)	25-150
DA742	Plate, Disneyland (signing)	25-150
DA743	Plate, Disneyland (crossing)	25-150
DA744	Plate, Disneyland (Betsy Ross)	25-150
DA750	Porcelain bisque	50-800
DA751	Music box (logo)	20-85
DA752	Music box (Minute Man Mickey)	20-85

Banks

DB140	Dumbo, Leeds	10-35
DB141	Mickey, Leeds	10-35
DB142	Donald, standing, Leeds	10-35
DB143	Donald, sitting, Leeds	10-35
DB150	*Alice In Wonderland*, Leeds	10-35
DB155	Marx 5¢, 10¢ and 25¢ Register, tin litho	50-175
DB156	2nd National Duck Bank	50-175
DB160	Mickey Mouse Club, figural, ceramic	18-45
DB168	Western Donald, plastic	10-35
DB170	Uncle Scrooge, in bed	20-65
DB171	Clock, available in red, blue and yellow	10-35
DB178	Mouseclubhouse Treasury Bank, w/Mousekey, Mattel	25-90
DB179	Mickey Mouse swimming underwater	50-75

Bells

Tinker Bell became the symbol of the Disneyland TV show and naturally appeared on a number of souvenir bells.

| DB161 | Disneyland ceramic Tinker Bell (1950s) | 70-125 |
| DB162 | Tinker Bell musical bell set | 45-110 |

Books — Art and Animation

DB250	*The Art of Animation*, 1958, Golden	25-100
DB252	*The Art of Walt Disney*, 1973, Abrams, 1st Ed w/mylar dust jacket	100-150
DB253	*The Fine Art of Walt Disney's Donald Duck*, 1981, Another Rainbow, bound folio of paintings by Carl Barks	100-350
DB254	*Walt Disney's Uncle Scrooge McDuck: His Life and Times*, 1981, Celestial Arts	75-150
DB255	*Disney Animation — The Illusion of Life*, 1981, Abbeville	45-75

Books — Cut or Punch Out

DB318	*Alice In Wonderland*, 1951, #2194	60-110
DB319	*Peter Pan*, 1952, #2112	65-120
DB322	*Davy Crockett*, 1955, #1943	45-95
DB325	*Let's Build Disneyland*, 1957, #1986	140-250
DB327	*Zorro*, 1957, Golden Funtime	25-45
DB346	*Sleeping Beauty*, 1959 Whitman	140-250
DB350	*Dell Disneyland Park*, 1960	45-100
DB385	*Disneyland, Walt Disney's* (Golden) 1963	35-75

Books — Reference

DB407	*The Story of Walt Disney*, 1957, Holt	15-40
DB413	*Uncle Scrooge*, 1979, Abbeville	40-75
DB450	*Disneyana*, 1974, Hawthorn	65-140
DB451	*A Celebration of Comic Art and Memorabilia*, 1975, Hawthorn	45-100
DB466	*The Disney Studio Story*, 1988, Crown Publishers Inc.	20-40

Chinaware

| DC615 | Peter Pan Tea Set | 175-375 |
| DC618 | Royal Orleans Mickey and Beanstalk Set | 75-140 |

Christmas

| DC635 | Paramount Figural Light Set | 75-150 |
| DC636 | Paramount Replacement Light Set | 150-100 |

Clocks

| DC650 | Allied Pluto, animated, plastic, 1953 | 145-300 |
| DC652 | Mickey or Lady Wall Clock, 1955 | 30-75 |

DD414

DD491

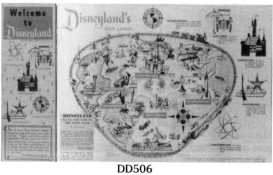

DD506

DD588

Disneykins

DD401	Castle Display of Original 34 Figures	200-450
DD402	Figures, original 34, boxed, ea	3-10
DD403	Disneykin Scene Boxes, 10 different, ea	5-20
DD413	Multi-Box of all 34 Figures, yellow	45-125
DD414	Multi-Box of 34 New Disneykins	800-1400

Disneykin Playsets, original figures only

DD415	Mickey Mouse Scene	25-75
DD416	Donald Duck Scene	25-75
DD417	Panchito Western Scene	25-75
DD418	*Dumbo* Circus Scene	20-65
DD419	*Pinocchio* Scene	20-65
DD422	*Babes In Toyland* Display	125-250
DD423	DisneyKings Display	150-350
DD424	New Disneykins Display	350-850

New Disneykins Playsets

DD425	*Sleeping Beauty*	55-300
DD426	*Alice in Wonderland*	75-400
DD427	Cinderella Mice, plus Wendy and Owl	25-125
DD428	*Peter Pan* Lost Boys, Smee plus Flower	25-125
DD429	Standing Lady & Tramp plus Clowns	25-125
DD430	Three Pigs plus Brer Fox	25-125

Larger and Special Packaging

DD431	*Lady and the Tramp* Kennel Box, 10 figures	200-600
DD432	RCA Premium Boxed Set	20-85
DD433	Ludwig Von Drake Playsets, 4 different, ea	15-55
DD434	*101 Dalmatians,* boxed sets of 8, ea	150-300
DD435	*The Jungle Book* Sets, 3 different, ea	40-175
DD436	*Snow White and the Seven Dwarfs* Figurine Picture Book, 1968	75-150
DD437	Blister Packs of 8 figures, w/new Disneykins (6), ea	20-100

Triple Playsets (DD438-DD439)

DD438	*Pinocchio*	75-175
DD439	Snow White	80-175
DD440	Combination of *Pinocchio,* Snow White and *Dumbo* sets	80-175
DD441	Disney on Parade Playset, J.C. Penney	50-125
DD442	*101 Dalmatians,* boxed sets of 8, ea	75-300
DD443	Disney Fun Pals, blister packs, ea	15-50
DD455	New Disneykins, ea	20-50
DD491	*101 Dalmations* characters, ea	20-60

Disneyland

DD501	*The Story of Disneyland Guide Book,* '55	150-300
DD502	*Disneyland in Natural Color,* 1955	200-400
DD503	*At Disneyland the Story of Aluminum,* '55	25-70
DD504	*Monsanto Hall of Chemistry,* fold out booklet, 1956	30-70
DD505	*Disneyland — A Complete Guide Book to ... ,* 1956	40-80
DD506	Give-away Map/Guide Folders	
	— 1955 or 56	15-45
	— 1957, 58 or 59	10-30
DD508	Same as DD503, but with 1957 in upper right corner	25-50
DD522	*Walt Disney's Guide to Disneyland,* 1961	20-40
DD524	*Walt Disney's Guide to Disneyland,* 1962	20-40
DD525	*Monsanto Home of the Future,* 1963, 4-color	10-28
DD526	*Walt Disney's Guide to Disneyland,* 1963	20-40
DD529	*Walt Disney's It's A Small World,* 1964	25-50
DD535	Disneyland USA Summer '67	30-60
DD536	Club 33, Royal Street, New Orleans Square, 1967	20-45
DD541	*W. Disney's Pirates of the Caribbean,* 1968	20-45

DD505

DD584

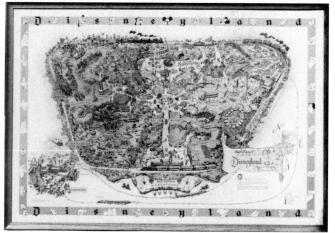

DD556

DD502

DD522

DD524

DD535

DD504

DD580

DD550 The Disneyland News-Monthly tabloid newspaper sold on Main Street. Vol 1 No 1, July 1955 to Vol 2 No 9, Mar 1957, ea ... 5-35

Disneyland maps have been available since 1958. They didn't change each year. Modifications were usually made every few years when major additions required new map art to be created. Maps from 1958 to 1964 show Edison Square and Liberty Street which were never built.

DD555	Map of Disneyland USA, 1958	45-125
DD556	Map of Disneyland USA, 1964	23-75
DD559	*Walt Disney's Guide to Disneyland*, 1968	20-60
DD560	Same as D5153, adds Bear Country, 1972	15-55
DD565	New Employee Package	15-50
DD570	Main Street Light Post Signs, various promotions	65-350
DD580	Opening Day Press Ticket	150-325
DD582	Declaration of Independence and Quill Pen, INA	45-100
DD584	Walt Disney Story, press giveaway	175-300
DD585	America Sings, Sam the Eagle, press giveaway, 1974	90-250
DD586	Space Mountain, press giveaway, 1977	50-125
DD588	Key to New Fantasyland and Booklet	20-45
DC654	Sleeping Beauty	50-110
DC665	Bradley Mini Size Alarm, Mickey, Minnie, Donald, Cinderella, ea	30-75

Coins and Medallions

DC681	Walt Disney/Mickey 8 oz bronze	80-175
DC682	Walt Disney World-Official Opening	40-75

DD642

DF350-1

DC684	Tokyo Opening Day	35-55

Crayon and Coloring Sets

DC940	Peter Pan Crayons and Stencils	25-110
DC949	Mickey Mouse Club-12 coloring books & crayons, 1955, Whitman, boxed set	40-90
DC955	Annette Coloring Box, 1962, Whitman	30-65
DC982	Davy Crockett Pencil Craft Painting Box, Hasbro	30-60
DD595	Old Coupon Ticket Books, complete w/admission ticket	25-100

Dolls

The post 1950 dolls can't begin to compare in value with the 1930s character dolls made by Charlotte Clark, Knickerbocker, Crown, Ideal, Madam Alexander, and others. *Cinderella*, however, was released in 1950 – followed by *Alice In Wonderland, Peter Pan, Lady and the Tramp,* and *Sleeping Beauty*-so there were plenty of new characters for dolls and many exceptional prices resulted.

DD625	Gus or Jaq, 1950, Gund, ea	35-75
DD626	Cinderella, 1950	80-180
DD629	Cinderella, 1950, story book	50-100
DD630	Cinderella, 2-headed topsy-turvy, 18"	75-150
DD640	Pinocchio and the Blue Fairy, 1951, Duchess	50-125
DD641	Snow White, 1951, Duchess	30-85
DD642	Cinderella, 1951, Duchess	25-70
DD643	Alice In Wonderland, 1951, Duchess	35-80
DD650	Alice in Wonderland, 1951, movie doll	80-145
DD651	Alice in Wonderland, 1951, story book	50-100
DD670	Peter Pan, 1952, Ideal	50-110
DD676	Tinker Bell, 1952-59, various sizes	25-75
DD690	Mickey or Minnie, 1952, Sun Rubber w/clothes, ea	30-60
DD660	Baby Princess Sleeping Beauty, 1959	45-85
DD662	Talking Ludwig Von Drake, w/tape & controls	80-250
DD665	Cinderella, removable heads, set, 1964, Horsman	70-150
DD666	Cinderella in ball gown, 1964, Horsman	30-70
DD675	Small World Dolls, 12" female characters from Japan, Africa, Mexico, France & others, 1963, ea	35-70
DD680	Mary Poppins, 1964, 36" walking doll	40-120
DD681	Mary Poppins, 1964, Horsman, 3 sets, ea	25-90
DD683	White Rabbit, promotional	50-110
DD687	Dolls by Jerri	200-500
DD688	Mickey & Minnie, w/stands, 1985,	

DF608

DF522   DF520

DF620   DF622   DF623   DF640   DF642

	Applause, ea	35-60	DF511	Lady and Tramp	40-85

EPCOT Center

DE613	Souvenir ticket paperweight	30-55
DE614	same as DE613, but embedded in lucite	40-70
DE618	Set of 2 opening day plates (Ltd. to 7500)	75-100
DE625	Dreamfinder and Figment figure, bronze	200-450
DE627	Dream Machine with Dreamfinder and Figment, selling price	3000-5000

Figures — Ceramic

Major ceramic makers such as Leeds China Company, Evan K Shaw, and Hagen-Renaker are listed in their own classifications. Bisque figures are also listed separately. Catalog stock numbers are shown for '70s and '80s figures, when available.

DF300	Enesco marked figures, ea	30-100
DF301	Snow White and Seven Dwarfs teapot	250-500
DF315	Alice (9016), White Rabbit (9001) or Cheshire Cat (9023), ea	25-60
DF318	Mad Hatter (9000) or March Hare (9003), ea	30-70
DF325	Snow White, lifting dress (0332)	35-75
DF340	Lady (9019) or Tramp (9020), ea	25-50
DF345	Pongo (9034) or Perdita (9035), 7", ea	150-400
DF347	Dalmatian Pups, six different (9036), 4" to 5", ea	45-100
DF350	Thomas O' Malley (Aristocats)	35-95
DF351	Duchess (Aristocats)	35-95

Figures — Plastic

Louis Marx & Co. started producing a line of rubberized plastic figures in 1953. These were used in a variety of Marx playsets. Durham, Multiple Products, Sutton and other toy makers have produced a wide variety of plastic figures for individual sale and as part of other toy products.

In addition, there were three large horse and rider sets — Zorro (also came in three smaller sizes), Johnny Tremain, and Sleeping Beauty and the Prince. There was a Peter Pan boxed set of 5 figures and other sets packaged in plastic bags. Linemar did a 12" Babes in Toyland soldier set and Auburn did some special sets for Disneyland. Vanity Fair Electronics Corp. produced StoryKins sets of plastic figures.

DF510	Peter Pan, boxed set	55-115

DF511	Lady and Tramp	40-85
DF512	Auburn Disneyland sets, ea	65-135
DF520	Zorro on horse w/all accessories	75-150
DF521	Johnny Tremain & Horse, w/all accessories	45-100
DF522	Sleeping Beauty and Prince, horse w/all accessories	60-130
DF524	Babes in Toyland Flexible Soldiers, Linemar	20-50
DF525	Zorro & Horse, 5"or 7", in package	25-45
DF530	Donald Duck's Express & Figures, 1968	30-65
DF531	Mowgli's Hut-Mobile & Figures, 1968	45-95
DF532	Mickey Mouse's Tin Lizzie & Figures, '68	35-70
DF533	Donald Duck's Whirlybird & Figures, 1968	35-70
DF534	Mickey Mouse's Hot Rod & Figures, 1968	40-0
DF537	StoryKins Snow White and Doc	50-100
DF538	StoryKins remaining 6 Dwarfs	50-100

Figures — Porcelain Bisque

There have been hundreds of bisque figures made in two periods: 1931-41 and 1971-present.

Christmas bisques from Grolier began in 1979 and theme parks began issuing a new series in 1985 based on the studio Christmas card 50 years previous.

Items marked Disney Gift-Ware were discontinued in 1977. The Spirit of '76 was sold mainly at Disneyland. (See **America on Parade**)

DF600	Disney Gift Ware Figures, ea	10-35
DF601	Theme Park, 6 figures, ea	18-40
DF606	Theme Park Multi Figures	30-60
DF608	Royal Orleans, Show White, Pinocchio or Cinderella, ea	40-80

Grolier Christmas bisques

DF620	Mickey, Minnie and Pluto at Lamppost, 1979	25-60
DF622	Santa and Mickey, (short run), 1981	75-150
DF623	Dumbo pulling sleigh, 1982	30-60
DF627	Musical We Wish You A Merry Christmas, 1986	25-45

Disneyland/Walt Disney World Christmas bisques

DF640	1985, based on 1934 Studio card	50-100
DF642	1986, based on 1935 Studio card	30-65
DF643	1987, based on 1937 Snow White card	75-100

DF942   DF941

DF943

DF939

DG675   DG680   DG601

DH130-38

Friction Toys

DF930	Donald's motorcycle (Line-Mar)	200-400
DF937	Donald's rocket	250-550
DF938	Mickey's airliner	260-600
DF939	Mickey's delivery wagon w/Donald	350-550
DF940	Mickey Mouse sparkling jet	300-600
DF941	Character moving vans, 3 different, ea	275-550
DF942	Gasoline Co. truck	300-650
DF943	Log Co. truck	300-650
DF945	Mickey Mouse racing kart (Marx)	150-275

Goebel Figurines

Goebel, the German company famous for Hummel figurines, produced a continuous series of Disney figures from 1950-67. The Goebel 50th Anniversary book lists them as being sold in the U.S. from 1952-54. The majority of the first 220 pieces were based on the film *Bambi*. Many merely used the same figures on different bases, bookends, ashtrays, or as salt and pepper shakers. The Goebel Disney figures sold in America had a "full bee" mark (a bee in the letter V) on the underside of each piece, along with the word "Germany." The full bee set of *Snow White and the Seven Dwarfs* did not include the Prince. This piece was added in a later remake of the set. A third and smaller Snow White set was issued in 1984, also without a prince.

Following is a list of Disney Goebel figures known to be sold in the U.S. Disney figures were numbered and each number was preceded by the letters DIS. The incised number is legible on some pieces.

Values listed are for "full Bee" marked figures.

DG501	Dwarf "Bashful", 1950	35-75
DG502	Dwarf "Sleepy"	35-75
DG503	Dwarf "Happy"	35-75
DG504	Dwarf "Grumpy"	35-75
DG505	Dwarf "Sneezy"	35-75
DG506	Dwarf "Dopey"	35-75
DG507	Dwarf "Doc"	35-75
DG508	Thumper, ashtray w/lip on tail	150-220
DG509	Bambi, ashtray	1200-180
DG512	Snow White	150-220
DG513	Small Bambi, w/its head turned backwards, a butterfly sitting on its tail	25 65
DG514	Small Flower, sitting on its hind legs	25-65
DG521	Lying Bambi, w/o base	20-55
DG528	Owl, spreading out its wings on ashtray	100-200
DG532	Thumper as salt shaker	35-60
DG533	Flower as salt & pepper shakers, set	70-120
DG534	Laughing Thumper as salt shaker	35-60
DG541	Stem & Bambi, looking right, vase	80-175
DG542	Stem & Bambi, looking left, vase	80-175
DG573	Donald Duck, as ice-hockey player	125-210
DG574	Nephew, as ice-hockey player	100-175
DG575	"Mickey Mouse", as hunter, beside tree trunk, as vase	200-350
DG577	Kneeling Mickey Mouse, going hunting	175-300
DG578	Mickey Mouse, w/book sitting on a log	120-200
DG579	Figaro, w/head raised	25-60
DG580	Figaro, w/head turned to left	25-60
DG599	Sitting Pinocchio	50-175

DH101-13

DH192-93

DH175-85

DM625

DM628

DM401   DM402

Disney theme parks in the mid-1980s.

DG600	Walking Pinocchio, w/plumed hat & apple in hand	250-400
DG601	Elmer Elephant & Tillie	85-250
DG602	J. Worthington Foulfellow	250-400
DG603	Gideon	90-275
DG604	Round weaved small basket w/Figaro on its cover	60 -195
DG611	Large Bambi & Frog, on an oval base	350-600
DG613	Standing Bambi & Sitting Thumper	200-350
DG619	Two Kissing Skunks	200-350
DG620	Two Sitting Rabbits, on oval base	200-350
DG622	Dumbo as single figurine	160-225
DG625	Figaro w/large ball	120-200
DG628	Large Playful Rabbits, w/o base	220-450
DG638	Figaro & basket, as salt & pepper shakers, set	145-225
DG650	Standing Bambi, as perfume spender, w/light, 1953	195-350
DG651	Rabbit standing on its hind legs as perfume spender	180-300
DG680	Tinkerbell	75-125

Hagen-Renaker Ceramics

Hagen-Renaker (Monrovia, CA) famous for miniature ceramic Disney figures, was licensed from 1955-61. *Lady and the Tramp* figures were sold exclusively at Disneyland the first year. In 1956 the company added figures from *Alice in Wonderland*, *Bambi*, *Cinderella*, *Dumbo* and "The Mickey Mouse Club." Larger figures were distributed nationally under the Designer's Workshop name: Snow White, the Seven Dwarfs, Jiminy Cricket and other characters. Banks and cookie jars were 1956 DW products. More miniatures were soon included. The *Peter Pan* and *Fantasia* figures were added in 1957; *Snow White and the Seven Dwarfs* miniatures in 1958; and *Sleeping Beauty* characters in 1959. A larger set of Hagen-Renaker *Fantasia* figures were produced for sale at

DH101	Lady (sold later as "non-Disney"), orig.	30-65
DH102	Tramp	150-300
DH103	Scamp, Ruffles or Fluffy, ea	45-75
DH106	Scooter, Jock or Trusty, (sold later as "non-Disney"), ea	65-125
DH109	Si or Am, ea	70-140
DH111	Pedro or Dachsie, ea	85-160
DH113	Peg or Bull, ea	95-175
DH115	Alice	200-375
DH116	Mad Hatter, March Hare or Caterpillar, ea	160-350
DH119	Cinderella	175-375
DH120	Gus or Jaq, ea	100-200
DH122	Bambi or Faline, ea	80-150
DH124	Flower or Thumper, ea	55-95
DH126	Dumbo or Timothy Mouse, ea	75-145
DH130	Mickey, as band leader	100-225
DH131	Pluto or Goofy	90-175
DH133	Donald Duck	100-210
DH134	Scrooge McDuck, w/dollar	100-200
DH135	Huey, Louie or Dewey, playing baseball, ea	65-110
DH138	Chip or Dale, ea	80-150
DH140	Peter Pan	120-220
DH141	Wendy or Michael, ea	100-200
DH143	John	170-300
DH144	Michael's Teddy Bear (sold later as "non-Disney") or Nana	125-195
DH146	Tinker Bell, flying	300-550
DH147	Tinker Bell, kneeling	150-300
DH148	Tinker Bell, shelf sitter	250-500
DH149	Reclining Mermaid, blonde or redhead, ea	100-200
DH151	Kneeling Mermaid, blonde or redhead, ea	120-220

DP050   DP205   DP051

DP470

DP201   DP204   DP203

DM627   DP475

DH155	Bacchus	100-200
DH156	Faun #1, #2 or #3, ea	75-150
DH159	Unicorn	150-240
DH160	Baby Unicorn or Baby Pegasus, ea	100-180
DH165	Snow White	100-185
DH166	Seven Dwarfs, set	150-300
DH175	Sleeping Beauty	120-250
DH176	Prince Phillip	100-175
DH177	Maleficent & Raven	400-700
DH178	Flora, Fauna, or Merryweather, ea	80-140
DH181	King Stefan or King Hubert, ea	140-250
DH183	The Queen	100-200
DH184	Samson	450-800
DH185	Rabbit, Squirrel, Owl, Cardinal or Bluebird, ea	60-125

Larger (about 3" to 4 1/2") Designer's Workshop Figures

DH190	Bambi or Flower, ea	60-175
DH191	Jiminy Cricket or Figaro, ea	115-350
DH192	Snow White (watch for broken arms)	200-600
DH193	Seven Dwarfs, ea	70-200
DH194	Dumbo	100-220
DH200	Practical Pig, Thumper, Dumbo or Figaro cookie jar, ea	200-400
DH203	Practical Pig, Thumper, Dumbo, Figaro or Lady bank, ea	150-350

3" Figures Circa 1985

DH320	Mickey, as the Sorcerer's Apprentice	75-140
DH321	Broom, w/water bucket	40-75
DH322	Bacchus	30-50
DH323	Baby Pegasus, pink, blue or black, ea	30-50
DH326	Ostrich	90-180

Maps

DM328	Peter Pan's map of Neverland (1952) (Colgate Peter Pan Beauty Bar)	50-150

Mickey Mouse club Magazines

DM401	Volume 1 — Number 1, Winter 1956	20-50
DM402	Volume 1 — Number 2, Spring 1956	20-45
DM403	Volume 1 — Number 3, Summer 1956	15-40
DM404	Volume 1 — Number 4, Fall 1956	15-40

Model Kits

DM625	Perri the Squirrel	25-65
DM627	Tomorrowland Rocket	75-150
DM628	Peter Pan's Pirate Ship, from Disneyland, 3 versions	18-75

Music Boxes

DM925	Disneyland "Melody Player" (1955) Chein	75-140
DM950	Wooden music boxes, ea (1970-71)	45-90
DM960	Musical blocks, ea	30-60
DM970	Ceramic revolving, Mickey (3 versions), Minnie,	

	Donald (3 versions), Bambi, Winnie the Pooh, Cinderella, Pinocchio, & Pluto, ea	25-65
DM980	Mickey or Pinocchio, wall hanging	50-95

Pinback Buttons, Pins and Badges

There were a number of buttons and tabs for the TV "Mickey Mouse Club" in the 1950s and a few theme park buttons in the 1950s-1960s period. By the time Walt Disney Productions celebrated its 50th year in 1973, pinback buttons had become a part of every promotion — Grad Nite, America on Parade, Mickey and Donald's 50th birthdays, The Disney Channel, new theme parks, park souvenir buttons, film buttons and the much sought after Walt Disney World Costuming Division buttons. Collecting post 1980 buttons and pins has achieved mania proportions.

DP050	Pinocchio at Hudson's	25-40
DP051	Peter Pan at Hudson's	25-40
DP070	Donald Disneyland Flasher Badge	50-120
DP075	Disneyland Yearly Anniversary Pins, plastic or metal, 1956 to date, ea	5-65
DP100	Cheerios Wiggle Picture Badge & 6 inserts, 1957	40-90
DP125	Golden Horseshoe Revue, 2 versions, ea	20-40
DP140	Walt Disney World Yearly Anniversary Pins, plastic, 1972 to date, ea	10-55
DP156	Liberty Square Medal	30-60
DP178	Mickey's Christmas Carol — Detroit Parade	18-35
DP190	30th — Parade Button	20-40
DP191	I Won a GM Car!	50-100

Costuming Division Cast Buttons Walt Disney World

DP200	Maleficent — You Want What Size!	100-200
DP201	Happiness is a New Spring Wardrobe!	100-200
DP202	Smile! It's a Nice Reflection on You!, round	95-200
DP203	When You're Lookin' Good, We're Lookin' Good!	100-175
DP204	Wardrobe Gets My Vote!	100-175
DP205	Snow White — Season's Greetings, 3D	65-135
DP225	Star Tours Aviator Wings, press pin	30-60
DP250	The Disney Channel, Mickey satellite	35-75
DP275	Walt Disney World 15th Anniversary Coke pins, set	100-175

DP405

Plates — Collectors'

Miniature collectors' plates have been available since the early days of Disneyland. Christmas plates began in 1973 and now different editions are marketed each year by Schmid, Grolier, and Disney theme parks. Grolier followed Schmid's Christmas series in 1979. Disney's own series premiered in 1985. Schmid closed the first Christmas series with 1982 and started over again in 1983. The Grolier plate illustrations are the same as used on each year's bisque figurine, bell and ornament. The Disney series is based on corporate Christmas cards issued 50 years previous. A 500 plate limited edition press giveaway was produced for the premiere of the "A Very Merry Christmas Parade" in 1977. Mother's Day plates began in 1974.

DP405	*Fantasia*, 1950s Disneyland souvenir	100-200

Schmid Collector's Plates

DP450	Christmas '73 "Sleigh Ride"	100-200
DP451	Christmas '74 "Decorating the Tree"	55-100
DP452	Christmas '75 "Caroling"	30-60
DP455	Mother's Day '74 "Flowers for Mother"	15-40
DP460	Bi-Centennial	10-40
DP470	*Snow White and the Seven Dwarfs*, Goebel, 1980	25-50
DP471	Wedgewood Sleeping Beauty Castle (Disneyland) or Cinderella Castle (Walt Disney World), 1st edition, theme park series, ea	35-70
DP473	2nd edition, Snow White and Dopey in Fantasyland	15-35
DP475	Very Merry Christmas Parade, limited to 500	150-350
DP480	Disneyland, 25 Years	20-40
DP481	Walt Disney World, 10 Years	20-45
DP482	Disneyland, 30 Years	20-45
DP484	Walt Disney World 15th Anniversary	20-35

Prints — Art and Framed Pictures

Disneyland marketing department artist Charles Boyer did a Walt Disney take-off painting of Norman Rockwell's "Self Portrait" for the cover of an employee magazine in 1978. Many recipients requested frameable copies, and Boyer did a signed/numbered edition of 1,800. Its success led to many other Boyer limited edition lithographs. Another Rainbow has produced a series of Carl Barks signed lithographs. Disney artist John Hench signed a 750 limited edition of the 25th and 50th Mickey Mouse birthday paintings he created. An employee drawing was held for the right to purchase a portfolio of the two prints for $50 each in 1978.

DP749	"Self Portrait", Boyer	700-1400
DP750	"Partners", Boyer	600-1000
DP752	"New Fantasyland", Boyer	45-100
DP753	"Tokyo Disneyland", Boyer	200-400
DP760	Another Rainbow Carl Barks prints, over 20 different, ea	800-1700
DP770	John Hench Mickey 50th Birthday Portfolio	500-1000

Radios, Phonographs and Tape Players

DR125	Alice in Wonderland Phonograph, 45 rpm, RCA	65-145
DR126	Snow White Phonograph, 45 rpm, RCA	65-145
DR127	Mickey Mouse Phonograph, 45 rpm, RCA	65-145
DR128	Donald Duck Electric Phonograph, Spears	150-300

Records — Phonograph

DR315	Fantasia, 3 record set w/program, Disneyland, 1st ed.	35-75
DR316	VISTA, 2nd ed.	15-35
DR320	Pop-up albums w/4 complete pop-up scenes. Titles include Dumbo and Sword in the Stone, ea	35-75
DR326	Walt Disney World Electric Water Pageant picture disk, 1973	10-35
DR330	Ronco's The Greatest Hits of Walt Disney, w/uncut cutouts & song sheets	20-35
DR335	The Magical Music of Walt Disney w/book	30-60

Rings

DR501	Donald Duck Living Toy ring w/Pep package magnet	150-275
DR502	Weather Bird Pinocchio ring	75-120

Evan K. Shaw Company Ceramics

DS340	Cinderella in rags	200-400
DS341	Cinderella or Prince, dressed for the ball, ea	175-300
DS344	Bruno, sitting or prone (repainted from Pluto mold)	75-150
DS346	Gus or Jaq, ea	35-125
DS348	Bluebirds, Mama Mouse or Baby Mouse, ea	50-150
DS351	Alice In Wonderland	175-450
DS352	Tweedledee or Tweedledum, ea	150-300
DS354	Walrus	150-300
DS355	March Hare, White Rabbit or Mad Hatter, ea	75-200
DS358	Doormouse	50-150
DS360	Alice in Wonderland Teapots, 4 diff, ea	200-400
DS361	Snow White & the Seven Dwarfs, set	800-1200
DS362	Peter Pan, sitting or standing, ea	200-400
DS364	Tinker Bell or Mermaid, ea	175-350
DS366	Wendy, Michael, or Nana, ea	75-150

DS355-60

DS384

DS340-48

DS369	Lady or Tramp, ea	50-100
DS371	Peg	75-150
DS372	Jock, Trusty, Dachshund, or Limey, ea	50-90
DS376	Si, Am or Scamp Pup, ea	50-100
DS378	Bambi, w/butterfly	40-90
DS379	Bambi, standing or prone, ea	35-80
DS381	Thumper, Flower w/flower, or Flower w/o flower, ea	40-60
DS384	Dumbo or Timothy, ea	60-150
DS386	Pinocchio, Figaro, or Jiminy Cricket, ea	60-150
DS389	Mickey or Donald, 2 sizes, ea	40-90
DS392	Pluto	60-120
DS393	Huey, Louie or Dewey, ea	30-50
DS396	Three Little Pigs, 3, ea	30-50
DS399	Stormy, standing or prone, ea	30-65

Toys — Battery Operated, Mechanical

DT750	Mickey Drummer	800-1500
DT755	Mickey Magician, light-up eyes	1200-2500
DT758	Pluto, lantern	100-200
DT760	Walking Pluto	200-400
DT765	Fire Truck w/Donald climbing ladder	1200-2500
DT770	Character Talking Bus	400-800

Trains and Handcars

Schuco made two models of the Disneyland-Alweg monorail system. These sets, licensed and produced in Germany, were imported and sold at Disneyland in 1962-63.

Pride Lines Ltd was licensed in 1982 to make character trolley cars and banks. They also reproduced Lionel handcars before creating handcars and trains of their own design.

DT947	Blue Monorail Set, Schuco	300-750
DT948	Red Monorail Set, Schuco	450-1000
DT909	Disneyland Santa Fe Railroad, HO, Tyco	300-500

Pride Lines, Ltd. has produced many electric motorized streetcars and handcars. They are listed here with the original retail price for each unit.

Streetcars—Walt Disney World Tencennial ($275), Minnie Mouse, green ($275), Minnie Mouse, ivory ($275), Mickey Mouse, orange ($275), Donald's 50th Birthday, limited to 1,000 ($350) and Disneyland 30th Year, limited to 750 ($395).

Handcars — Mickey/Minnie Lionel repro ($250), Donald/Pluto Lionel repro ($250), Mickey Fantasia ($250), Uncle Scrooge "Gold Mobile" ($250) and Donald's 50th Birthday, limited to 1,000 ($295).

Commemorative pieces were limited and are no longer produced. Resale experience is limited, but the Tencennial Streetcar realized over twice its selling price at one auction.

Wind-Up Toys

Marx and Linemar made most post-1950 metal windups. The other companies featured plastic items. Values are naturally higher if the toy is in good working condition.

DW701	Mickey, Donald or Pluto Gym Toy Acrobat, celluloid figures w/pupil eyes, Linemar, ea	200-400
DW702	Walt Disney's Rocking Chair, celluloid Donald w/pupil eyes on litho tin Dumbo	

DT947

Streetcars by Pride Lines

DW701

DW735   DW722   DW765

DW706

DW733

DZ518

	rocker. Activated by pulling string anchored	
	by solid plastic Pluto, Linemar	250-500
DW703	Merry-go-round w/4 celluloid figures	275-550
DW704	Disney Parade Roadster, Marx	150-300
DW706	Pecos Bill Ridin' Widowmaker,	
	Marx, plastic	100-225
DW708	Donald Duck & his nephews,	
	Marx, plastic	150-300
DW709	Donald the Skier, Marx, plastic	200-450
DW710	Donald the Drummer, plastic w/metal	
	drum, 2 sizes, Marx	160-300
DW711	Donald Duck, Mavco	125-175
DW712	Donald Duck the Gay Caballero, Mavco	125-175
DW713	Mickey Mouse Scooter Jockey, Mavco	135-185
DW715	Mickey the Musician (xylophone), no key	
	came in the center, plastic, Marx	100-185
DW717	Fuzzy Walking Donald	100-200
DW719	Mickey w/rotating wire tail,	
	plastic, Marx	95-200
DW720	Pluto w/rotating wire tail,	
	plastic, Marx	75-180
DW722	Mickey w/rotating wire tail,	
	metal, Linemar	125-250
DW724	Mickey's Disney Jalopy, Linemar	185-375
DW725	Dancing Cinderella & Prince, Irwin	60-120
DW726	Mechanical Donald w/rotating tail	100-200
DW727	Mechanical Goofy w/rotating tail	100-200
DW728	Mechanical Pluto w/rotating tail	100-200
DW729	Pluto pulling cart, Linemar	275-450
DW730	Mickey riding rocking horse Pluto,	
	Linemar	350-700
DW730	Partying Pluto, Linemar	95-195
DW731	Climbing Fireman Donald, Linemar	200-350
DW732	Stretchy Pluto, Linemar	125-260
DW733	Mickey on roller skates, Linemar	450-900
DW735	Minnie on rocker, knitting, Linemar	140-275

DW738	Mickey, Pluto or Goofy on unicycle,	
	Linemar, ea	200-350
DW740	Big Bad Wolf Jumper, Linemar	200-360
DW741	Jumping Three Little Pigs, Linemar, ea	200-360
DW745	Mickey or Donald Crazy Car, Linemar, metal	
	figures, ea	135-200
DW747	Mickey or Donald Crazy Car, Linemar, plastic	
	figures, ea	120-195
DW750	Donald Drummer, metal, Linemar	200-425
DW755	Remote squeeze action Donald, Pluto,	
	Jiminy Cricket or Bambi, Linemar, ea	75-165
DW760	Disneyland Ferris Wheel, Chein	180-375
DW761	Disneyland Roller Coaster, w/both cars,	
	Chein	200-400
DW765	Pinocchio, Toy Soldier or Ludwig Von	
	Drake Walker, 1961, Linemar, ea	150-245

Zorro

Zorro offered adventure, excitement, mystery and a great identity for our own alter-egos when he first burst upon the TV screen Oct 10, 1957. The program aired for two years on ABC-TV, on Walt Disney Presents, for years in syndication and on The Disney Channel in the mid-1980s.

DZ512	Polo Shirt Pack w/mask &	
	cardboard stand-up	50-100
DZ515	Whip Set w/mask, whip, ring & lariat,	
	Shimmel	45-95
DZ518	Action Set w/hat, mask, whip, lariat,	
	pistol, 2 fencing foils & sheath knife,	
	Marx, set	100-225
DZ520	Cap Pistol, Marx	30-65
DZ522	Target Set, 2 guns, 4 darts & target, Lido	35-70
DZ524	Target Game & Water Pistol,	
	Knickerbocker Plastic Co.	40-80
DZ530	Plastic Figures, Zorro on horse,	
	Lido, 3 sizes	50-150
DZ536	Bookends, pair	75-125
DZ540	Oil Painting by Numbers, Hassenfeld	30-50
DZ575	Lunch Box w/thermos (blue sky),	
	Aladdin, 1958-59	65-120
DZ560	Zorro Game, Whitman	20-45

See also: **Action Figures; Animation Art; Bicycles; Books; Buttons, Pinback; Cereal Boxes; Character & Promotional Glasses; Comic Books; Dakin; Golden Books; Happy Meals; Lunch Boxes; Magazines; Marx Playsets; Movie Posters; Non-Sports Trading Cards; Paper Dolls; PEZ Dispensers; Picture Discs; Toy Trains**

ELVIS PRESLEY   consultant Harry Johnson

"The King of Rock 'N Roll" was born Elvis Aaron Presley in

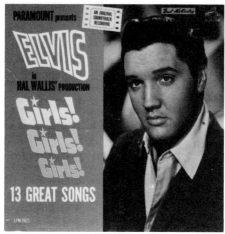

EP500

Tupelo, Miss on Jan 8, 1935. His recording of a blues song, "That's All Right, Mama," on Sun Records started him on the road to international success. This led to a recording contract with RCA Victor and one hit after another. Even a stint in the Army didn't slow his career. He returned from overseas to embark on a movie career and continue his hit parade.

In his later years Elvis's following stayed loyal. His death on Aug 16, 1977 cemented this devotion. His Memphis mansion "Graceland" remains a major tourist attraction.

"The King's" enduring popularity created an extremely wide variety of collectible merchandise before and after his death. Any original 45 rpm or 78 rpm Sun Label record is valuable, but beware of fakes. Special editions of his RCA records are among the most valuable Elvis items, but the differences between extremely valuable and common is often slight. Popular editions of Elvis hits remain available so this section concentrates only in merchandise. The key to value where records are concerned is usually the picture jacket or premium items distributed with the record albums.

In 1956, Elvis Presley Enterprises created a line of merchandise ranging from perfume and silk-like scarfs to drinking glasses and wallets. This special fan merchandise operation lasted little more than a year. All items are © Elvis Presley Enterprises and lead the most valuable collectibles list. RCA distributed pocket calendars starting in 1963 up to the 1980s. The first year is particularly scarce and all years are welcomed by collectors. A one sheet wall calendar was produced in 1963 only. Most items made after Elvis's death are common.

EP100	*Country And Western Music Stars* magazine, Fawcett 1958	25-50
EP105	*Elvis Presley Hero or Heel?* magazine, Whitestone, 1957	50-75
EP110	"Fun In Acapulco" movie booklet Paramount, 1963	50-75
EP115	*Rock-N-Roll Stars* magazine, Fawcett, 1956	50-75
EP120	"Young Lovers" Charlton Comic with Elvis Story, May 1957	75-100
EP125	Diary, 1956	450-600

Full size McCormick music box whiskey bottles EP126-31

EP126	Platinum	150-300
EP127	Gold	150-300
EP128	White	75-150
EP129	Black	50-100
EP130	Pink	50-100
EP131	Hawaiian	75-150
EP200	Emenee Official Elvis Presley Guitar, given one per theatre to the first girl entering to see *Love Me Tender*.	700-1400
EP250	Record player	800-1000
EP251	Record case w/Elvis' name	300-500
EP300	Charm Bracelet, with guitar, breaking heart, hound dog, & photo charm	150-300

EP305	Dog Tag Bracelet with etching of Elvis	75-100
EP306	Dog Tag Bracelet with Elvis serial # and blood type	50-100
EP309	Love Me Tender heart necklace, 1956	75-150
EP310	Elvis Photo Charm	50-75
EP315	Elvis Photo Ring	100-200
EP400	Bust of Elvis (Limited Edition)	400-700
EP405	Figural Clock, Elvis in white suit holding small microphone, clock in guitar	100-400
EP410	Drinking Glass, 1956	200-400
EP415	"Love Me Tender" picture frame w/ "Sincerely Elvis Presley" at bottom in gold & color photo of Elvis, 1956	200-400
EP420	Elvis Presley's "Teddy Bear" Perfume	100-400
EP425	"Elvis Presley Permits" good for 1 hour with Elvis for any girl who could catch him	25-50
EP430	Pillow, 1956	250-400
EP435	Pocket calendar, 1963	300-500
EP436	Pocket calendars, 1964-1980, ea	25-300
EP440	"Elvis" 1961 color postcard with "Aloha, Elvis Presley" facsimile autograph, "From Elvis and the Colonel,"	25-50
EP445	Hound Dog overnight case	300-500
EP450	Scarf, silk-like, 1956	200-400
EP455	"Don't Be Cruel" Sheet Music	25-50
EP456	"Love Me Tender" Sheet Music	25-50
EP460	Wall calendar, 1963	400-750
EP465	"Best Wishes Elvis Presley" glazed ceramic wall tile	200-400
EP470	Illustrated Wallet marked "Elvis Presley Rock n' Roll," 1956	200-700
EP500	Girls, Girls, Girls LP2621 w/calendar (RCA)	50-75

See also: **Autographs; Buttons; Non-Sports Cards; Records**

FF130   FF135

FEMMES FATALE   **Tom Tumbusch**

In 1950, sex was a hushed subject and the most risque photo in magazines featured a woman in a two piece bathing suit. Hollywood and magazines like *Playboy* forged a new sexual awareness. Aspiring actresses and models bowed to nude and sometimes sexually explicit photographs as a means to get publicity...or simply to survive. Marilyn Monroe's nude calendar pose launched her career and legitimized the practice within limits. Her success was mirrored to a lesser degree by Jayne Mansfield, Stella Stevens, and Carroll Baker. In the case of Marilyn Chambers the limits were crossed into porno movie-making after she had posed as the perfect mother for Ivory Snow soap boxes. Procter and Gamble was upset to learn their carefully chosen mother-next-door had turned her image blue...and pulled her product boxes from the shelves. Later, Vanessa Williams, the country's first black Miss America, was forced to surrender her crown due to posing for art study photographs in the zeal of her youth and not fully understanding the implications of the photograph's release she signed. The Kellogg's company had printed millions of Corn Flakes boxes which were due to be packaged just after the scandal broke. All but a few were shredded. The curiosity surrounding established or momentary femmes fatale makes grist for the tabloids and conversation pieces for collectors who managed to save production objects or acquire a withdrawn item before they were all destroyed.

FF100	Jayne Mansfield figural hot water bottle, in box	50-100
FF130	Marilyn Chambers Ivory Snow box	30-60
FF135	Vanessa Williams Kellogg's Corn Flakes box	60-90

GAMES, CHARACTER & TV SHOW   by Ted Hake

Games of all sorts have long been a staple of the toy industry. With the proliferation of newspaper comic strips in the early 1900s, manufacturers were quick to develop games that featured America's many cartoon stars. In the 1930s, animated cartoon characters sparked the creation of still more character games. Television, however, proved to be the game manufacturer's best friend. Throughout the 1950s and 1960s a huge variety of games were produced. Virtually the first licensed item for a new TV series was a game featuring the characters and/or theme of the show. Games based on space subjects, Hanna Barbera characters, horror, James Bond, and TV legends seem to outpace the market. Some games appear and disappear as fast as a quickly cancelled TV series, but rarity is secondary to the popularity of the characters on which the game is based.

Collectible values are based on a combination of popularity, scarcity and condition. Games in excellent condition must be complete and show only the slightest traces of wear on the box and playing parts. Fine condition games must also be complete but boxes may have some rub marks or split corners. Tape or writing on the box or game parts, unless very minor, reduces a game's value below the "fine" price.

The prices in this section are for games in fine to excellent condition. The manufacturer and year are listed if known.

GA100	The Addams Family Game, 1964, Ideal Toy	25-50
GA101	Adventures of Lassie, 1955, Lisbeth Whiting	20-40
GA102	Adventures of Popeye, 1957, Transogram	20-40
GA103	Adventures of Robin Hood, 1958, Bettye-B Products	30-65
GA104	All-Star Baseball, 1955	20-40
GA105	Aquanauts, 1961, Transogram	20-40
GA106	Atom Ant Saves the Day, 1966, Transogram	20-40
GA107	Barney Google An' Snuffy Smith Time's A Wastin', 1963, Milton Bradley	20-40
GA108	Beatles Flip Your Wig, 1964, Milton Bradley	60-125
GA109	Beverly Hillbillies, 1963, Standard Toykraft	25-45

GA108

GA116

GA117

GA104

GA110	Bewitched, 1965, Game Gems	30-60
GA111	Burke's Law - The Game of Who, 1963, Transogram	20-40
GA112	Cannonball, 1959 (based on U.S. TV show about truckers), Bell Toys & Games Ltd, London	30-60
GA113	Captain Gallant of the Foreign Legion Adventure, 1955, Transogram	25-50
GA114	Captain Video - An Exciting Space Game, 1950s, Milton Bradley	35-75
GA115	Car 54, Where Are You? 1961, Allison Toys	60-125
GA116	Charlie Brown's All-Stars, 1965, Parker Bros.	25-50
GA117	Dino the Dinosaur, 1961, Transogram	20-40
GA118	Dondi Prairie Race, 1960s, Hasbro	20-40
GA119	Dragnet, 1955, Transogram	30-60
GA120	Eliot Ness & The Untouchables, 1961, Transogram	35-75
GA121	Flintstones Mitt-Full - A Game of Skill, 1962, Whitman	25-50
GA122	Fugitive, 1964, Ideal Toy	25-50
GA123	Gidget Fortune Teller, 1966, Milton Bradley	20-40
GA124	Green Hornet Quick Switch, 1966, Milton Bradley	40-85

GA125

GA162

GA176

GA125	Groucho's You Bet Your Life, 1955, Lowell Toy	50-100
GA126	Hawaii Five-O, 1968, Remco	20-40
GA127	Hawaiian Eye, 1963, Lowell Toy	20-40
GA128	Hogan's Heroes Bluff Out, 1966, Transogram	25-50
GA129	Howdy Doody's Adventure, 1951, Milton Bradley	30-60
GA130	Howdy Doody's T.V. Game, 1952, Milton Bradley	35-70
GA131	Huckleberry Hound "Bumps", 1961, Transogram	20-40
GA132	Huckleberry Hound Western, 1959, Milton Bradley	25-50
GA133	"I Spy", 1965, Ideal Toy	20-50
GA135	Jackie Gleason's TV Fun, 1956, Transogram	60-125
GA140	James Bond 007 Goldfinger, 1966, Milton Bradley	20-40
GA141	James Bond Message for M, 1966, Ideal Toy	60-125
GA143	Jan Murray's Treasure Hunt, 1950s, Gardner Games	35-75

GA163	Legend of Jesse James, 1966, Milton Bradley	35-70
GA164	Lippy The Lion Flips, 1962, Transogram	20-40
GA166	Lost In Space, 1965, Milton Bradley	30-65
GA168	Lost in Space 3-D Action Fun, 1966, Remco	125-250
GA170	Lucky Show, 1962, Transogram	60-125
GA172	Major MATT MASON Space Exploration Game, The, 1968, Mattel	75-150
GA174	Mighty Mouse Game With His Pals Heckle and Jeckle, 1957, Milton Bradley	40-75
GA176	Mister Ed The Talking Horse, 1962, Parker Brothers	25-50
GA178	Munsters Drag Race, 1965, Hasbro	100-250
GA179	Munsters Masquerade Party, 1964, Hasbro	100-200
GA180	Munsters Picnic, 1965, Hasbro	100-200

GA145

GA145	Jetsons Fun Pad, 1963, Milton Bradley	45-90
GA146	Jetsons Out of This World, 1962, Transogram	60-125
GA147	Jetsons Rosie The Robot, 1962, Transogram	40-75
GA153	Joe Palooka Boxing, 1950s, Lowell Toy	35-75
GA155	John Drake Secret Agent, 1966, Milton Bradley	20-40
GA156	Justice League of America - Wonder Woman, 1967, Hasbro	20-40
GA157	KISS On Tour, American Publishing Corp.	25-45
GA158	Land of the Giants, 1968, Ideal Toy	25-50
GA160	Leave It To Beaver Ambush 1959, Hasbro	25-50
GA162	Leave It To Beaver Rocket To The Moon, 1959, Hasbro	40-75

GA178

GA184

GI150	GI241	GI341	GI431

GA245

GA182	Mushmouse & Punkinpuss, 1964, Ideal Toy		25-50
GA184	My Favorite Martian 1963, Transogram		20-40
GA186	Outer Limits, 1964, Milton Bradley		75-150
GA188	Peanuts, 1959, Selchow & Righter		25 50
GA190	Perry Mason, 1959, Transogram		20-40
GA192	Peter Gunn Detective, 1960, Lowell Toy		30-60
GA194	Phantom, 1966, Transogram		40-75
GA196	Prince Valiant A Game of Valor, 1950s, Transogram		25-50
GA198	Quick Draw McGraw Private Eye, 1960, Milton Bradley		25-50
GA200	Ramar of the Jungle, ©1953, Dexter Wayne Co.		40-75
GA202	Rat Patrol, 1966, Transogram		35-70
GA204	Ripcord Skydiving, 1962, Lowell Toy		25-50
GA206	Rocky and His Friends, 1960, Milton Bradley		35-75
GA208	Route 66 Travel, 1962, Transogram		30-60
GA210	Space:1999, 1974, Omnia (England)		20-40
GA212	Spiderman & The Fantastic Four, 1978, Milton Bradley		20-40
GA214	Steve Canyon, 1959, Lowell Toy		25-50
GA216	Superman & Superboy, 1967, Milton Bradley		25-50
GA218	Surf Side 6, 1960s, Lowell Toy		20-40
GA220	12 O'Clock High, 1965, Ideal Toy		35-75
GA222	Talk To Cecil Talking Adventure, 1961, Mattel		50-100
GA224	Thunderbirds, 1967, Parker Brothers		20-40
GA226	Time Tunnel, 1966, Ideal Toy		25-50
GA228	Tiny Tim Game of Beautiful Things, 1970, Parker Brothers		20-40
GA230	Tom & Jerry, 1962, Selchow & Richter		30-60
GA232	Travel With Woody Woodpecker, 1956, Cadaco-Ellis		25-50
GA234	Video Village, 1960, Milton Bradley		25-50
GA236	Virginian, 1962, Transogram		25-50
GA238	Wally Gator, 1962, Transogram		25-50
GA240	What's My Line? 1956, Lowell Toy		25-50
GA245	Who Framed Roger Rabbit?, Milton Bradley		30-60

See also: **Beatles; James Bond; Kiss; Peanuts**

G.I. JOE (1964-76)   by Carol Markowski

G.I. Joe was the brainstorm of Hasbro employee Donald Levine. Joe made his debut in February of 1964. Instead of calling the figures "dolls", Hasbro promoted them as "poseable action figures for boys." The 12" figures were a smashing success, spawning numerous costumes and accessories. Joe's outfits were modeled after World War II and Korean War uniforms, with the exception of a few pilot outfits and the Vietnam Green Beret outfit in 1966.

There were originally four G.I. Joe figures, one for each branch of military service (army, navy, air force, marines). Accessories and playsets were produced for each version of the figure. A black G.I. Joe was first sold in 1965. Talking Joes

were introduced in 1967. A nurse figure was also sold the same year, but sales were extremely low (the figure looked too much like a "doll").

Flocked hair and a beard were added to the figures, and by 1970 the G.I. Joe Adventure Team was created. Joe was now a Jungle Explorer, Aquanaut, Polar Explorer, etc. instead of a soldier, marine, or pilot. The "Kung Fu Grip" was introduced in 1974.

The Arab oil embargo of 1973 increased the cost of plastic. By 1976, Joe was reduced to a smaller 8" size, and was called Super Joe. From 1977 to 1981 no figures were produced.

Hasbro stock numbers are listed in parentheses. All of the original series figures were named G.I. Joe with the exception of the nurse, foreign combat series and futuristic villains.

Prices are for "Complete No Package" (CNP), "Mint in Package" (MIP), and "Mint in Mint Package" (MIMP). Complete definitions are in the Action Figures section.

Tomart's Price Guide to Action Figure Collectibles includes a complete listing of G.I. Joe items, plus a details of each item's contents. See page 150 for ordering information.

G.I. JOE ACTION SOLDIER AND ACCESSORIES

GI101	G.I. Joe Action Soldier (7500)	100	150	225
GI105	Green Beret Figure (7536)	275	1000	1450
GI111	Field Jacket Set (7501)	40	100	130
GI112	Command Post Poncho Set (7517)	50	90	150
GI113	Command Post Small Arms Set (7518)	40	60	90
GI114	MP "Ike" costume (7521)	90	170	200
GI119	MP "Ike" Jacket (7524)	35	60	80
GI121	MP Helmet & Small Arms (7526)	35	50	80
GI122	Combat Field Pack Set (7502	40	85	130
GI123	Bivouac Sleeping Bag Set (7512)	45	110	140
GI124	Mountain Troops (7530)	45	125	150
GI131	Bivouac-Pup Tent Set (7513)	50	160	200
GI132	Sabotage Set (7516)	150	275	400
GI133	Ski Patrol (7531)	125	225	300
GI134	Special Forces Bazooka (7532)	50	250	350
GI135	Heavy Weapons Set (7538)	150	275	400
GI136	Military Police Set (7539)	100	190	250
GI138	Jungle Fighter (7522)	20	85	115
GI139	Ski Troops Set (7527)	40	60	90
GI140	Rocket Firing Bazooka (7528)	40	65	110
GI141	Snow Troop Set (7529)	30	60	80
GI150	Talking Action Soldier (7590)	125	200	350
GI153	Action Soldier Negro (7900)	550	900	1400
GI155	West Point Cadet (7537)	200	350	500
GI164	Military Police Set (7521)	40	75	125
GI165	Green Beret (7533)	20	100	130
GI172	Combat Engineer (7571)	75	200	275
GI173	Combat Construction (7572)	80	210	300
GI174	Combat Demolition (7573)	30	125	225

G.I. JOE ACTION SAILOR AND ACCESSORIES

GI201	G.I. Joe action sailor (7600)	75	250	350
GI211	Sea Rescue Set (7601)	40	150	250
GI217	Dress Parade (7619)	35	75	100

GI131   GI132   GI133

GI221

GI225

GI111   GI122   GI123   GI124

GI227

GI218	Deep Sea Diver (7620)	65	175	300
GI221	Shore Patrol Set (7612)	135	230	400
GI222	Shore Patrol (7613)	40	90	120
GI224	Shore Patrol Helmet Set (7616)	25	60	85
GI225	Deep Freeze Set (7623)	200	450	600
GI226	Breeches Buoy (7625)	300	550	750
GI227	Navy Frogman Underwater Demolition Set (7602)	135	350	500
GI228	Sea Rescue (7622)	50	200	300
GI229	LSO Set (7626)	35	55	85
GI241	Talking Action Sailor (7690)	160	500	750
GI242	Annapolis Cadet (7624)	250	650	1000
GI243	Navy Attack Set (7607)	50	120	185
GI244	Navy Attack Work Shirt (7608)	20	45	80
GI247	Landing Signal Officer Set (7621)	90	325	475

GI354	Weapons Pack (7727)	50	125	165
GI355	Tank Commander Set (7731)	80	140	300
GI356	Jungle Fighter Set (7732)	80	150	325

G.I. JOE ACTION PILOT AND ACCESSORIES

GI401	G.I. Joe Action Pilot (7800)	85	250	350
GI411	Survival Set (7801)	45	140	245
GI412	Dress Uniform (7803)	145	275	400
GI413	Survival Life Raft Set (7802)	20	60	85
GI414	Scramble Equipment Set (7807)	100	225	350
GI415	Flight Suit (7808)	20	60	100
GI416	Scramble Air Vest (7809)	20	50	80
GI417	Scramble Crash Helmet (7810)	40	75	100
GI418	Scramble Parachute Pack (7811)	25	55	80
GI419	Communications (7812)	30	65	95
GI420	Air Police Set (7813)	120	185	225
GI421	Air Force Accessories Set (7814)	35	75	110
GI422	Air Security Set (7815)	195	275	400
GI424	Crash Crew Set (7820)	75	250	350
GI425	Working Parachute Set (7823)	300	650	850
GI426	Astronaut Suit (7824)	30	250	325
GI427	Air Sea Rescue (7825)	165	425	675
GI431	Talking Action Pilot (7890)	200	650	850
GI441	Air Cadet (7822)	300	550	800
GI442	Action Pilot Dress Jacket (7804)	50	85	110

GI228   GI226

GI218

G.I. JOE ACTION MARINE AND ACCESSORIES

GI301	G.I. Joe Action Marine (7700)	80	275	350
GI311	Communications Post G.I. Joe Poncho Set (7701)	45	100	175
GI312	Combat Paratrooper Special Parachute Set (7705)	40	95	160
GI314	Communications Post-Flag (7704)	50	155	235
GI318	Dress Parade Set (7710)	60	155	225
GI319	Beachhead Assault Tent (7711)	55	125	195
GI321	Beachhead Aslt. Fatigue Shirt (7714)	45	65	85
GI325	Marine Medic (7719)	75	175	220
GI326	Medic Set (7720)	25	40	80
GI327	First Aid Set (7721)	30	45	85
GI328	Bunk Bed (7723)	55	125	200
GI330	Mortar Set (7725)	60	140	190
GI331	Automatic Machine Gun (7726)	65	150	200
GI332	Weapons Rack (7727)	95	175	250
GI333	Demolition (7730)	70	225	350
GI341	Talking Action Marine (7790)	200	450	625
GI351	Communications Poncho (7702)	55	125	175
GI352	Paratrooper Set (7709)	60	165	200
GI353	Beachhead flame thrower (7716)	50	120	160

GI319   GI318   GI325

GI355   GI332

Action Soldiers of the World

GI501	German set (8100)	400	1200	2000
GI502	Japanese set (8101)	500	1400	2200
GI503	Russian set (8102)	350	1100	1900
GI504	French set (8103)	280	1180	1800
GI505	British set (8104)	300	1150	2000
GI506	Australian set (8105)	255	1050	1650
GI511	German Soldier (8200)	215	675	950
GI512	Japanese Soldier (8201)	275	775	1150
GI513	Russian Soldier (8202)	235	675	950
GI514	French Soldier (8203)	220	575	900
GI515	British Soldier (8204)	225	675	950
GI516	Australian Soldier (8205)	220	575	900
GI521	German Equipment (8300)	200	350	450
GI522	Japanese Equipment (8301)	185	275	325
GI523	Russian Equipment (8302)	105	225	275
GI524	French Equipment (8303)	50	150	225
GI525	British Equipment (8304)	135	200	300
GI526	Australian Equipment (8305)	55	175	250
GI530	Foreign Soldier Set (8111.89) includes GI511-16	-	1500	2500

Heavy Equipment/Games/Other Items

GI601	Five Star Jeep Set (7000)	135	215	325
GI605	Action Nurse (8060)	1200	1850	3000
GI611	Foot Locker gift set	70	155	225
GI612	Adventure Locker	165	235	300
GI614	Astro Locker	80	220	280
GI631	Desert Patrol Set (8030)	700	1400	1800
GI632	Same as GI631, w/o figure	500	1100	1400
GI634	Crash Crew Fire Truck (8040)	700	1400	1800
GI635	Same as GI634, w/o figure	500	1000	1400
GI636	Astronaut Suit and Space Capsule Set (8020)	225	425	500
GI637	Same as GI636, w/o figure	150	250	425
GI640	Frogman and Sea Sled (8050)	160	280	400
GI641	Military Staff Car	500	900	1200
GI642	Motorcycle	150	225	325
GI643	Side Car	250	300	450
GI644	Navy Jet	450	700	1000
GI650	Machine Gun Set (Sears)	150	375	500
GI651	Forward Observer Set (Sears)	160	375	500
GI652	Green Beret Set (Sears)	400	700	900
GI653	Scuba Outfit Set (Sears)	230	425	600
GI654	Capsule and Space Outfit (Sears)	150	250	300
GI655	Recovery of the Lost Mummy (Sears)	50	90	140
GI657	Giant Helicopter and Amphicat Set (Sears)	60	110	160
GI659	Mystery of the Boiling Lagoon	45	64	85

The Adventure Team

GI701	G.I. Joe Man of Action (7500)	75	160	240
GI702	Land Adventurer (7401)	70	150	200
GI703	Sea Adventurer (7402)	70	160	210
GI704	Air Adventurer (7403)	65	135	190
GI705	Negro Adventurer (7404)	110	170	240
GI711	Talking Man of Action (7590)	90	155	240
GI712	Talking Astronaut (7405)	150	235	300
GI713	Talking Commander (7400)	95	175	250
GI721	Land Adventurer w/Kung Fu Grip (7280)	75	140	240
GI722	Sea Adventurer w/Kung Fu Grip (7281)	80	145	185
GI723	Air Adventurer w/Kung Fu Grip (7282)	80	154	185
GI724	Black Adventurer w/Kung Fu Grip (7283)	130	180	265
GI725	Man of Action w/Kung Fu Grip (7284)	80	130	180
GI730	Talking Commander w/Kung Fu Grip (7290)	90	140	190
GI731	Talking Black Commander (7291)	180	225	350
GI732	Talking Man of Action (7292)	90	155	225
GI734	Eagle Eye G.I. Joe	55	125	175
GI735	Bullet Man	55	125	175

G.I. Joe Adventures

GI800	Hidden Missile Discovery (7415)	35	75	100
GI822	Secret Mission to Spy Island (7411)	30	60	80
GI823	Danger of the Depths (7412)	30	60	80
GI824	Revenge of the Spy Shark (7413)	60	90	130
GI825	Black Widow Rendezvous (7414)	50	80	130
GI826	Peril of the Raging Inferno (7416)	50	85	135
GI827	Search for the Stolen Idol (7418)	62	115	140
GI828	Helicopter (7380)	40	65	80
GI829	Attack at Vulture Falls (7420)	50	85	135
GI830	Jaws of Death (7421)	60	130	160
GI831	Eight Ropes of Danger (7422)	100	140	200
GI832	White Tiger Hunt (7436)	100	140	200
GI833	Capture of the Pygmy Gorilla (7437)	50	85	135
GI834	Devil of the Deep (7439)	50	77	115
GI835	Sky Dive to Danger (7440)	70	100	135
GI836	Secret of the Mummy's Tomb (7441)	90	120	220
GI837	The Fate of the Trouble Shooter (7450)	68	112	130
GI838	Sky Hawk (7470)	50	75	105
GI839	Sea Wolf Submarine (7460)	45	60	105
GI840	Adventure Team Headquarters (7490)	60	80	110

GI412

GI414

GI511-16 and GI516-26

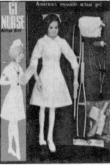

		GI356		GI605			GI831	
GI841	Sandstorm Survival (7493)				85	125	210
GI843	Training Center (7495)				75	115	200
GI844	Secret Mountain Outpost (8040)				50	75	105
GI845	Spacewalk Mystery (7445)				110	175	275
GI850	The Shark's Surprise (7442)				110	175	275
GI851	Hidden Missile Discovery (7415)				80	140	200
GI852	Fantastic Freefall (7423)				100	170	235
GI853	Adventure Set (7480) w/GI822, GI823, and GI859				90	150	200
GI855	Turbo Copter (7363)				25	55	105
GI857	Drag Bike (7364)				25	55	105
GI859	Flying Space Adventure (7425)				95	200	300
GI861	Mobile Support Vehicle (7499)				60	80	120
GI862	Adventure Team Vehicle (7005)				40	70	90
GI863	Talking G.I. Joe w/command post items (90517)				100	185	275
GI864	Talking G.I. Joe w/special force items (90532)				175	400	650
GI865	Talking G.I. Joe w/LSO items (90621)				250	450	600
GI866	Talking G.I. Joe w/field pack items (90712)				95	225	300
GI875	Emergency Rescue playset				25	50	85

GI721-24

G.I. JOE — A REAL AMERICAN HERO (1982-92)
by Bill Sikora

Many things were different when G.I. Joe reappeared in 1982. The figures were only 3-3/4", and each character had a code name. No longer was every figure a G.I. Joe. In fact, none were called Joe. Descriptive names like Bazooka, Snake Eyes, Grunt, and Cover Girl added new depth to the play value. Each figure came with small weapons and a back pack. An element of futuristic fantasy was added to figures beyond the first series. COBRA was the enemy force from the outset.

For a complete guide to G.I. Joe and action figure collecting in general, check out *Tomart's Price Guide to Action Figure Collectibles*. The book lists more than 300 action figure lines, with nearly 4,000 color and b&w photographs. It is regularly updated in *Tomart's Action Figure Digest*. For ordering information, see page 150.

3-3/4" FIGURES
First Series, 1982 (straight arms)

GI910	Snake Eyes (commando)	15	50	75
GI911	Scarlet (counter-intelligence)	15	50	75
GI912	Cobra Commander (straight arm, mail in premium)	18	38	60

GI850

GI832

GI833

GI711

GI713

GI910

GI911

Circus Time

LITTLE BENNY WANTED A PONY

A LITTLE GOLDEN BOOK plus a real MASK
And here is an ANGRY FROWN for you.

ANIMAL PAINT BOOK

Doctor Dan THE BANDAGE MAN

DOCTOR DAN The Bandage Man
by Helen Gaspard
pictures by Corinne Malvern
SIMON AND SCHUSTER NEW YORK

Doctor Dan AT THE CIRCUS

Nurse Nancy

TEX AND HIS TOYS

Little Lulu AND HER MAGIC TRICKS
KLEENEX TISSUES
Things to make and do with Kleenex Tissues

GINGER PAPER DOLL

Ginger

THE PAPER DOLL WEDDING

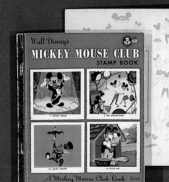
Walt Disney's MICKEY MOUSE CLUB STAMP BOOK
A Mickey Mouse Club Book

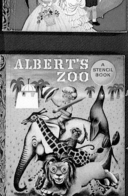
1961
JULY

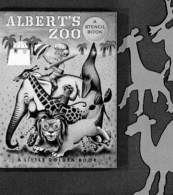
ALBERT'S ZOO
A STENCIL BOOK
A LITTLE GOLDEN BOOK

FUN WITH DECALS
A very special LITTLE GOLDEN BOOK with a page of real DECALS

A LITTLE GOLDEN ACTIVITY BOOK
Walt Disney's Sleeping Beauty
A Little Golden Story Book with dolls to punch out and dresses to cut out

Little Red Riding Hood
A STORY BOOK, WITH DOLLS TO CUT OUT AND DRESS

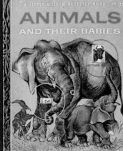
ANIMALS AND THEIR BABIES

LET'S SAVE MONEY

TRIM THE Christmas Tree
A story with 10 cut-out ornaments to use on your own Christmas tree!

MIKE and MELISSA PAPER DOLLS
Two pendant dolls with clothes and accessories to cut out and a storybook to read and to play

McDonald's
STAR TREK
MEAL

5 NEW BOXES! 5 STAR TREK PRIZES!

With Hamburger .... $1.30 each
With Cheeseburger .... $1.35 each

INCLUDES:
• A Regular size Hamburger ... or Cheeseburger (slight additional charge)
• Regular size order of French Fries • Regular size Soft Drink
• McDonaldland Cookie Sampler and a Star Trek prize!

Offer ends February 3, 1980 or while supply lasts.

Hot Wheels
MATTEL

HAPPY MEAL

Available NOW

COLLECT ALL 12
One in each Hot Wheels
Happy Meal

While supplies last. This toy has been safety tested for children age 3 and over.
CAUTION: May contain small parts and is not intended for children under
3 years of age. Ask about special toys for kids under 3.

McDonald's Happy Meal featuring
Jim Henson's
FRAGGLE ROCK

Boober & Wembley Fraggle

Collect all 4
While supplies last.

CAUTION: May contain small parts. Not intended for children under 3.
Ask about special toys for kids under 3!

McDonald's Happy Meal
FEATURING
Jim Henson's
MUPPET KIDS

THE MORE THE BETTER

TO SNAP TOGETHER

WHILE SUPPLIES LAST.

CAUTION: May contain small parts. Not intended for children under 3!
ASK ABOUT SPECIAL ITEMS FOR KIDS UNDER 3!

McDonald's
HAPPY MEAL
featuring
TINY TOON
Adventures

There's a different car and driver on the flip side.
Collect all 4, and get all 8!

FLIP CARS

McDonald's Happy Meal presents
LEGO MOTION
COLLECT ALL 8 BUILDING SETS WHILE SUPPLIES LAST

McDonald's
Sport Ball
HAPPY MEAL

Catch 'em all!
while supplies last.

Basketball and hoop are safety-tested for children age 3 and over.
CAUTION: May contain small parts. Not intended for children under 3.
Ask about special toys for kids under 3!

ALL ABOARD!

McDonaldland EXPRESS
HAPPY MEAL

THIS WEEK'S CAR

COLLECT ALL 4 CARS

HAPPY MEAL INCLUDES:
• regular size Hamburger or Cheeseburger
• regular size order of fries
• regular size soft drink
• decals featuring McDonaldland characters!

McDino CHANGEABLES
HAPPY MEAL

Happy Meal!

COLLECT ALL 8
While supplies last.

Safety-tested for children age 3 and over. CAUTION: May contain small parts.
Not intended for children under 3. Ask about special toys for kids under 3.

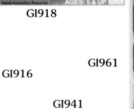

GI918

GI916

GI961

GI941

GI914	Mobat w/Steeler	18	45	55
GI916	Motorized Crimson Attack Tank (CAT)	20	60	80
GI918	Cobra Missile Command Headquarters (Sears Exclusive)	75	115	150
Second Series, 1983 (swivel arm)				
GI921	Snake Eyes	15	50	75
GI923	Scarlet	15	50	75
GI925	Falcon Glider w/Grunt	15	45	60
GI927	Viper Glider w/Viper Pilot	15	45	60
GI929	Headquarters Command Center	25	60	85
Third Series, 1983-84				
GI930	Cobra Sentry and Missile System (Sears exclusive)	20	60	80
Fourth Series, 1984				
GI941	USS Flagg w/Admiral	30	55	75
Fifth Series, 1985				
GI958	Terror Dome w/Firebat	35	85	125
Sixth Series, 1986-87				
GI961	Defiant: Space Vehicle Launch Complex w/Payload & Hard Top	50	88	125
GI961	Crossfire w/Rumbler (Alpha)	20	35	60
GI962	Crossfire w/Rumbler (Delta)	20	35	60

GOLDEN BOOKS   by Rebecca Greason

A quick search through almost every yard sale book box will yield any number of Golden Books, especially the ubiquitous Little Golden Books, easily identified by their bright golden spines. Also to be found are Big, Giant, and De Luxe Golden Books, as well as books from a myriad of other Golden series, both hard and soft-cover. What began as an experiment in 1942 to produce an inexpensive series of children's books has

GO401

89   GO402

GO406

GO407

GO408

more than 3,000 color and b&w photos of Little Golden Books, Big Golden Books, Giant Golden Books and the rest of the Golden Books family with detailed descriptions and prices. See page 150 for ordering information.

Abbreviations used in the listings are: adp—adapted; c—copyright; GPI—Golden Press, Inc.; illus—illustrated; LG—Little Golden; LGB—Little Golden Book; pp—pages; trans—translated; vol—volume; WD—Walt Disney; WDP—Walt Disney Productions; WDS—Walt Disney Studios. Prices are for good to mint or "as new" condition.

Big Golden Books

Large format Golden Books were introduced in 1944, with the designation "Big Golden Book" appearing around 1947. Although a variety of sizes and binding styles have been used, the books are generally 9" X 12". The number of pages varies. Most books are marked "Big Golden Book" on the cover.

GO401 *Baby's Mother Goose*
(Nursery Rhymes) illus by Eloise Wilkin,
©1958, 24pp   10-30

GO402 *Caroline at the Ranch*
written & illus by Pierre Probst, trans by
Debra Dabrowska, ©1968 by Librairie
Hachette, 28pp   10-40

GO403 *Caroline in Europe*
written & illus by Pierre Probst, trans by
Susan Witty, ©1961 by Librairie
Hachette, 28pp   10-40

GO404 *Funny Bunny*
by Rachel Learnard, illus by Alice & Martin
Provensen, ©1950. 28pp. Pop-up inside
front cover.   12-30

GO405 *Golden Treasury of Caroline & Her Friends*
written & illus by Pierre Probst, ©1953 by
Librairie Hachette. Printed in France by
Brodart/Topan. Unpaged thick quarto.   30-85

GO406 *Little Black Sambo*
by Helen Bannerman, illus by Bonnie & Bill
Rutherford, ©1961, 20pp. First Golden Press
printing (1976). Previously published as a
Top-Top Book.   10-35

GO407 *Roy Rogers, King of the Cowboys*
by Elizabeth Beecher, illus by Peter Alvarado,
©1953 by Roy Rogers Enterprises, 112pp   15-45

GO408 *Santa Claus Book, The*
complied by Kathryn Jackson, illus by Retta
Worcester, ©1952, 128pp   15-30

Big Golden Books - Disney

GO409 *Alice in Wonderland*
based on the Lewis Carroll story, illus by WDS,
adp by Al Dempster, ©1951 by WDP, 28pp,
1st edition has gilt decorations on cover
and specially bordered pages.   10-40

evolved into a publishing colossus, with Golden emerging as the world's largest producer of children's books. In 1986, Western Publishing Company, the parent organization of Golden Books, published their billionth Golden Book. Now into their third generation of young readers, with new series being introduced yearly, production shows no sign of abating as Golden rounds the half-century mark.

Interest in Golden Books ranges from the nostalgic ("This was my favorite book when I was a child") to specialized collector categories. Thanks to licensing contracts with companies like Disney, Warner Bros., Hanna-Barbera, and Mattel, a list of Golden Book titles reads like a "who's who" of cartoon characters. Favorite authors and artists are another collectible area.

General condition guidelines for other collectible categories also apply to Golden Books. Collectors are especially cautioned to check for missing pages. Title pages and last pages are favorite tear-outs with young folks. And except for a child's name in the front, crayon or pencil markings within a book will greatly reduce the value. Books missing either front or back covers are not considered collectible. The edition or printing is also important. Although not all books are marked, the majority of Golden Books have some indication of edition. For Little Golden Books, edition is generally noted with the copyright notice on the front or back of the title page or as a letter code in the lower right corner of the last page (a = first, c = third, etc.) Larger Golden Books may show the edition in the same manner, or on the inside of the back or front cover as a letter code followed by a double price code (A100100 = first, $1.00).

Tomart's Price Guide to Golden Book Collectibles includes

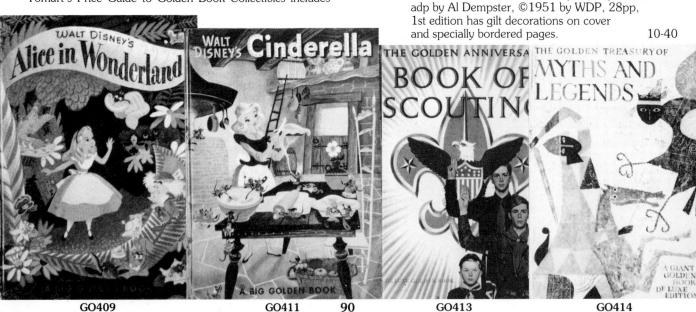
GO409   GO411   **90**   GO413   GO414

GO16

GO17

GO20

GO415

GO421

GO422

GO423

GO430

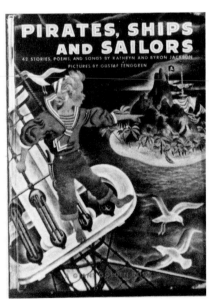

GO424

GO433

GO434   GO436   GO438   GO441   GO442

GO410 Same as above, later editions without gilt
on cover & page borders.   3-12

GO411 *Cinderella*
adp by Jane Werner, illus by WDS, adp by Retta
Worcester, ©1950 by WDP, 28pp, 1st
edition has gilt decoration throughout, honeycomb pumpkin inside front cover.   10-35

GO412 Same as above, later editions without gilt
decorations and honeycomb pumpkin.   3-12

De Luxe Golden Books

A special series of educational books designed to widen the
young readers' horizons was developed in the sixties. Books
are generally several hundred pages in length.

GO413 *Golden Anniversary Book of Scouting*
by R. D. Bezucha, Illus by Norman Rockwell,
et al., ©1959 by the Boy Scouts of America
and GPI, 166pp, issued with dust jacket.   15-35

GO414 *Golden Treasury of Myths & Legends*
adapted by Anne Terry White from the
world's great classics, illus by Alice &
Martin Provensen, ©1959, 166pp.   10-35

GO415 *Golden Treasury of Poetry, The*
selected by Louis Untermeyer, illus by Joan
Walsh Anglund, ©1959, 324pp.   12-40

Funtime Books

One of many soft cover series produced by Golden, the
Funtime books featured cut and paste activities, such as punch-
out and paper dolls, making complete books hard to find
today. Books that feature popular cartoon characters are especially sought after.

GO416 *Charmin' Chatty* (GF237)
1964, paper doll   12-25

GO417 *Disneyland, Walt Disney's* (GF230)
©1963, punch-outs   35-75

GO418 *Popeye* (GF177)
©1961, punch-outs   15-45

GO419 *Pollyanna, Walt Disney's* (GF163)
©1960, paper doll   15-30

GO420 *Sleeping Beauty, Walt Disney's* (GF195)
©1959, punch-outs   15-50

Giant Golden Books

Introduced in 1944, these books are identified as both
"Giant" and "Giant De Luxe" and were originally 10-1/4" X
13", although the size many vary considerably on later books.
Editorial content of these larger format books drew not only on
the story content of the Little Golden series, but also fostered a
developing concept for providing quality educational books for
younger readers.

GO421 *Animal's Merry Christmas, The*
by Kathryn Jackson, illus by Richard Scarry,
©1950, 96pp. Early editions w/pop-up
Santa inside cover only.   15-50

GO422 *Fairy Tale Book, The*
trans by Marie Ponsot, illus by Adrienne Segur,
©1958, 156pp   12-45

GO423 *Giant Golden Book of Elves and Fairies*
selected by Jane Werner, illus by Garth Williams,

©1951, 76pp   35-75

GO424 *Pirates, Ships and Sailors, Tenggren's*
by Kathryn Jackson, illus by Gustaf Tenggren,
©1950, 96pp   15-60

Golden Books (General)

Books in this listing are general titles produced by Golden
but not related to a specific series.

GO430 *Chinese Fairy Tales*
trans by Marie Ponsot, illus by Serge Rizatto,
©1960 by Fabbri, Milan, 156pp   15-40

GO431 *Golden Puppet Playhouse*
©1961. A "talent kit" w/complete
accessories for a puppet show, including
a stage & 3 hand puppets.   18-45

GO432 *Pinocchio*
by Carlo Collodi, illus by Sergio Rizzato,
©1963 by Golden Press, illus ©1963 by
Fratelli Fabbri Editori, 118pp   15-35

GO433 *Russian Fairy Tales*
trans by Marie Ponsot, illus by Benvenuti,
©1960 by Fabbri, Milan, 66pp   15-40

Little Golden Books

Since they first appeared on the market in 1942, over 1100
individual titles have been published in the Little Golden Series.
Collector interest is almost as varied as the titles. Some people
collect all the books with "Golden Backs," some are seeking to
assemble the first 600 titles, others want all 1100+. Highest
interest is reserved for books that have activities (paper dolls,
puzzles, etc.) and books that feature cartoon characters, westerns and TV show personalities. Early books in the series (1-
28, 30, and 34) were issued in dust jackets, and copies that
still have them are eagerly sought.

GO434 *Pets for Peter* (82)
by Jane Werner, illus by Aurelius Battaglia,
©1950, 28pp, 1st edition w/puzzle. One
of at least 13 Little Golden Books published
with a puzzle in the inside back cover.   20-35

GO435 Same as above without puzzle   5-10

GO436 *Doctor Dan, The Bandage Man* (111)
by Helen Gaspard, illus by Corinne Malvern,
©1950, 28pp w/a strip of 6 Band-Aids®
on the title page   15-30

GO437 Same as above without the Band-Aids®   6-12

GO438 *Paper Doll Wedding, The* (193)
written & illus by Hilda Miloche & Wilma Kane,
©1954, 28pp. Complete & uncut.   18-40

GO439 Same as above, complete but cut.   15-30

GO440 Same as above without paper dolls.or clothes   2-6

Ten paper doll books were included in the regular LGB
series and the LG Activity series. The books were so popular
that some of the titles were repeated several times within the
series.

GO441 *It's Howdy Doody Time* (223)
by Edward Kean, illus by Art Seiden,
©1955 by Kagran Corp., 24pp   12-30

GO442 *Twins, The* (227)
by Ruth & Harold Shane, illus by Eloise

GO443

GO444

GO445

GO446

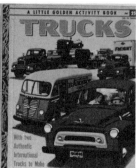

GO448

Wilkin, ©1955, 28pp   12-25

Collector interest in any books illustrated by Eloise Wilkin runs high. *The Twins* is one of the most difficult titles to find.

GO443 *Roy Rogers and the Mountain Lion* (231)
by Ann McGovern, illus by Mel Crawford,
©1955 by Frontiers, Inc., 24pp   12-28

GO444 *Jetsons, The* (500)
by Carl Memling, illus by Hawley Pratt
& Al White, ©1962 by Hanna-Barbera
Productions   12-25

GO445 *Good Humor Man, The* (550)
by Kathleen N. Daly, illus by Tibor Gergely,
©1964, 24pp   12-40

Little Golden Books - Activity Series

Books that included activities were so popular in the regular LGB series that a special series was developed. Thirty-three books were produced between 1955 and 1963, featuring wheels, stamps, punch-outs, and other activities.

GO446 *Clown Coloring Book* (A5)
illus by Art Seiden, ©1955, 20pp. With
crayon box attached to cover.   15-35

GO447 Same as above without crayons   6-15

GO448 *Trucks* (A6)
by Kathryn Jackson, illus by Ray Quigley, ©1955,
24pp, w/two punch-out trucks.   25-50

GO449 Same as above without trucks   8-12

GO450 *Mickey Mouse Club Stamp Book, Walt Disney's* (A10)
by Kathleen N. Daly, illus by WDS, adp by
Julius Svendsen, ©1956 by WDP, w/
unused stamps in front of book   15-35

GO451 Same as above w/stamps glued in.   6-12

GO452 *Mike and Melissa* (A31)
by Jane Werner Watson, illus by Adriana Mazza
Saviozzi, ©1959, 20pp. Two punch-out paper
dolls on heavy board, clothes were on
outside half of each page.   25-40

GO453 Same as above, complete but cut   15-25

GO454 Same as above, no dolls or clothes   3-8

GO455 *Sleeping Beauty, Walt Disney's* (A33)
based on the Walt Disney movie, illus adp by
Julius Svendsen, et al., ©1959 by WDP, 20pp.
Sleeping Beauty & Prince Phillip paper dolls
on heavy board.   30-75

GO456 Same as above, complete but cut   25-60

GO457 Same as above, no dolls or clothes   5-12

GO458 *Gordon's Jet Flight* (A48)
by Naomi J. Glasson, illus by Mel Crawford,
©1961, 20pp. w/an American Airlines
Astrojet punch-out.   25-50

GO459 Same as above without Astrojet   6-10

GO463

Tiny Golden Books

Each set of 12 Tiny Golden Books (2-1/4" X 3-1/4") was housed in a "bookshelf box," protected by a slipcase. The sets were later combined to form "Tiny Golden Libraries" of 24 and 36 books.

GO460 *Tiny Movie Stories, Walt Disney's*
by WDS, ©1950 by WDP, twelve 24 pp books in
a Movie Theater box, w/slipcase   35-70

GO461 Same as above without slipcase   25-60

GO462 Individual volumes   2-6

GO463 *Tiny Golden Library, The*
(Animal, Movie, & Nonsense Stories) ©1964,
36 books in a wood-pattern box.   40-80

GO464 *Tiny Golden Library, The*
(Animal and Nonsense Stories) ©1968,
24 books in Nonsense Town Box.   35-60

Slipcase Sets

Specially boxed sets of books have been produced in many Golden Series. While most boxes were meant mainly for presentation (and were discarded later), other sets came in decorative slipcases designed for storage. Sets contained original material as well as stories previously published by Golden

GO465 *Golden Treasure Chest, The*
Edited by Bryna & Louis Untermeyer,

GO450

GO452

GO455

GO458

©1968, 4 vols, 256pp each, in Treasure
Chest slipcase. Classic tales & legends.　25-50
GO466　Individual volumes　4-10
GO467　*Little Golden Book Library*
©1969, 4 vols, 384pp each, in slipcase, 58
all-time classic stories from the LGB series　35-60
GO468　Individual volumes　8-14
GO469　*Walt Disney Parade*
by WDS, ©1970 by WDP, 4 vols, 256pp each,
in Disney slipcase. A Disney showcase.　40-60
GO470　Individual volumes　8-12

HAPPY MEALS (MCDONALD'S)
by Meredith Williams

Since Ray Kroc bought the rights to the McDonald's brothers operation and opened his first restaurant in Des Plaines,
Illinois, on April 15, 1955, many collectible items have come
from this company...pins, buttons, uniforms, cups, mugs, glasses, jewelry, postcards, advertising pieces, special convention
pieces, retail items, and many more. With over 11,000 stores
worldwide the volume of collectibles being produced is fantasti-
cally high.

In 1977 McDonald's began their kids' meal program called
Happy Meals. The promotion has been very successful and the
toys, boxes, and advertising pieces have become some of the
most sought after McDonald's collectibles. Nearly two hundred
different Happy Meals have been made available to the public.

But not all Happy Meals have been available nationwide;
many were regional or local promotions. Plus there were items
test marketed but not released in quantity. This makes collecting Happy Meal items a real challenge. Contact with collectors
in other parts of the country is a must. The greatest difficulty is
finding the toys McDonald's produced especially for children
under three. Quantities were limited because each store
received only a small number of these compared to the other
toys.

The items listed include some Happy Meals distributed
regionally. Prices reflect the condition most likely to be found
at a garage sale - in good condition but showing some use. The
item should be complete; it's common to find toys missing
small parts. The highest prices are paid for Mint In Package
(MIP) items. These have never been used and include the promotional package. MIP items can go for two to four times what
a non-MIP item would. Prices also vary widely from one part of
the country to another. The price for an item in a region
where a Happy Meal was offered could be less than in a region
where these items were not available.

*Tomart's Price Guide to McDonald's Happy Meal
Collectibles* is a complete guide to Happy Meals, with extensive listings and photographs. See order form on page 150.

Astrosniks 1983
Boxes
HA501　Rover/One Wheel Drive　5
HA502　Round Spaceship/Robo/Astralia　5
HA503　Space Ship/Moon Golf Course　5
HA504　Space Vehicle/Volcano/Dinosaur　5
Figurines, 2-3" tall molded hard plastic w/yellow M
HA505　Astralia, Laser, Robo-Robot, Scout,
　　　　Skater, Snikapotamus, Sport or Thirsty　3
HA513　Astrosniks Happy Meal Translite menu
　　　　board sign　10
Astrosniks 1984
Boxes
HA515　Snik Station/Perfido　5
HA516　McStore/Racer/Driller/Ski　5
Figurines, 2"-3" tall molded hard plastic w/yellow M
HA517　Commander, Copter, Drill, Perfido,
　　　　Racing or Ski　3
HA523　Astrosniks Happy Meal Translite menu
　　　　board sign　10

HA517-22

Barnyard 1986 (Also called Old McDonald's Farm)
Boxes
HA525　Old McDonald's BARN　5
HA526　Old McDonald's HOUSE　5
Figurines, plastic, made by Playmates Company
HA527　Man, Wife, Cow, Hen, Pig, Rooster or Sheep　3
HA534　Barnyard Happy Meal Translite menu board sign　10
Chip 'n Dale 1989
Boxes
HA535　Framed, A Whale of a Time, The Yolk's On Him,
　　　　or Rollin' In Dough　1
Figurines
HA539　Chip's Rockin' Racer (red rocket) under 3　3
HA540　Gadget's Rockin Rider (pink cup) under 3　2
HA541　Set 1, Chip's Whirly-Copter (blue-orange)　2
HA542　Set 2, Dale's Roto-Roadster (yellow)　2
HA543　Set 3, Gadget's Rescue Racer (pink)　2
HA544　Set 4, Monterey Jack's
　　　　Propel-A-Phone (turquoise)　2
HA545　Chip 'n Dale Happy Meal Translite
　　　　advertising sign
HA546　Counter display (includes four premiums)　50
Dukes of Hazard 1982
Food Containers
HA547　Boss Hogg Caddy, white plastic/decals　5
HA548　Bronco Car, white plastic/decals　5
HA549　General Lee Car, orange plastic/decals　5
HA550　Pick Up Truck, white plastic/decals　5
HA551　Police Car, white plastic/decals　5
Cups, white plastic
HA552　Bo, Boss Hogg, Daisy, Luke, Rosco, or
　　　　Uncle Jesse　3
HA558　Dukes of Hazard Translite menu board sign　10
E.T. 1985
Boxes
HA560　E.T. Makes Friends or The Great Adventure　3
Posters
HA562　Boy/Girl and Spaceship, Boy on Bike/E.T.
　　　　Flying, E.T. Raising Finger, or E.T. w/Phone　3
HA566　E.T. Happy Meal Translite menu board sign　10
Funny Fry Friends 1990
Boxes
HA567　City Sights, Cool Day at School, Ski Holiday,
　　　　Snowy Day Play　1
Figurines and figure sets
HA571　Lit' Chief Indian Chief (orange)
　　　　under 3 premium　3
HA572　Little Darling cow girl (yellow)
　　　　under 3 premium　3
HA573　Hoops, Rollin Rocker, Matey, Gadzooks,

HA583

HA594

HA670

	Tracker, ZZZ's, Tootall, or Sweet Cuddles, ea	2	
HA581	Funny Fry Friends Translite, large	8	
HA582	Funny Fry Friends Translite, drive-thru sign	6	
HA583	Counter Display (includes all 8 premiums)	60	

Garfield 1989
Boxes
HA584	Cat With a Mission, Mischief - What a Great Morning, Picnic Basket, Plane/Ahh Vacation	1	

Figurines
HA588	Garfield on Scooter, Garfield on 4 Wheeler, Garfield on Skateboard, or Garfield on Scooter	1	
HA592	Garfield Happy Meal Translite, large	8	
HA593	Garfield Happy Meal Translite, drive-thru	6	
HA594	Counter Display (includes the four premiums)	50	

Good Sports 1984
Boxes
HA595	Basketball, Gymnastics, Skiing, Sled Run	3	

Puffy Stickers
HA601	Birdie the Early Bird w/soccer ball, Grimace on red toboggan, Hamburglar w/hockey stick, Mayor McCheese on skis, Ronald McDonald w/ice skates, Sam the Olympic Eagle w/basketball	3	
HA607	Good Sports Happy Meal Translite	10	

High Flying Kite 1987
HA608	Box High Flying Kite	5	

Kites
HA609	Birdie string, Hamburglar string, Ronald string	8	
HA612	High Flying Kite Translite	10	

Kissyfur 1987
HA613	Kissyfur box (shows the 8 premiums)	5	

Figurines
HA614	Beehonie/Rabbit furry finish	5
HA615	Duane/Pig furry finish	5
HA616	Lennie/Hog furry finish	5
HA617	Toot/Beaver furry finish	4
HA618	Floyd/Alligator smooth finish	3
HA619	Gus/Big Bear smooth finish	3
HA620	Floyd/Alligator smooth finish	3
HA621	Kissyfur/Little Bear smooth finish	3
HA622	Kissyfur Happy Meal Translite	10

Mix 'Em Up Monsters 1988
HA623	Box Mix 'Em Up Monsters	3

3 Piece Figurines
HA624	Blibble, Corkle , Gropple , or Thugger, ea	2
HA628	Mix 'Em Up Monsters Translite	10

Moveables 1988
HA629	Box Move into Homes	10

Figurines, hard rubber/painted
HA630	Birdie, Captain Crook, Fry Girl, Hamburgler, Professor, or Ronald ea	5
HA636	Moveables Translite	10

Music 1985
Boxes
HA637	Audience Clapping, Can You Find, Fill in the Letters, or McDonaldland Friends	5

45 RPM Fisher-Price Records (ea came w/dust jacket)
HA641	Coming Around the Mountain, If You're Happy, Great to be Crazy, or Hokey Pokey, ea	4
HA645	Music Translite	10

HA601-06

HA614-21

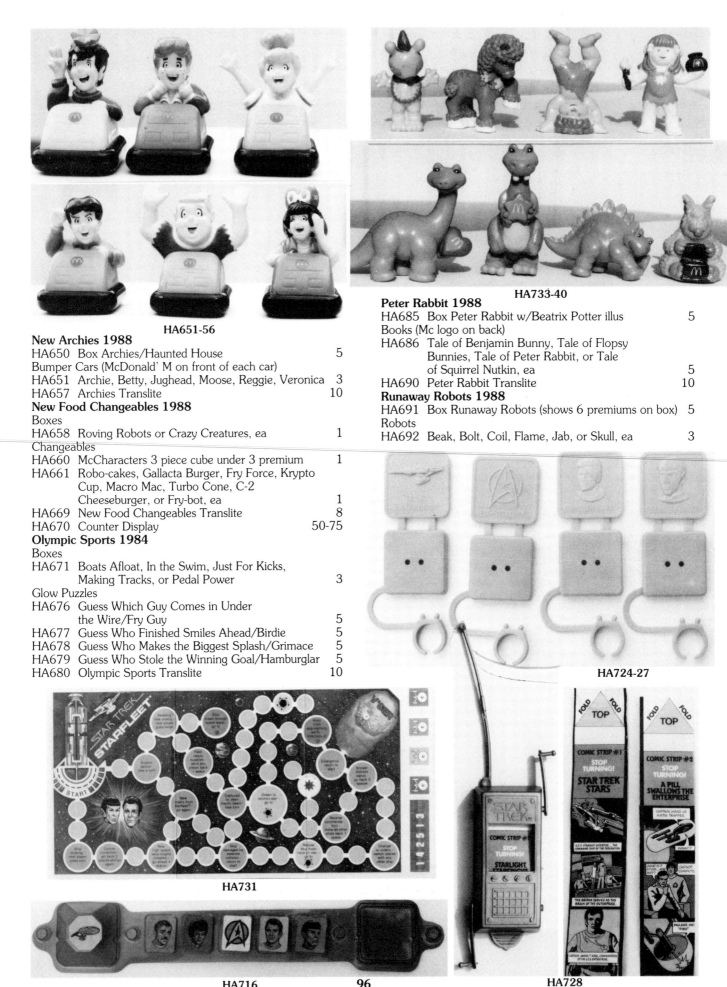

HA651-56

New Archies 1988
HA650	Box Archies/Haunted House	5

Bumper Cars (McDonald' M on front of each car)

HA651	Archie, Betty, Jughead, Moose, Reggie, Veronica	3
HA657	Archies Translite	10

New Food Changeables 1988
Boxes
HA658	Roving Robots or Crazy Creatures, ea	1

Changeables
HA660	McCharacters 3 piece cube under 3 premium	1
HA661	Robo-cakes, Gallacta Burger, Fry Force, Krypto Cup, Macro Mac, Turbo Cone, C-2 Cheeseburger, or Fry-bot, ea	1
HA669	New Food Changeables Translite	8
HA670	Counter Display	50-75

Olympic Sports 1984
Boxes
HA671	Boats Afloat, In the Swim, Just For Kicks, Making Tracks, or Pedal Power	3

Glow Puzzles
HA676	Guess Which Guy Comes in Under the Wire/Fry Guy	5
HA677	Guess Who Finished Smiles Ahead/Birdie	5
HA678	Guess Who Makes the Biggest Splash/Grimace	5
HA679	Guess Who Stole the Winning Goal/Hamburglar	5
HA680	Olympic Sports Translite	10

HA733-40

Peter Rabbit 1988
HA685	Box Peter Rabbit w/Beatrix Potter illus	5

Books (Mc logo on back)
HA686	Tale of Benjamin Bunny, Tale of Flopsy Bunnies, Tale of Peter Rabbit, or Tale of Squirrel Nutkin, ea	5
HA690	Peter Rabbit Translite	10

Runaway Robots 1988
HA691	Box Runaway Robots (shows 6 premiums on box)	5

Robots
HA692	Beak, Bolt, Coil, Flame, Jab, or Skull, ea	3

HA724-27

HA731

HA716

HA728

Sand Castle 1987   HW150
Sand Mold Food Containers
HA701 Cylindrical, Domed, Rectangle, or Square, ea   4
HA705 Sand Castle Translite   10

Star Trek 1979-80
Boxes Star Trek Meal
HA710 The Bridge - Draw the Alien   15-18
HA711 The Bridge - Planet Faces   15-18
HA712 Federation   15-18
HA713 Klingons   15-18
HA714 Spacesuit   15-18
HA715 Transporter Room   15-18
HA716 Bracelet, Starfleet (blue plastic, decals/chart)   6
HA717 Ceiling Dangler, U.S.S. Enterprise/5 boxes   50
HA718 Tri-level cardboard sign w/Capt. Kirk/Mr. Spock   50
HA719 Crew Badge, round paper w/stick-on tape at top   5
HA720 Iron-On Transfers: Kirk, McCoy, Ilia or Spock, ea 5
HA724 Rings (red, blue, or yellow) Kirk, Spock,
       Star Trek, or Enterprise, ea   6
HA728 Video Communicator (silver or black), Comic
       Strips 1 thru 5 (one strip w/2 comics back
       to back came with each communicator)   5
HA729 Translite (shows one box)   75
HA730 Translite (shows 4 food items)   75
HA731 Starfleet Game (die-cut punch-out paper)   5

Tinosaurs 1986
HA732 Box Tinosaurs shows 8 premiums   5
Figurines
HA733 Bones, Dinah, Fern, Jad, Knobby, Link,
       Spell, or Tiny, ea   3
HA741 Tinosaurs Translite   10

Turbo Macs 1988, 1990
HA742 Box Turbo Macs featuring the Mountain
       Launch Ramp   2
Cars (1988 set; 1990 set only slightly different)
HA743 Ronald (soft rubber) under 3 premium   2
HA744 Birdie, Grimace, Hamburglar, or Ronald   2
HA748 Turbo Macs Translite   10
HA750 Other' Happy Meal Premium Displays   50-75

HOT WHEELS by Paul Wallace and Randy Thoreen

Mattel introduced the first 16 Hot Wheels cars, eight play-sets, and two collector's cases in 1968. Few playsets and accessories have achieved value. The real value is in the cars themselves. The most valuable cars were produced between 1970 and 1978. The toughest to find were produced in 1973. The name and year of most vehicles appear on the bottom. The quickest way to spot the best cars is to look at the wheels. If the racing slick tires have a red line, they were made in the years 1968 to 1978. Virtually any mint "red line" is worth $10 to $15. Several black walls have exceptional value, too, but the red stripe is a quick visual signal to the most collectible Hot Wheels. Black wall tires occurred on some earlier models and became standard in 1979. From 1983-1987 Mattel produced a line of Hot Wheels called Real Riders that have rubber Goodyear tires and either white or grey hubs. They are very popular with collectors.

Most vehicles achieving the highest valuable status were made for a single year or less. There are cases where different versions of the same vehicles were repeated in other years. In other instances, value is due to a rare color. The value range listed is for Hot Wheels in near mint to mint condition in the original package. Damage in any form would substantially reduce the value of most items.

Playsets
HW150 Military Pak w/Staff Car, 1976   300-400
HW151 Staff Car only   200-300
HW160 Road King Set, 1974   400-500
HW175 Sky Show Set, 1970   300-400
HW180 Thrill Driver Set, 1977   75-100

Red Line Wheels   HW175
HW200 Alive '55, blue, 1973   35-50
HW202 Breakaway Bucket, 1974   50-75
HW204 Buzz Off, blue, 1974   35-50
HW206 VW Beach Bomb, 1969   35-50
HW208 Classic Cord, 1971   75-150
HW209 Custom Corvette, 1968   25-50
HW210 Double Header, 1973   50-75
HW218 El Rey Special, blue, 1974   75-100
HW222 GMC Motor Home, orange, 1977   50-75
HW226 Heavy Chevy, yellow, 1974   35-50
HW228 Heavyweights, all models, 1970   35-50
HW230 Hiway Robber, 1973   35-50
HW236 Letter Getter, U.S. mail truck, 1977   50-75
HW240 Mongoose, funny car, 1970   50-75
HW244 Motocross 1, motorcycle, 1975   75-100
HW246 Mustang Stocker, yellow, 1975   50-75
HW248 Odd-Job, 1973   35-50
HW250 Olds 442, 1971   75-150
HW252 Paddy Wagon   35-50
HW254 Pit Crew Car, 1971   50-75
HW256 Police Cruiser, 1969   35-50
HW260 Prowler, 1973   50-75
HW262 Rear Engine Dragsters, each, 1972   75-150
HW264 Red Baron, 1973   35-50
HW266 Seasider, 1970   25-75
HW267 Sidekick, 1972   50-75
HW268 S'Cool Bus, 1970   75-150
HW270 Show-Off, 1973   35-50
HW272 Snake, funny car, 1970   50-75

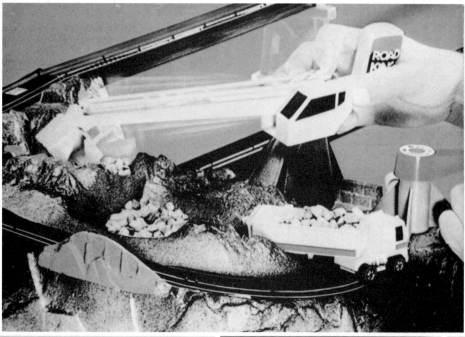

#8262 BREAKAWAY BUCKET™

HW202

#6976 BUZZ OFF™

HW160   HW204

Classic Cord #6472

HW208

HW210   #5880 DOUBLE HEADER®

#8273 EL REY SPECIAL™

HW218

25. #9645
GMC MOTOR HOME

HW222

HW236

#7619 HEAVY CHEVY

HW226

HW273 Snake, funny car, 1973	HW236	
HW276 Street Eater, motorcycle, 1975	150-250	
HW278 Street Snorter, 1973	75-100	
HW280 Superfine Turbine, 1973	35-50	
	35-50	

HW282 Sweet 16, 1973	50-75
HW284 Toys "Я" Us Van, 1975	50-75
Black Wall Tires	
HW300 Alien, blue, 1988	5-10
HW302 A-OK, grey hub Real Riders	50-75

12 Joiners
1 Clamp
2 Matching Collector's Buttons
1 International Collector's Catalog
Std. Pack: ½ Doz.   Wt: 8 Lbs.

HW180

6969 SNAKE®

#6979 HIWAY ROBBER®
HW230

34. #9203
HW246

#6981 ODD JOB®
HW248

#6966 PADDY WAGON™
HW252

#6963 POLICE CRUISER
HW256

#6965 PROWLER™
HW260

54. #9120

55. #9186
HW262

Rear Engine MONGOOSE® #5699

#6968 ALIVE '55™
HW200

#6982 SHOW-OFF™
HW270

#6971 STREET SNORTER™
HW278

6004 SUPERFINE TURBINE™
HW280

6007 SWEET "16"®
HW282

58. #9649
'31 DOOZIE
HW306

32. #2014
HOT BIRD™
HW316

HW304 Cadillac Seville, gold w/purple sides	20-30	
HW306 Doozie, orange w/green fenders, 1977	50-75	
HW308 Datsun 200SX, purple, 1984	15-20	
HW310 Flat Out 442 (green), 1984	15-20	
HW312 Frito Lay Delivery Van, 1984	10-25	
HW314 GT Racer, blue,1990	20-40	
HW316 Hot Bird, brown	50-75	
HW318 Pontiac J2000, green, 1984	25-50	
HW320 Railroad Tanker, yellow,1990	25-50	
HW322 Talbot Lago, maroon, 1988	5-10	
HW324 Toys "Я" Us Bronco, 1982	25-50	
HW326 Toys "Я" Us Pickup Truck, 1979	25-50	
HW328 '57 T-Bird, black, white hub Real Riders	50-75	

HW330 '65 Mustang Convertible, black, 1984   10-15
HW332 3 Window '34, black, white hub Real Riders   50-75

JAMES BOND   by Stephen Kulakoski

One by-product of the Cold War was a public fascination with espionage and covert operations among rival power blocs. The most popular secret agent...and perhaps the character most responsible for this interest in all matters clandestine...was James Bond, Agent 007 from Great Britain. But Bond was purely fictional, springing entirely from the fertile imagination of writer Ian Fleming (1908-1964). At various times a journalist, stockbroker, and British naval intelligence officer, Fleming developed a successful formula by combining intrigue, gadgetry, sex and a hero with endearing idiosyn-crasies. Fans followed Bond's exploits against the conspiracies of diabolical international villains through 14 Fleming novels. Bond's greatest fame has come from the seeming unending series of movies, beginning with the 1963 release of *Dr. No.*

Price ranges listed are for pieces in Fine to Mint condition. Items which are incomplete or missing the original package bring substantially lesser values.

JB450

Gilbert Toy Company 1965-66
12" Action Figures
JB101	James Bond 007 (Sean Connery)	100-200
JB102	Odd Job 12"	225-325

Rubber Hand Puppets
JB111	James Bond	75-150
JB112	Oddjob, w/hat	75-150

JB125	JB126	JB129

3-1/2" Figures and accessories JB121-43
JB121	#1 Bond w/Beretta pistol	10-15
JB122	#2 Bond w/rifle	10-15
JB123	#3 Bond in scuba suit w/spear gun	10-15
JB124	#4 Oddjob	10-15
JB125	#5 Bond's Boss "M"	10-15
JB126	#6 Goldfinger	10-15
JB127	#7 Miss Moneypenny	10-15
JB128	#8 Largo	10-15
JB129	#9 Domino	10-15
JB130	#10 Dr. No	10-15
JB135	Boxed set, includes JB121-30	100-175
JB141	Dr. No's Dragon Tank & Largo's Hydrofoil Yacht	35-50
JB142	Spin-Top Pool Table & Deadly Laser Table w/Bond	35-50
JB143	Secret Agent Gun Case & Bullet Shield "M's" Desk	25-40
JB150	Aston Martin, battery operated	350-500

Milton Bradley 1964-66
JB201	James Bond Secret Agent 007 Game, 1964	30-45
JB202	James Bond 007 Thunderball Game, 1965	35-50
JB203	James Bond 007 Goldfinger Game, 1966	35-50
JB211	Goldfinger puzzle	55-80
JB212	Thunderball—Spectre's Surprise puzzle	25-40
JB301	Aston Martin model kit (Airfix)	150-250
JB351	James Bond Figure model (Aurora) 1966	150-250
JB352	Oddjob Figure model (Aurora) 1966	150-250

JB202

Dazya Toy Co. 1966
JB401	M-101 Aston Martin Secret Ejector Car	250-350

JB453

Multiple Toymakers
JB450	SA Automatic Pistol	200-300
JB451	Bond-X Automatic Shooting Camera	150-250
JB452	007 P.A.K. (Personal Attack Kit)	125-200
JB453	Shooting Attache Case (w/JB454-55)	350-500

JB455	JB454

JB454	007 BoobyTrap Exploding Code Book	35-50
JB455	007 Code-O-Matic	50-75

Corgi Toy Cars
JB501	Aston Martin First Issue Gold Car, 1965	150-225
JB503	Toyota 2000 GT	175-250
JB505	Moonbuggy	175-250
JB507	Lotus Esprit	55-80
JB509	Citroen 2CV6	25-50

Corgi Jr. Cars (Blister Pack)
JB521	Aston Martin	10-20
JB523	Space Shuttle	10-20
JB525	Lotus Esprit	10-20
JB527	Jet Ranger	10-20
JB529	Citroen 2CV6	10-20

U.S. Game Systems 1973
JB551	Tarot Game	20-35

KI503

KI540

JB451

Mego Toy Co. 1979

JB601	James Bond (Roger Moore)	50-100
JB602	James Bond w/accessories	250-300
JB603	Drax	85-125
JB604	Holly Goodhead	90-125
JB605	Jaws	325-400

Revel Model Co. 1979

| JB651 | Moonraker Space Shuttle | 25-40 |

Matchbox Toy Cars 1985

| JB701 | Renault 11 Taxi | 10-20 |
| JB702 | Rolls Royce Silver Cloud II | 10-20 |

See also: **Books; Non-Sports Trading Cards**

KISS by Bob Gottuso (BOJO)
Photos by John Caracci

Perhaps there is nothing really unique about the concept of the rock star as a slightly surreal comic book superhero. But no rock group before or since has personified the concept better than KISS, whose first album in 1974 fueled a frenzy of devotion so intense it led to the formation of the Kiss Army, the official KISS fan club, a year later.

If a superhero identity was their trademark, then the mystery surrounding their individual identities was the touch of genius that catapulted them beyond mere stardom. Paul Stanley, the star child; Gene Simmons, the demon from hell; Ace Freleigh, the space traveler; and cat-man Peter Criss maintained their secret until their last full-costume concert in Brazil in 1983.

Manager Bill Aucoin supervised one of the heaviest merchandising efforts for a rock group in all of rock 'n roll history and the Kiss Army's demand for more kept it coming. From the first rock pinball machine to the KISS comic books, KISS memorabilia remains in demand around the world.

The prices in the following listing are a general guide for memorabilia in near mint condition (unless otherwise noted). Words in quotes actually appear on the item.

KI500	Back Pack, "Super Pack", Thermos 1979	30-60
KI501	Beach Towel, group picture, Franco, 1978	55-110
KI502	Breadspread, AQ Industries, sealed	60-125
KI503	Clock, wall, 30" X 20", Bob Wolfe, 1977	60-125
KI504	Colorforms Set, Colorforms 1979, w/flyer	30-55

Comic Books

| KI505 | Marvel Super Special #1 | 25-50 |
| KI506 | Marvel Super Special #2 | 20-40 |

Dolls, 12 1/2", Mego 1978 KI507-16

KI507	Ace, boxed	40-75
KI508	Ace, unboxed	20-35
KI509	Gene, boxed	40-75
KI510	Gene, unboxed	20-35
KI511	Peter, boxed	40-75
KI512	Peter, unboxed	20-35
KI513	Paul, boxed	40-75
KI514	Paul, unboxed	20-35
KI515	Complete Set, boxed	140-300
KI516	Draperies, A.Q. Industries, in pkg.	40-75
KI517	Game	25-45

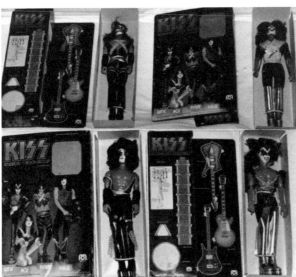

KI507-15

KI520

101

KI522

KI526

KI504   KI518

KI517

KI518	Guitar, plastic toy, in pkg.	50-100
KI519	same as above, unpackaged	25-45
KI520	Halloween Costume, 4 different, 1978, ea	20-45
KI521	Halloween mask only	9-18
KI522	KISS Your Face make-up kit Remco, 1978	40-75
KI523	Pen, 4 diff, on card, Wallace, 1978, ea	25-50
KI524	Pencils, 4 in package, Wallace 1978 (set)	25-45
KI525	Pendant, KISS logo, 3-D, GRT design	6-12
KI526	Pendant w/promotional store box	30-55
KI527	Pillow	40-75
KI528	Pinball Machine, arcade size	200-600
KI529	7-11 Plastic Cups, 8 diff, Munford, 1978, ea	20-35
KI530	"Have a Pepsi Day", scream mask, 1977	20-35
KI531	Poster Art set, Craftmaster 1977	20-35
KI532	Radio-controlled Van, Azrak-Hamway 1978	90-175
KI533	Record Player, Tiger, boxed	125-250
KI534	same as above, unboxed	90-175
KI535	Colorforms Transfer Set, 1979	20-40
KI536	Shoelaces w/logos, 1977	20-35
KI537	Showbeam/Cartridge w/viewer	25-45
KI538	Sleeping Bag, Washington Quilt 1978	100-200
KI539	Transistor Radio, 1977, w/box	35-70
KI540	Trash Can, P&K Products, 1978 2 diff, ea	50-100

| KI550 | Windbreaker, sold thru fan club | 55-110 |

See also: **Character & Promotional Glasses; Comic Books; Games; Model Kits; Non-Sports Trading Cards**

LUNCH BOXES   by Ted Hake

From 1985 to 1990, the number of lunch box collectors (sometimes called "boxers") has grown tremendously. The brightly-colored graphics and depictions of favorite cartoon, cowboy, and other entertainment-related characters and personalities appeal to many nostalgia-oriented collectors.

The lunch box concept originated in the 1800s with tin boxes for farm and factory workers. The child's lunch box first appeared during the 1930s. Steel eventually became the preferred material. The bright, multi-color lithographed designs of steel boxes are real works of art. Some vinyl boxes were made from the late 1950s until the early 1980s. Not as durable as steel, their value has been rising in proportion to their increasing scarcity. Lately the material of choice has become injection-molded plastic.

One especially collectible design is the box with the rounded top, or dome. This functional style, with the bottle fitting inside the dome, is both aesthetically pleasing and comparatively rare. Tall oval vinyl boxes with zippered tops, "brunch bags," are also popular.

The following prices are for boxes only in fine to excellent condition. Most boxes came with bottles which are generally worth about one-third the value of the box. Excellent condition means the box shows only slight traces of paint wear inside and out. Fine condition boxes may have some inside soiling or missing paint on 15% or so of the surfaces. The outside rims may have some paint wear and the illustrated surfaces may have scattered scratches but the wear must not be so evident as to make the box unattractive for display. The manufacturers and years are listed when known; Aladdin and King Seeley Thermos (KST) were the two main manufacturers. Boxes are made of steel unless otherwise noted.

LB020	Annie Oakley, 1956, Aladdin	150-300
LB030	Astronaut (dome), 1960-66, KST	100-200
LB040	Banana Splits (vinyl), 1970, KST	100-250
LB050	Barbie & Midge (vinyl dome), '64-67, KST	125-275
LB051	Barbie and Midge (vinyl), 1964-65, KST	50-80
LB060	Batman and Robin, 1966-67, Aladdin	60-150
LB070	Beany and Cecil (tan vinyl), 1963, KST	150-250
LB071	Beany and Cecil (white vinyl), '62-63, KST	175-275
LB080	Beatles Brunch Bag (vinyl), 1966, Aladdin	300-500
LB081	Beatles Kaboodle Kit, The (vinyl), 1965-66, Standard Plastic Products	400-750
LB082	Beatles, The, 1966-67, Aladdin	150-350
LB083	Beatles, The (vinyl), 1965, Air Flite	200-400
LB090	Bozo the Clown (dome), 1964-65, Aladdin	100-250
LB100	Brave Eagle, 1957-58, American Thermos	75-200
LB110	Buccaneer (dome), 1957-58, Aladdin	125-250
LB120	Bullwinkle & Rocky, 1962, Universal	150-300
LB121	Bullwinkle (in a balloon) (vinyl), 1962, KST	150-300

LB082

LB310

LB350

LB390

LB400

LB410

LB122	Bullwinkle (on the moon) (vinyl), '63, KST	150-300
LB130	Cable Car (dome), 1962, Aladdin	125-250
LB140	Captain Kangaroo (vinyl), 1964-66, KST	200-400
LB150	Cartoon Zoo Lunch Chest, 1962-63, Universal	150-300
LB160	Casey Jones (dome), 1960-61, Universal	200-400
LB170	Charlie's Angels Brunch Bag (vinyl), 1978-79, Aladdin	50-100
LB180	Chuck Wagon, 1958, American Thermos	75-175
LB190	Circus Wagon, 1958, American Thermos	100-250
LB200	Civil War, The (plastic), 1961, Universal	100-200
LB210	Cowboy, In Africa, 1968, KST	70-150
LB220	Daniel Boone, 1965, Aladdin	60-125
LB230	Davy Crockett Indian Fighter, 1955-56, ADCO Liberty	60-110
LB240	Deputy Dawg, 1961-62, (vinyl) KST	150-300
LB250	Disneyland (Castle), 1957-59, Aladdin	75-175
LB251	Disneyland (Monorail), 1960-62, Aladdin	90-175
LB260	Dr. Seuss (vinyl), 1970, Aladdin	60-125
LB270	Dudley Do-Right, 1962, Universal	150-350
LB280	Dutch Cottage (dome), 1958, American Thermos	175-400
LB290	Fess Parker/Daniel Boone Kaboodle Kit (vinyl), Standard Plastic Products	150-300
LB300	Flintstones & Dino, The, 1962-63, Aladdin	60-125
LB301	Flintstones, The, 1964-65, Aladdin	75-150
LB310	Gene Autry, 1954-55, Universal	80-200
LB320	Go-Go (vinyl), Aladdin	75-150
LB321	Go-Go Brunch Bag (vinyl), '66-67, Aladdin	75-150
LB330	Gomer Pyle, 1966, Aladdin	75-200
LB340	Great Wild West, 1954-55, Universal	150-300
LB350	Green Hornet, The, 1967, KST	100-250
LB360	Grizzly Adams (dome), 1978, Aladdin	40-100
LB370	Guns of Will Sonnet, The, 1968, KST	50-150
LB380	Gunsmoke, 1959-61, Aladdin	60-150
LB390	Hector Heathcote, 1964, Aladdin	150-300
LB400	Hogan's Heroes (dome), 1966, Aladdin	75-200
LB410	Home Town Airport (dome), 1960, KST	400-1000

LB420	Hopalong Cassidy (scalloped decal), 1950-51, Aladdin	60-150
LB421	Hopalong Cassidy (square decal), 1951-53, Aladdin	50-125
LB422	Hopalong Cassidy, 1954-56, Aladdin	90-200
LB430	Howdy Doody, 1954-55, ADCO Liberty	125-300
LB440	It's a Small World (vinyl), '68-69, Aladdin	125-250
LB450	It's About Time (dome), 1967, Aladdin	100-250
LB460	James Bond - 007, 1966, Aladdin	100-200
LB470	Jet Patrol, 1957-58, Aladdin	150-300
LB480	Jetsons, The (dome), 1963, Aladdin	400-1000
LB490	Land of the Giants, 1969-70, Aladdin	60-150
LB500	Lawman, 1961-62, KST	60-125
LB510	Linus, The Lion Hearted (vinyl), 1965, Aladdin	100-250
LB520	Lone Ranger, The, '54-55, ADCO, Liberty	125-300
LB530	Looney Tunes TV Set, 1959-61, American Thermos	100-225
LB540	Lost in Space (dome), 1967-68, KST	200-400
LB550	Ludwig Von Drake, 1962, Aladdin	75-150
LB560	Man From U.N.C.L.E., The, 1966-67, KST	75-175
LB570	Mary Poppins (vinyl), 1973, Aladdin	75-150
LB571	Mary Poppins Brunch Bag (vinyl), 1966-67, Aladdin	75-150
LB580	Mickey Mouse/Donald Duck, 1954-55, ADCO Liberty	125-300
LB590	Monkees, The (vinyl), 1967, KST	125-300
LB600	Munsters, The, 1965-66, KST	75-175
LB610	Paladin, 1960, Aladdin	75-200
LB620	Pathfinder, 1959, Universal	150-300
LB630	Pebbles & Bamm-Bamm, 1972, Aladdin	40-100
LB631	Pebbles & Bamm-Bamm (vinyl), '72, Aladdin	75-150
LB640	Pink Poodle Brunch Bag	90-175
LB650	Pop Art Bread Box (dome), 1968, Aladdin	125-275
LB660	Popeye, 1962, Universal	125-300
LB670	Porky's Lunch Wagon (dome), 1959-61, American Thermos	100-250
LB680	Rifleman, The, 1961-62, Aladdin	125-300

LB480

LB610

LB760

MG090

MG118

MG124

LB690	Roy Rogers Chow Wagon (dome), 1959-61, American Thermos	100-250	
LB691	Roy Rogers Saddlebag (off-white vinyl), 1960, KST	125-300	
LB692	Roy Rogers Saddlebag (tan vinyl), 1960, KST	75-200	
LB700	Shari Lewis (vinyl), 1963, Aladdin	125-250	
LB710	Sleeping Beauty (vinyl), 1970, Aladdin	100-200	
LB720	Smokey The Bear (vinyl), 1965, KST	125-250	
LB730	Snow White (vinyl), 1975, Aladdin	75-150	
LB740	Soupy Sales (vinyl), 1965, KST	200-400	
LB750	Space Explorer, 1960, Aladdin	150-300	
LB760	Star Trek (dome), 1968-69, Aladdin	250-500	
LB770	Steve Canyon, 1959, Aladdin	125-250	
LB780	Supercar, 1962	125-300	
LB790	Superman, 1954-55, Universal	150-350	
LB791	Superman, 1967-68, KST	100-200	
LB800	Tom Corbett: Space Cadet (blue), 1952-53, Aladdin	75-200	
LB801	Tom Corbett: Space Cadet (red), 1952-53, Aladdin	75-200	
LB802	Tom Corbett: Space Cadet, 1954-56, Aladdin	125-300	
LB810	Treasure Chest (dome), 1961-62, Aladdin	100-200	
LB820	Trigger, 1956, American Thermos	75-200	
LB830	Twiggy (vinyl), 1967-68, KST	100-200	
LB831	Twiggy Brunch Bag (vinyl), 1967-68, KST	75-175	
LB840	U. S. Space Corps, 1961-62, Universal	100-250	
LB850	Underdog, 1974, Okay Industries	350-800	
LB860	Voyage to the Bottom of the Sea, 1967, Aladdin	75-200	
LB870	Wagon Train, 1964-65, KST	75-200	

LB880	Westerner (vinyl), 1960, Universal	75-150
LB890	Wild Bill Hickok, 1956-58, Aladdin	75-200
LB900	Wild, Wild West, 1969, Aladdin	75-200
LB910	Wrangler (vinyl), 1962, Aladdin	100-200
LB920	Yellow Submarine, 1969, KST	150-400
LB930	Yogi Bear & Friends, 1963, Aladdin	50-150
LB940	Yosemite Sam (vinyl), 1971-72, KST	100-200
LB950	Zorro (blue sky), 1958-59, Aladdin	65-150
LB951	Zorro (red sky), 1966, Aladdin	75-175

See also: **Batman; Beatles; Disney; Star Trek; Western Heroes**

MAGAZINES by Frank Miller

People collect magazines because of a fascination with a person, place, or special topic. Magazines provide the picture and word histories that make them popular with a wide variety of collectors. People buy lots of magazines of particular dates to use as birthday gifts. All magazines are collectible. The key is finding the right topic. The most popular topics are:

Sports — We are a society who likes heroes. Because of this hero worship it's the individual (not the team) who's in demand by collectors. Also remember the "Rule of Regionalism." This means there is more interest for a magazine about the Cincinnati Reds in Cincinnati than in Denver. Further, the magazine's cover usually "makes it or breaks it" as a collectible. This is why *Sports Illustrated* is collected and *Reader's Digest* is not. Eight out of ten collectors judge by the cover, especially with regard to sports magazines.

Baseball rules over all other sports. Our national pastime has ten times the number of collectors than all other sports combined. Look for titles with the word "Baseball" or "Sport" in them, or players on the covers of general interest magazines.

MG159

MG158

MG170

MG172

Several magazine issues have become valuable because they contain card inserts. The most valuable *Life* magazine is the April 13, 1962 issue, because of a Mickey Mantle/Roger Maris card insert as part of a Post cereal promotion.

If baseball is a "10" in desirability, basketball is a "5" and football a "3." Any member of a basketball team can become a hero and thus demand the interest of collectors. There is lively interest in some college heroes, but football is more restrictive. Its heroes are usually quarterbacks, running backs, or receivers. Look for magazines with "foot" or "basket" in the title, especially the annuals.

Golf has definite boundaries for collectors. There are the pre-World War II and the post-World War II collectors. Golf is dominated by individuals like no other sport. Look for names like Ben Hogan, Jack Nicklaus, Arnold Palmer, Sam Sneed, and Nancy Lopez. Collectors' interest has mushroomed worldwide in the last five years, but most interest is in the pre-1970 era. Watch for *Sports Illustrated* and *Sport* magazine, along with *Golf*, *Golf Illustrated*, and *Golf Digest*.

Hockey has gained a large increase in interest. Two superstars to look for are Bobby Hull and Wayne Gretsky.

Boxing in the 1960s and 1970s was dominated by Mohammed Ali (Cassius Clay). Most other heavy and light-heavyweight champions are also worth gathering up.

Auto racing is extremely popular with many good magazines covering this field. (Pre-1968 issues of *Road & Track*, *Speed Age*, *Car & Driver*, and *Automobile Quarterly*.) The digest size custom car magazines of the 1951-1961 period (of which there are hundreds of titles) have had a resurgence of interest.

Adult — This market is one of the few collected for the inside instead of the cover. *Playboy* refined a marketplace previously dominated by semi-sleazy men's magazines. It's the predominant collector's magazine, the most desirable being any issues from 1953-1959. For other magazines of this type, the most collectible period is the 1950s. A few, such as *Rogue* and *Cavalier*, were influenced by *Playboy* and changed format to prolong their existence. Some changed their content and faced prosecution. This led to their demise, but it also added to their collectibility. Some issues are highly prized for the artwork of two outstanding artists. Alberto Vargas's illustrations appeared in the post war editions of *Esquire*, *Cavalier*, and *Playboy*. George Petty also appeared in *Esquire* in the 1940s and 1950s, as well as *True Magazine* in most of the 1955 issues.

Science Fiction and Fantasy — This is a vast field to cover. The most collected appeared in the 1920-1940 period. Some lived on into the 1950s. They include *Amazing Science Fiction*, *Amazing Stories*, *Analog*, *Avon Fantasy Reader*, *Fantastic Science Fiction Stories*, *Galaxy Science Fiction*, *Magazine of Fantasy and Science Fiction*, and *Planet Stories & Weird Tales*.

Counter Culture — A strange thing has happened to most counter culture magazines. Society has changed, so in some cases they are now general culture or mainline, or have been re-tagged as "alternative lifestyle" magazines. This doesn't sound so subversive as counter culture. They probably have their roots in the adult theme periodicals. Magazines such as *Playboy* and *Rogue* featured such anti-establishment writers as Kerouac and interviewed such extreme personalities as Lennie Bruce. The magazines being sought by collectors are early issues of *Rolling Stone*, *Creem*, *Mother Earth News*, and most of the "Biker" magazines that featured the girl next door on a Harley. Again, covers play a major part in what is being collected. The Beatles, Rolling Stones, Bob Dylan, and other rock stars are always in demand.

Another (and possibly more long term) collectible area are those periodicals issued by and in support of the Civil Rights movement (pro and con). Two mainline black magazines also deserve mention. *Jet* and *Ebony* documented the social structure of black America.

Some topics seem to be timeless. Marilyn Monroe, Judy Garland, *Gone with the Wind*, *The Wizard of Oz*, Elvis, or The Beatles are good examples.

The preceding topics should give you a good idea of what is collectable and which magazines to search for. But you will encounter many interesting magazines which are not listed here. Here are some basic guidelines to follow. All affect the value of any magazine.

First and foremost is condition. Second is...condition! This cannot be stressed enough! Evaluating a magazine's condition is extremely important. Here are our definitions:

Mint - Looks like it just came off the press. No bends, folds, or mutilations of any kind. Still glossy.

Excellent - Has been handled. May have minor bends or folds and may show some wear. No creases. The gloss is still there, but has a few scuffs or dull spots.

Very Good - Has had minimal handling, corners may be bent or folded. There's some loss of gloss or brightness. Slight creasing is tolerable.

Good - Shows bends, corners may be rounded and there are fold marks. May be creased. Minor tattering on edges, some yellowing (aging) of paper. May have some foxing (brown spots) from dampness. Some internal pages may have minor tears.

Poor - Cover or pages have major tears or discolorations. A major insert is missing. The cover or pages may be missing.

Next, focus on the cover. Is it a "Famous Face"? Was it created by a collectible illustrator such as Norman Rockwell or Maxfield Parrish?

Examine article content. Check the index for those topics which fit the collectible categories.

Flip through the magazine for full page color advertisements. Are there any cowboy/movie star/early TV star endorsement ads or any of the other major topics? Remember the power of advertising to sell a magazine as a collectible is one of the major reasons dealers sell to collectors. Also, color sells.

Copies without address labels are preferred. This is especial-

MG176	MG180

MG188	MG198

ly true for *TV Guide.*

Consider distribution. Is this a nationally distributed periodical, or was it only sold in a few localities? Universities typically publish great magazines locally, but they have little collectible value.

Don't forget availability. If the magazine is less than five years old, back issues may still be available from the publisher close to the original cover price.

Finally, remember supply - demand. A good rule of thumb is buy it if the demand exists, no matter how many copies are available.

The prices listed are for magazines in good to excellent condition. Mint condition is usually worth 20-25% above excellent.

American Heritage (hardcover)
MG040	Apr 1968 (Mickey Mouse)	7-15

Esquire
MG055	Sep, 1951 (color print of Marilyn Monroe)	18-60
MG060	Jan, 1954 (holiday issue)	8-35
MG065	July, 1954 (Sylvana Mangano)	8-30

Eye
MG090	Feb, 1969 (Spider-Man comic on cover)	20-40

Life
MG105	Jun 12,1950 (Hopalong Cassidy)	15-25
MG118	Apr 7, 1952 (Marilyn Monroe)	8-35
MG122	Apr 6, 1953 (Lucille Ball & family)	5-20
MG124	May 25, 1953 (Marilyn Monroe & Jane Russell)	8-25
MG126	Jul 20, 1953 (President & Mrs. Kennedy)	7-15
MG133	Sep 13, 1954 (Judy Garland)	4-15
MG137	Aug 8, 1955 (Ben Hogan)	13-25
MG143	Jun 25, 1956 (Mickey Mantle)	8-25
MG152	Apr 28, 1958 (Willie Mays)	3-15
MG157	Apr 20, 1959 (Marilyn Monroe)	8-25

MG158	Aug 15, 1960 (Marilyn Monroe/Yves Montand)	8-25
MG159	Nov 9, 1959 (Marilyn Monroe)	8-25
MG164	Dec 26, 1960 ("25 Years of Life-Special Double Issue")	3-12
MG168	Aug 18, 1961 (Mickey Mantle & Roger Maris)	3-12
MG170	Jan 5, 1962 (Lucille Ball)	5-20
MG172	Apr 13, 1962 (Richard Burton/ElizabethTaylor; must have both baseball cards inside)	2-150
MG176	Aug 17, 1962 (Marilyn Monroe)	8-25
MG178	Nov 29, 1963 (Kennedy assassination)	3-12
MG180	Aug 7, 1964 (Marilyn Monroe)	8-25
MG182	Aug 28, 1964 (The Beatles)	8-25
MG184	May 7, 1965 (John Wayne)	3-15
MG186	Jan 1, 1966 (Sean Connery as James Bond)	3-15
MG188	Mar 11, 1966 (Adam West as Batman)	3-15
MG190	Sep 13, 1968 (The Beatles)	3-15
MG195	Oct 15, 1971 (Walt Disney World opens)	3-12
MG198	Sep 8, 1972 (Marilyn Monroe)	8-25

Look
MG204	Aug 29, 1950 (Hopalong Cassidy & boy)	15-30
MG212	May 22, 1951 (Joe DiMaggio)	3-15
MG214	Oct 23, 1951 (Marilyn Monroe)	8-25
MG217	Jun 3, 1952 (Lucille Ball & Marilyn Monroe)	8-25
MG222	Apr 21, 1953 (Lucille Ball & family)	4-15
MG224	Nov 17, 1953 (Marilyn Monroe)	8-25
MG227	Sep 9, 1954 (Clark Gable)	4-15
MG232	Jul 26, 1955 (Fess Parker; Disney article)	4-15
MG238	Oct 16, 1956 (James Dean)	8-25
MG244	Oct 27,1959 (Wagon Train)	5-15
MG251	Apr 6, 1971 (Mickey Mouse, 9 page article on Walt Disney World)	3-12

Mechanix Illustrated
MG275	May, 1954 (Creature From The Black Lagoon)	8-35

MG227	MG244	106	MG480	MG532

Newsweek

MG304	May 15, 1950 (Groucho Marx)	4-15
MG306	Jul 10, 1950 (Gen. MacArthur)	3-12
MG310	Nov 5, 1951 (Winston Churchill)	3-12
MG314	Dec 22, 1952 (Illustrator John Falter)	3-12
MG318	Jan 19, 1953 (Lucille Ball)	4-15
MG322	Feb 16, 1953 (Disney's Peter Pan)	4-15
MG326	May 17, 1954 (Grace Kelly)	4-15
MG330	Oct 4, 1954 (Bob Feller & Jim Lemon)	3-12
MG334	Oct 3, 1955 (World Series)	4-15
MG338	Jun 25, 1956 (Mickey Mantle)	5-20
MG342	Jul 1, 1957 (Stan Musial)	5-20
MG350	Jun 18, 1962 (Arnold Palmer)	8-15
MG354	Feb 24, 1964 (The Beatles)	7-25
MG358	Oct 11, 1965 (Sandy Koufax)	4-15
MG375	Dec 22, 1980 (John Lennon killed)	3-15

Our Sports Negro Athlete Magazine

MG401	May 1953 (No. 1; edited by Jackie Robinson)	13-50

Playboy

MG451	Dec 1953 (No.1; w/Marilyn Monroe)	300-1200
MG452	Jan 1954 (No. 2)	150-500
MG453	Feb 1954 (No. 3)	50-200
MG462	Feb 1955 (Playmate Jayne Mansfield)	10-75
MG468	Sep 1955 (Marilyn Monroe pictorial)	10-75

Police Gazette

MG480	Personality issues	15-25

Saturday Evening Post

MG500	Most issues w/Norman Rockwell or John Falter covers	4-20
MG514	May 19, 1956 (Norman Rockwell cover; Marilyn Monroe by Pete Martin)	5-15
MG517	Oct 6, 1956 (Adlai Stevenson cover by Norman Rockwell; Kim Novak)	3-12
MG519	Dec 29, 1956 (Norman Rockwell cover)	3-12
MG525	Jun 28, 1958 (Norman Rockwell cover)	3-12
MG531	Feb 13, 1960 (Norman Rockwell cover; Rockwell's story)	5-15
MG532	Mar 21, 1964 (The Beatles)	5-25
MG536	Aug 8, 1964 (The Beatles)	5-25
MG544	Aug 27, 1966 (The Beatles)	8-25

Sport

MG561	Jul 1950 (Stan Musial)	3-20
MG565	Special 1950 Annual	5-25
MG574	Jun 1951 (Sugar Ray Robinson)	3-20
MG576	Sep 1951 (Ted Williams)	3-20
MG578	Oct 1951 (Jackie Robinson)	3-20
MG586	Apr 1953 (Mickey Mantle)	5-25
MG590	1962 (Special issue on Mickey Mantle & Willie Mays)	25-50

Sports Illustrated

MG601	Aug 16, 1954 (No. 1; baseball card insert)	100-200
MG602	Aug 23, 1954 (No. 2; baseball card insert)	100-200
MG612	Apr 11, 1955 (Willie Mays; baseball card insert)	15-75
MG613	Apr 18, 1955 (Al Rosen; baseball card insert)	15-75
MG626	Oct 1, 1956 (Mickey Mantle; World Series issue)	5-25

Time

MG701	Jan 2, 1950 (Winston Churchill)	5-20
MG703	Apr 10, 1950 (Ted Williams)	8-25
MG708	Nov 27, 1950 (Hopalong Cassidy)	8-25
MG716	Mar 3, 1952 (John Wayne)	8-25
MG718	May 26, 1952 (Lucille Ball)	8-25
MG722	Jun 8, 1953 (3-D Movies)	5-20
MG723	Jun 15, 1953 (Mickey Mantle)	5-20
MG727	Jun 7, 1954 (Humphrey Bogart)	5-20
MG728	Jun 21, 1954 (Sam Snead)	8-15
MG729	Jul 26, 1954 (Willie Mays)	5-20
MG737	May 14, 1956 (Marilyn Monroe)	8-25
MG746	Mar 30, 1959 (TV's Western Heroes)	3-15
MG749	Oct 26, 1959 (TV's Private Eyes)	3-15
MG757	Mar 22, 1963 (Cassius Clay)	3-15
MG761	May 21, 1965 (Rock & Roll Singers)	3-15

MG884   MG885   MG886   MG887

MG767	Sep 22, 1967 (The Beatles)	5-25
MG772	Mar 1, 1968 (Bobby Hull)	5-10
MG785	Dec 22, 1980 (John Lennon killed)	3-15

TV Digest

MG802	Feb 11, 1950 Philadelphia ed (Nancy Franklin)	10-30
MG805	Aug 19, 1950 Philadelphia ed (Jackie Gleason)	10-30
MG809	Dec 30, 1950 Philadelphia ed (Ed McMahon)	10-30
MG813	Mar 31, 1951 Philadelphia ed (Jerry "Beanbag" Lester)	10-30
MG816	Jul 21, 1951 Philadelphia ed (Jackie Gleason)	10-30
MG819	Oct 20, 1951 Philadelphia ed (Lucille Ball)	15-35

TV Guide, Regional - higher priced magazines, best prices in Los Angeles

MG832	Feb 11, 1950 (Ed Sullivan)	13-25
MG835	Aug 5, 1950 (Fred Allen & Jack Haley)	14-42
MG836	Aug 12, 1950 (Grace Kelly)	15-55
MG838	Sep 2, 1950 (Howdy Doody)	17-65
MG840	Sep 16, 1950 (Jimmy Durante, Kate Smith, Groucho Marx, Frank Sinatra, Jack Benny, Fred Allen)	14-38
MG842	Oct 14, 1950 (Miss TV of 1950)	14-38
MG844	Nov 11, 1950 (Dean Martin & Jerry Lewis)	13-37
MG846	Nov 25, 1950 (Howdy Doody & Rootie Tootie [later Rootie Kazootie])	16-65
MG850	May 26, 1951 (Frank Sinatra)	14-34
MG852	Jun 9, 1951 (Groucho Marx)	14-35
MG856	Aug 31, 1951 (Howdy Doody & other kid show characters)	15-50
MG860	Jan 4, 1952 (Sid Caesar, Ed Sullivan, Arthur Godfrey, Milton Berle, Perry Como & Groucho Marx)	15-50
MG862	Mar 14, 1952 (Dean Martin & Jerry Lewis)	16-60
MG864	May 16, 1952 (Gene Autry)	14-43
MG866	Jun 20, 1952 (previous covers)	14-34
MG868	Jul 25, 1952 for Greater New York area w/Howdy Doody Show ticket contest	15-45
MG870	Oct 10, 1952 (Al Capp & L'il Abner)	15-55
MG872	Oct 31, 1952 for Greater New York area w/Howdy Doody Presidential ballot	15-45
MG880	Jan 2, 1953 (Jackie Gleason)	13-38
MG882	Jan 23, 1953 (Marilyn Monroe)	14-43

TV Guide, National

MG884	Apr 3, 1953 (1st national issue; 1st glossy cover: Lucille Ball; Lucille's baby; headline "Lucy's $50,000,000 Baby")	35-350
MG885	Apr 10, 1953 (Jack Webb)	15-55
MG886	Apr 24, 1953 (Ralph Edwards)	10-40
MG887	May 1, 1953 (Eve Arden)	14-40
MG889	Sep 25, 1953 (George Reeves/Superman)	50-170
MG891	Mar 19, 1954 (Groucho Marx)	13-38
MG893	May 14, 1954 (Frank Sinatra)	14-38
MG895	Jun 25, 1954 (Howdy Doody & Buffalo Bob Smith)	15-47
MG897	Sep 25, 1954 (Fall Preview Issue)	30-85
MG899	Oct 23, 1954 (Walt Disney & characters)	14-40
MG901	Dec 24, 1954 (The Nelson Family)	15-48
MG904	Sep 24, 1955 (Fall Preview Issue)	15-48
MG906	Dec 10, 1955 (Lucille Ball)	15-45
MG908	May 19, 1956 (Phil Silvers)	12-25

MARILYN MONROE   by Howard Lowery

Marilyn Monroe was more than a movie star; she became, in her lifetime, an American icon. Her early death made her a legend, and a sad reminder of the price fame and fortune can demand.

Born Norma Jean Mortonson in 1926 to an unwed mother, she spent many years in foster homes separated from her mother, who suffered from mental illness. She first attracted attention when she was photographed for the armed services magazine *Yank* while working in a defense plant. This led to modeling jobs, and during the mid-to-late 1940s she appeared, often unidentified, in several magazines.

Her film career began at 20th Century Fox where she adopted her famous name and appeared in *Scudda Hoo! Scudda Hey!* (1948) and *The Dangerous Years* (1948). Her career blossomed in the early 1950s, during which time she was often cast as the typical "dumb blonde" until she fought for, and received, more significant and demanding roles in *Bus Stop* (1956), *Some Like It Hot* (1959) and *The Misfits* (1961).

Marilyn's personal life brought her as much attention as her film roles, especially her marriages to baseball great Joe DiMaggio and playwright Arthur Miller, and her association with other famous men. In 1962, she was fired from the never-completed *Something's Got to Give* and later fell victim to an overdose of sleeping pills. Her early death shocked the world.

Collectors focus on Marilyn Monroe the person as much as Marilyn Monroe the star. Her films were, in general, more respectable than critics have given them credit for, and collectors value the one-sheet posters, lobby cards, still photographs and other publicity items associated with them. Equally sought-after are the movie fan magazines with covers featuring her likeness.

However, most highly prized are Marilyn Monroe's personal effects — items she owned, or which were associated with her. Following her unexpected death, a surprising number of friends, servants, former boyfriends, movie industry associates and others visited her house and took home souvenirs. Although these may be difficult to identify, they have found their way into the collectors' market and command respectable prices. These can be as commonplace as a signed check or autographed photograph, or as unusual as her favorite purse or a box made from a brass shell casing by a soldier stationed in Korea and sent to her as a gift.

Items listed in this section come from actual sales at public auction from 1989-91.

Magazines

MA101	*Avante Garde*, Mar 1968, photos from last photo session	80
MA102	Collection, 1953-54, w/Monroe stories	200
MA103	*Marilyn*, 84 page Dell devoted to Monroe	66
MA104	*Modern Screen*, Mar 1954, Monroe cover	185
MA105	*Modern Screen Pin-Ups #1*, 1955, Monroe cover	102
MA106	*Movieland*, Jan 1953, Monroe Cover	44
MA107	*New York Mirror Magazine*, Jun 23, 1957, Monroe cover	94
MA108	People, Dec 2, 1953	
MA109	*3D Movie Magazine #1*, 1953, Monroe cover	122

Movie Memorabilia

MA110	collection of lobby cards & one-sheets, most in average condition, 1954-60	250
MA111	linen-backed Italian reissue 37" x 54" poster for Niagara	300

Lobby Cards

The Seven Year Itch, 1955

MA113	title lobby card	134
MA114	featuring Monroe	88
MA115	full set of 8	325
MA116	*There's No Business Like Show Business*, 1954, featuring Monroe	39

One-Sheet Posters

MA117	set: *Bus Stop, Let's Make Love, & Marilyn,* 1950s-60s	300
MA118	set: *Love Nest, O'Henry's Full House, &*	

MA146

MA108

MA103

MA109

MA122

MX125

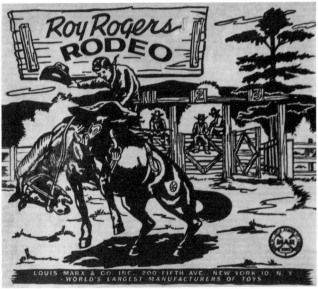

MX140

	As Young As You Feel, 1951-52	275
MA119	*Don't Bother to Knock*, 1952	450
MA120	*Gentlemen Prefer Blondes*, 1953	400
MA121	*The Misfits*, 1961, Monroe-Clark Gable	332
MA122	*The Seven Year Itch*, 1955	325-534

Miscellaneous

MA123	21-1/2" x 14" x 4-1/2" wooden box filled w/newspaper clippings & magazine covers, 1950s-1980s	638
MA124	revised shooting script for TV movie *Marilyn: The Untold Story* based on Norman Mailer's book, 1980	88
MA125	*The Marilyn Monroe Story*, early (first?) paperback book about Monroe, 1953	94
MA126	jigsaw puzzle of famous nude photo (rare)	225
MA127	limited edition full-color print, 1970s	55
MA128	limited edition full-color print taken from photographer's original negative	71
MA129	plastic draftsman's aid w/reclining figure of Monroe carved into it	105
MA130	serving tray w/famous nude photo	198

Personal Items

MA131	box made from brass shell casing sent by soldier stationed in Korea as gift, 1950s	479
MA132	Bulova watch engraved "Love, Marilyn", 1950's, gift from Monroe	643
MA133	cigarette case w/engraved message on lid, late 1950s, gift from Monroe	3000
MA134	evening gown worn during publicity appearances for *Gentlemen Prefer Blondes*	7500
MA135	Mexican-made letter opener engraved "Love, Marilyn," 1950's, gift from Monroe	369
MA136	dainty handkerchief embroidered w/ flowers & initials, 1950s	2145
MA137	William Morris Agency payroll statement for 6 days' work at 20th Century Fox, Jan 28, 1954	585
MA139	alligator-hide purse w/initials engraved on top snap, 1950s	1126
MA140	signed check for $1286.23 to Beverly Hills Hilton, 1960	4400
MA141	silver plated food warmer engraved w/initials, 1950s	757

Photographs

MA145	3 signed photos (signatures very faint)	1452
MA146	reproductions of famous nude shot, all on calendar-type paper, early 1950s	239
MA147	100+ b&w scene photos featuring Monroe from *Gentlemen Prefer Blondes*, 1953	475
MA148	pin-up calendar w/famous nude photo, unused	850
MA149	8" x 10" of Monroe in flimsy negligee	36
MA150	8 b&w wardrobe test shots of Monroe, 1950s	425

See also: **Autographs; Books; Character and Promotional Glasses; Magazines; Movie Posters; Paper Dolls; Playboy**

MARX PLAYSETS — by Rick Koch

There were basically 60-75 Marx playsets manufactured from the early 50s until the company was dissolved in 1982. Some sets had many variations with over 200 different box and content variations on the Fort Apache set alone. In the early years there was a lithograph tin building or other structure central to the playset. All other pieces were non-painted, flexible plastic, molded in different colors. Most sets had 1 to 10 key figures. A Roy Rogers, The Lone Ranger and Wagon Train set, for example, may have had the same Indians, but it was Roy and Dale, Lone Ranger and Tonto, or the Wagon Masters molded after the TV or film characters which are the most desirable figures in the set. Likewise, there were campfires, covered wagons, horses, and similar figures which were used from set to set.

Each Marx playset came with an inventory of the pieces included along with instructions for those components requiring assembly. Each set usually contained over 100 different pieces. These were packaged in paper bags, stenciled with a word like "COWBOYS" and an inventory number for that particular group of cowboys. Leading collectors of Marx playsets insist on having every component which came in the box, even the cardboard dividers and packing.

All the normal factors such as condition, an original box, etc. are important in evaluating Marx playsets. However, with so many different pieces involved, the degree of completeness becomes the leading factor in determining value. Because playsets are rarely found 100% complete or in mint condition, the values in this section are presented differently than the ranges found for other categories ... the reason being the tremendous difference in values depending on the completeness.

The Louis Marx Toy Company was the leading producer of this type of toy and was responsible for most of the higher valued sets in this category. The two major exceptions are the Batman playset from Ideal and the Captain Video Space Port produced by Superior. Multi-Products and several other toy companies have produced similar figures by the pound, but none have measured up to the most valuable sets found here.

Playsets marked with an * also contain the word "Authorized" in the title.

		60%	90%	Mint
MX101	Alamo	200	350	500
MX102	Alaskan	300	550	900
MX103	Battle Ground	75	150	275
MX104	Ben Hur*	500	1000	1800
MX105	Boy's Camp	250	500	750
MX106	Cape Canaveral	50	125	250

MX114

MX107	Cape Canaveral w/Train	125	350	550
MX108	Captain Gallant*	400	900	1700
MX109	Castle Set	75	150	250
MX110	Construction Company	75	200	350
MX111	D-Day	75	200	350
MX112	Daktari*	150	500	800
MX113	Disney TV Playhouse*	150	350	600
MX114	Disneyland*	300	600	1000
MX115	Farm	50	125	200
MX116	Fire House	250	600	1000
MX117	Fort Apache Stockade	75	150	300
MX118	Flintstones*	150	350	650
MX119	Gallant Men*	125	300	550
MX120	Giant Civil War	400	1200	2000
MX121	Gunsmoke*	500	2500	4000
MX122	IGY (Int'l Geophysical Year)	350	750	1200
MX123	Iwo Jima	100	250	400
MX124	Johnny Ringo*	400	1500	2500
MX125	Johnny Tremain*	250	700	1250
MX126	Jungle Jim*	300	900	1500
MX127	Lone Ranger Ranch*	50	150	300
MX128	Lone Ranger Rodeo*	45	100	200
MX129	Official Davy Crockett at Alamo	150	400	750
MX130	Operation Moon Base	200	450	750
MX131	Prehistoric Times	125	300	550
MX132	Prince Valiant*	150	350	600
MX133	Revolutionary War Set	250	550	800
MX134	Rex Mars	150	350	600
MX135	Richard Greene Robin Hood*	350	900	1500
MX136	Rifleman*	250	700	1300
MX137	Rin Tin Tin*	100	400	700
MX138	Robin Hood	125	300	550
MX139	Roy Rogers Double-R-Bar Ranch Set*	50	150	300
MX140	Roy Rogers Rodeo*	45	100	200
MX141	Roy Rogers Mineral City Set	200	550	750
MX142	School House	100	250	450
MX143	Sears Store	250	600	1000
MX144	Service Station	50	100	200
MX145	Sky Scraper	250	600	1000
MX146	Space Patrol*	500	900	1500
MX147	Super Circus*	125	350	500
MX148	Tales of Wells Fargo*	350	600	850
MX149	Tales of Wells Fargo w/train*	400	650	1000
MX150	Tom Corbett*	150	350	600
MX151	Untouchables*	500	2200	3000
MX152	Wagon Train (Large)*	300	900	1500
MX153	Wagon Train (Small)*	250	550	800
MX154	Wyatt Earp*	350	600	850

MX155	Yogi Bear at Jellystone Park*	150	350	650
MX156	Zorro*	400	1200	1800

Other High Valued Playsets

MX157	Batman (Ideal)	200	600	1000
MX158	Captain Video (Superior)	150	350	550
MX159	Gerry Anderson's Fireball XL5 (MPC)	200	450	750

MEGO FIGURES   by Mark Huckabone

Mego figures were made from 1972 to 1982. The line started with DC and Marvel super heroes. Eventually it was expanded to include "Star Trek" and other TV shows.

In 1973 Mego introduced figures based on the famous *Planet of the Apes* film series. *The Wizard of Oz*, the Universal Monsters and *Star Trek: The Motion Picture* were other films used as sources for figures.

Mego was the first company to produce a smaller, all plastic version with the "Comic Action" figure line in 1975. Four limited edition die-cast metal super heroes were offered by 1977. Mego turned to historic characters for their collections of knights, western heroes, pirates, and Robin Hood figures.

The predominant Mego size was 8" tall figures with cloth costumes. Larger 12-1/2" *Star Trek*, *Buck Rogers*, *Black Hole*, and super hero figures were also produced. Smaller figures were normally 3-3/4". Playsets and vehicles were available for most 8" series. Some were Ward's exclusives and today are exceptionally valuable.

Figures were originally packaged in boxes, but were released later on blister cards. There are a number of variations with Batman with the removable cowl being the most sought after. Figures of Clark Kent, Peter Parker, Bruce Wayne, and Dick Grayson were offered exclusively by Montgomery Ward's in 1974 and are probably the rarest figures to find.

Price ranges are divided into three categories: "Complete No Package," "Mint in Package," and "Mint in Mint Package." See the Action Figure section on page 5 for a full description of these categories.

For a complete guide to Mego figures and action figure collecting in general, check out *Tomart's Price Guide to Action Figure Collectibles*. The book lists more than 300 action figure lines, with nearly 4,000 color and b&w photographs. It is regularly updated in Tomart's *Action Figure Digest* magazine. For ordering information, see page 150.

	CNP	MIP	MMP
Greatest American Hero, The 3-3/4" 1981			
MF100 Convertible bug w/Ralph and Bill	95	175	200
Mad Monster Series, The 1974			
MF101 The Dreadful Dracula	50	115	175
MF102 The Human Wolfman	40	95	150
MF103 The Monster Frankenstein	40	50	75

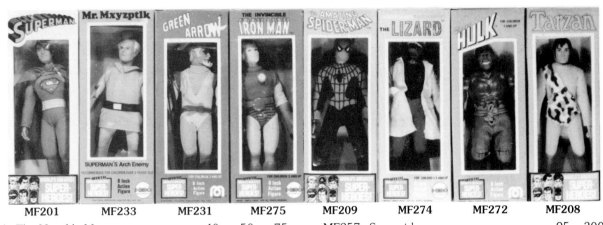

MF201	**MF233**	**MF231**	**MF275**

MF209	**MF274**	**MF272**	**MF208**

MF104	The Horrible Mummy	40	50	75
MF110	Mad Monster Castle, vinyl	90	175	225

Official World's Greatest Super Heroes 1972-78

1972, boxed figures

MF201	Superman	35	80	125
MF202	Batman (removeable mask)	150	225	275
MF203	Batman (painted mask)	40	95	140
MF204	Robin (removeable mask)	175	250	300
MF205	Robin (painted mask)	35	80	125
MF206	Aquaman	40	125	175
MF207	Captain America	50	145	195
MF208	Tarzan	40	95	150
MF209	Spider-Man	12	75	100
MF210	Shazam	65	125	175

1972, S.S. Kresge carded figures

MF211	Superman	35	200	250
MF212	Batman (removeable mask)	150	325	375
MF213	Batman (painted mask)	40	200	250
MF214	Robin (removeable mask)	175	350	400
MF215	Robin (painted mask)	35	200	250
MF216	Aquaman	40	225	275
MF217	Captain America	50	250	275
MF218	Tarzan	40	200	250
MF219	Spider-Man	12	250	275
MF220	Shazam	65	250	275

1973, boxed figures

MF231	Green Arrow	95	200	250
MF233	Mr. Mxyzlptlk	40	60	90
MF234	Riddler	75	225	275
MF235	Penguin	45	100	150
MF236	Joker	50	125	175
MF237	Supergirl	95	275	400
MF238	Batgirl	75	250	300
MF239	Wonder Woman	75	250	300
MF240	Catwoman	75	175	200

1973, S.S. Kresge carded figures

MF251	Green Arrow	95	350	400
MF252	Mr. Mxyzlptlk	40	200	250
MF254	Riddler	75	325	375
MF255	Penguin	45	200	250
MF256	Joker	50	200	250

MF257	Supergirl	95	300	425
MF258	Batgirl	75	300	350
MF259	Wonder Woman	75	300	350
MF260	Catwoman	75	300	350

1974, boxed figures

MF271	Green Goblin	95	200	250
MF272	The Hulk	25	65	90
MF273	The Falcon	60	100	150
MF274	The Lizard	75	150	200
MF275	Iron Man	50	125	165
MF281	Clark Kent (Ward's exclusive)	250	300	400
MF282	Peter Parker (Ward's exclusive)	250	300	400
MF283	Bruce Wayne (Ward's exclusive)	250	300	400
MF284	Dick Grayson (Ward's exclusive)	250	300	400

1975, boxed figures

MF301	Fist Fighting Batman	75	350	375
MF302	Fist Fighting Robin	75	350	375
MF303	Fist Fighting Joker	75	425	450
MF304	Fist Fighting Riddler	75	425	475
MF311	Mr. Fantastic	25	100	150
MF312	Invisible Girl	40	125	175
MF313	Human Torch	25	75	125
MF314	The Thing	25	100	150
MF315	Thor	125	250	350
MF316	Conan	100	225	275

1975, carded figures

MF321	Green Goblin	95	200	250
MF322	Falcon	60	100	150
MF323	Lizard	75	150	200
MF324	Iron Man	50	125	165
MF325	Thor	125	250	350
MF326	Conan	100	225	275

1976, carded figures

MF331	Kid Flash	150	250	300
MF332	Aqualad	150	250	300
MF333	Wonder Girl	150	250	300
MF334	Speedy	195	325	400
MF338	Isis	50	95	125
MF339	Isis, boxed	50	175	250

1978

MF350	Aquaman vs. Great White Shark	175	275	350

MF217

MF220

MF513   **111**

MF325

MF331

	MF239	MF237	MF238	MF240		

Accessories and playsets

MF421	Mobile Bat Lab (1975)	100	200	250
MF422	Jokermobile (1975)	100	225	300
MF432	Captain Americar (1976)	75	175	225
MF433	Green Arrowcar (1976)	100	200	250
MF440	Hall of Justice, vinyl (1976)	100	200	250
MF451	Batman's Wayne Foundation Penthouse, vinyl (1977)	300	650	800

Star Trek (television) 1974-76, 1979

MF506	Gorn	65	175	225
MF507	Cheron	50	110	130
MF508	The Keeper	50	125	150
MF509	Neptunian	70	175	225
MF510	Andorian	175	350	400
MF511	Mugato	150	300	335
MF512	Romulan	200	400	450
MF513	Talos	100	250	300
MF550	Vinyl *Enterprise* Bridge	50	100	140

Star Trek: The Motion Picture 12" figures

MF517	Decker	40	100	125
MF518	Klingon	40	88	120

Star Trek: The Motion Picture 3-3/4" figures

MF526	Klingon	50	100	150
MF527	Arcturian	50	100	150
MF528	Betelgeusian	65	100	150
MF529	Megarite	65	100	150
MF530	Rigellian	50	100	150
MF531	Zaranite	65	100	150
MF561	Command Bridge	30	75	110

Super Softies, 19"

MF600	Batman, talking	75	135	150
MF601	Batman, non-talking	50	100	125
MF610	Lone Ranger, talking	75	135	150
MF611	Lone Ranger, non-talking	50	100	125
MF620	Spider-Man, talking	75	135	150
MF621	Spider-Man, non-talking	50	100	125
MF630	Superman, talking	75	135	150
MF631	Superman, non-talking	50	100	125

Wizard of Oz 1974

MF706	Wicked Witch	40	75	100
MF708	Mayor Munchkin	50	75	125
MF709	General Munchkin	75	125	150
MF710	Dancer Munchkin	75	125	150
MF711	Flower Girl Munchkin	75	125	150
MF721	Emerald City playset w/Wizard	40	75	100
MF722	MF721 w/7 figures	-	175	225
MF725	Munchkinland playset	150	300	350
MF735	Witch's Castle (Sears exclusive)	250	350	400

World's Greatest Super Knights 1975-76

MF801	King Arthur	50	75	100
MF802	Sir Galahad	65	90	110
MF803	The Black Knight	75	100	125
MF804	Sir Lancelot	65	90	110
MF805	Ivanhoe	50	80	110
MF811	Jousting Horses, ea	50	85	100
MF812	Castle Playset	75	175	250

World's Greatest Super Pirates 1974

MF901	Captain Patch	50	100	125

	MF334	MF333	MF331	MF332		

MF902	Jean Lafitte	50	100	125
MF903	Long John Silver	65	125	150
MF904	Black Beard	50	100	125

MODEL KITS, CHARACTER by P. David Welch
Special thanks to Greg Roccano & Mark Karpinski

The 1960s are considered the "Golden Age" for kits with Aurora far ahead in both product diversity and demand. Aurora's line-up of original and glow issue Universal Studios monsters are today's most sought-after kits.

Rating a kit's condition can be difficult because factors such as assembled parts, painted parts, missing pieces, missing instructions, box condition, and country of origin drastically affect value. The following are generally accepted determinations of condition.

Mint in Box (MIB) Sealed: Mint in box with box shrink wrap; most kits had factory wraps on boxes. Provided the boxes are not damaged, collectors may pay a 10-20% premium over MIB price. Beware of bogus re-sealing by dishonest individuals.

MIB: A complete, unused kit with an excellent box and instructions and no glue or paint on pieces. Most collectors insist the plastic "trees" which hold pieces be intact. This is the condition upon which the values in this section are based.

Partial Assembly: A partially built kit with excellent box/instructions and no painting prices at 85 percent of MIB at best. The more assembly, the more the price decreases. Old styrene glues actually "melted" pieces together. White glues (such as Elmer's) do not decrease value as much as styrene glues because they can be removed.

Partial Painting: A complete, partially painted kit with excellent box/instruction and no glueing prices at 85 percent of MIB at best. Painting is not as serious as glueing because most experienced modelers know how to strip paint. Again, the more painting, the more the price decreases because stripping takes time and is not always completely successful.

Partial Assembly/Painting: Together, these two factors can make pricing very difficult. A general guideline would be 70 percent of MIB with excellent box/instructions.

Built-Up: A fully assembled, complete kit with no box/instructions has a value of 15-45 percent of MIB. The more expensive the MIB kit, the more desirable the built-up. If a kit was issued several times, built-up value decreases. Vehicles such as Batmobiles and UFOs go toward low percentages because of low visual appeal. Further, without instructions, an inexperienced person will find it virtually impossible to determine if a built-up is complete. Except for very high-priced kits, incomplete built-ups have little value.

Missing Pieces: Missing pieces cause a big decrease in value regardless of all other factors. Even a MIB kit missing one piece is worth only 80 percent at best of a truly complete MIB kit! Some collectors will not buy a kit missing pieces.

Instructions: Deduct 5-10 percent of MIB price for missing instructions. Instructions sheets alone sell at $5-10. Sheets for rare, expensive kits such as Aurora's Giant Frankenstein can bring over $35!

Boxes: The market for empty kit boxes is almost exclusive to Aurora boxes. Generally, an excellent condition box has no split corners, tape, paint, glue punctures, severe creases, or

| MK560 | MK562 | MK685 | MK691 | MK345 | MK346 | MK301 |

scuffs. Excellent boxes alone have maximum value of 40 percent MIB price. These box defects decrease value on MIB kits by 20 percent or more.

Foreign Issue: This factor applies primarily to Aurora kits. Aurora had branches in Canada, England, and Holland which issued boxes and instructions worded in other languages and plastic parts in colors other than U.S. issues. Foreign issue kits are rare, but some collectors devalue MIB foreign issue kits to about 75 percent of U.S. MIB prices.

Kit values also vary due to region of the country and local collector demand. There is strong interest in American kits in Europe and Japan.

In sum, the values listed here are conservative, mid-range price guidelines indicative of what most collectors would be willing to pay.

AMT

MK100	Dragula, Munsters' TV Car, #905, 1964	165
MK110	Exploration set, #958, 1974	75
MK120	KISS van, 1977	75
MK130	Munsters' Koach, 1964	175
MK140	Klingon Cruiser, #922, 1967	120
MK141	Klingon Cruiser, #952	65
MK145	Mr. Spock w/Snake, #956, 1973	60
MK146	Mr. Spock Without Snake, #973, 1979	30
MK150	Spaceship Set, #953, 1975	60
MK155	USS Enterprise w/lights, #931, 1967	175
MK156	USS Enterprise without lights, #951, 1976	50

Aurora

Some information about the Aurora monster line-up may be confusing. For example, Frankenstein was issued first in 1961 in a long, rectangular box. The Frightening Lighting 1969 issue was the same kit with duplicate glow parts that were optional. The box was the same shape with a lightning bolt added to the art. In 1969 and 1972, the optional glow format continued and square boxes with altered artwork were introduced. The 1969 glow boxes were thicker and sturdier than the 1972 glows. In many cases, the color of the plastic was different between original and glow issues. The kit itself will always carry the date of original issue. The Monster Scenes and Monsters of the Movies Frankensteins are completely different kits than the 1961, 1969, and 1972 issues. For the Aurora line in general, dates listed may vary a year either way. It is the kit name and kit number that are most relevant. Please note that different kits carried identical numbers.

MK200	Addams Family House, #805, 1965	450
MK205	Alfred E. Neumann, #802, 1965	120
MK210	Allosaurus, #736, 1972	50
MK212	Ankylosaurus, #744, 1974	60
MK215	Apache Warrior, #401, 1961	150
MK220	Aramis, #K10, 1958	75

MK225	Archie's Car, #582, 1969	50
MK230	Athos, #K8, 1958	75
MK235	Babe Ruth, #862, 1965	135
MK240	Banana Splits Buggy, #832, 1969	90
MK250	Batboat, #811	285
MK251	Batcycle, #810, 1967	270
MK252	Batman, #467, 1964	135
MK253	Batmobile, #486, 1966	200
MK254	Batplane, #487, 1966	135
MK260	Black Beauty ("Green Hornet"), #489, 1967	330
MK265	Blackbeard, #463, 1965	110
MK270	Bride of Frankenstein, #482, 1964	375
MK275	Captain Action, #480, 1966	165
MK280	Captain America, #476, 1966	135
MK282	Captain America, Comic Scenes #192, 1974	50
MK285	Captain Kidd, #464, 1965	60
MK287	Chamber of Horrors Guillotine	90
MK290	Confederate Raider, #402, 1959	225
MK295	Crusader, #K7, 1959	100
MK300	Creature, The (From the Black Lagoon), #426, 1963	250
MK301	Creature, The (From the Black Lagoon), Glow, #483, 1969/1972	90
MK302	Creature, The (From the Black Lagoon), Monsters of the Movies, #654, 1975	90
MK305	Customizing Monster Kit No. 1, #463, 1963	90
MK306	Customizing Monster Kit No. 2, #464, 1963	90
MK310	D'Artagnan, #410, 1966	90
MK315	Dick Tracy, #818, 1968	120
MK318	Dick Tracy Space Coupe, #819, 1968	85
MK320	Dr. Deadly's Daughter (The Victim), Monster Scenes, #632, 1971	50
MK322	Dr. Deadly, Monster Scenes, #631, 1971	75
MK325	Dr. Jekyll, #460, 1965	135
MK327	Dr. Jekyll, Glow, #482, 1969/1972	50
MK330	Dracula, #424, 1962	180
MK331	Dracula's Dragster, #466, 1966	210
MK332	Dracula, Frightening Lightning, #424/454, 1969	240
MK333	Dracula, Glow, #454, 1969/1972	60
MK334	Dracula, Monsters of the Movies, #656, 1975	120
MK340	Flying Sub, #817, 1968	110
MK345	Forgotten Prisoner of Castel-Maré, The, #422, 1966	240
MK346	Forgotten Prisoner of Castel-Maré, The, Frightening Lightning, #422/453, 1969	300
MK347	Forgotten Prisoner of Castel-Maré, The, Glow, #453, 1969/1972	110
MK350	Frankenstein, #423, 1961	195
MK351	Frankenstein, Frightening Lightning, #423/449, 1969	225

| MK510 | MK425 | MK287 | MK680 | MK390 | MK470 |

MK352	Frankenstein, Glow, #449, 1969/1972	60	MK525	Napoleon Solo, #411, 1966	135
MK353	Frankenstein, Monster Scenes, #633, 1971	110	MK530	Nutty Nose Nipper, #806, 1965	90
MK354	Frankenstein, Monsters of the Movies, #651, 1975	120	MK535	Odd Job, #415, 1966	210
MK356	Frankenstein's Flivver, #465, 1964	240	MK540	Pain Parlor, 635, 1971	55
MK360	Frog, The, #451, 1966	180	MK545	Pan Am Space Clipper (2001: A Space Odyssey) #148, 1968	105
MK365	George Washington, #852, 1965	75	MK550	Pendulum, Monster Scenes, #636, 1971	60
MK370	Ghidrah, Monsters of the Movies, #658, 1975	210	MK555	Penguin, #416, 1967	275
MK375	Giant Woolly Mammoth, #743, 1972	60	MK560	Phantom of the Opera, The, #428, 1963	150
MK380	Gigantic Frankenstein ("Big Frankie"), #470, 1964, w/3 bottles paint & brush	700	MK561	Phantom of the Opera, The, #451, 1969/1972	55
MK385	Gladiator, w/sword, #405, 1959	120	MK562	Phantom of the Opera, The, Frightening Lightning, #428/451, 1969	210
MK386	Gladiator, w/trident, #406, 1959	120	MK565	Porthos, #K9, 1958	75
MK390	Godzilla, #469, 1964	360	MK570	Pushmi-Pullyu, (Dr. Doolittle), #814, 1968	50
MK391	Godzilla, Glow, #466, 1969/1972	105	MK575	Rat Patrol Diorama, #340, 1967	60
MK393	Godzilla's Go-Cart, #485, 1966	750	MK580	Robot ("Lost in Space"), #418, 1968	475
MK395	Gold Knight on Horseback, #K5, 1957/475, 1965	150	MK585	Rodan, Monsters of the Movies, #657, 1975	180
MK400	Green Beret, #413, 1966	75	MK590	Sabre Tooth Tiger, #722, 1972	50
MK405	Gruesome Goodies, Monster Scenes, #634, 1971	50	MK595	Seaview, #707, 1966	150
MK407	Guillotine, The Chamber of Horrors, #800, 1964	240	MK597	Seaview, #253, 1975	50
MK409	Hanging Cage, Monster Scenes, #637, 1971	50	MK600	Spartacus, #405, 1965	180
MK415	Hercules, #481, 1965	210	MK605	Spiderman, #477, 1966	150
MK420	Hulk, #421, 1966	135	MK610	Spindrift, #255, 1975	55
MK425	Hunchback of Notre Dame, The, #461, 1964	135	MK615	Steve Canyon, #404, 1966	75
MK430	Illya Kuryakin, #412, 1966	105	MK620	Superboy, #478, 1965	135
MK435	James Bond, #414, 1966	180	MK622	Superman, #562, 1963	135
MK440	Jerry West, #865, 1965	90	MK625	Tar Pit, #735, 1971	55
MK445	Jesse James, #408, 1966	150	MK630	Tarzan, #820, 1967	90
MK450	Jimmy Brown, #863, 1965	90	MK635	Tonto, #809, 1967	80
MK455	John F. Kennedy, #851, 1964	90	MK640	Tyrannosaurus Rex, #746, 1974	100
MK460	Johnny Unitas, #864, 1965	90	MK645	U.S. Marshall, #408, 1959	120
MK465	Jungle Swamp, #740, 1972	60	MK650	U.F.O., #813, 1968	75
MK470	King Kong, #468, 1964	300	MK655	Undertaker's Dragster, #570	150
MK472	King Kong's Thronester, #484, 1966	700	MK657	Vampire, #452, 1966	150
MK473	King Kong, Glow, #465, 1969/1972	80	MK658	Vampirella, Monster Scenes, #638, 1971	90
MK475	Land of the Giants, Snake Scene, #816, 1968	210	MK660	Viking, #K6, 1959	120
MK477	Land of the Giants Spaceship, #830, 1968	265	MK665	Voyager (Fantastic Voyage), #831, 1969	300
MK480	Lone Ranger, #808, 1967	75	MK670	Wacky Back Whacker, #807, 1965	120
MK485	Lost in Space, #419, 1966	550	MK675	Willie Mays, #860, 1965	110
MK487	Lost in Space, #420, 1966	750	MK680	Witch, The, #483, 1965	180
MK490	Mad Barber, #455	500	MK681	Witch, The, Glow, #470, 1969/1970	50
MK495	Mod Squad Woodie, #583, 1970	60	MK685	Wolfman, #425, 1962	165
MK500	Moon Bus (2001: A Space Odyssey), #829, 1968	210	MK690	Wolfman's Wagon, #458, 1965	270
MK510	Mummy, The, #427, 1963	150	MK691	Wolfman, Frightening Lightning, #425/450, 1969	210
MK512	Mummy's Chariot, #459, 1965	300	MK692	Wolfman, Glow, #450, 1969/1972	50
MK514	Mummy, The, Frightening Lightning, #427/452, 1969	210	MK694	Wolfman, Monsters of the Movies, #652, 1975	110
MK516	Mummy, The, Glow, #452, 1969/1972	50	MK696	Wonder Woman, #479, 1965	285
MK520	Munsters, The (family), #804, 1965	550	MK698	Zorro, #801, 1965	95

Hawk

MK710	Wierdsville Customizing Kit, #301, 1964	135

Lindberg

MK740	Big Wheeler, #277, 1965	75
MK745	Creeping Crusher, #273, 1965	60
MK750	Green Ghoul, #274, 1965	60
MK755	Krimson Terror, #272, 1965	60
MK760	Mad Maestro, #284, 1965	135
MK765	Mad Mangler, #275, 1965	60
MK770	Road Hog, #276, 1965	75
MK775	Satan's Crate, #279, 1965	120
MK780	Scuttle Bucket, #278, 1965	75

Monogram

MK800	Flip Out, Fred Flypogger, #105, 1965	100
MK805	Speed Shift, Fred Flypogger, #104, 1965	100
MK810	Super Fuzz, Fred Flypogger, #104, 1965	150

MPC (Modern Plastics Corp.)

MK820	Barnabas Collins, TV "Dark Shadows," #1550, 1969	150
MK822	Barnabas Vampire Van, TV "Dark Shadows," #1626, 1969	90
MK825	Ghost of America w/Stroker McGurk, #104, 1964	110
MK830	Raiders' Coach, Paul Revere & Raiders, #0622, 1969	90
MK835	Stroker McGurk and Surf Rod, #100, 1964	65
MK840	Tall T w/Stroker McGurk, #102, 1964	65
MK845	Werewolf, TV "Dark Shadows," #1552, 1969	210
MK850	Yellow Submarine, Beatles, #617, 1968	150

Multipile

MK860	Iron Maiden, #981, 1966	120
MK864	Torture Chair, #980, 1966	120
MK868	Torture Wheel, #979, 1966	120

Pyro

MK870	Rawhide, #276, 1958	60
MK874	Restless Gun, #277, 1958	60
MK878	Wyatt Earp, #278, 1958	60

Remco

MK880	Flintstones' Sports Car, #450, 1961	90
MK882	Flintstones' Yacht, #451, 1961	90
MK884	Flintstones' Paddy Wagon, #452, 1961	90

Revell

MK900	Angel Fink, #1307, 1965	90
MK905	Beatnik Bandit, #1279, 1963 (Ed Roth)	50
MK910	Birthday Bird, #2051, 1960 (Dr. Seuss)	60
MK915	Bonanza, #1931, 1966	60
MK920	Busby The Afghan Yak, #2006, 1959 (Dr. Seuss)	60
MK922	Cat In The Hat, #2000, 1958 (Dr. Seuss)	60
MK923	Cat In The Hat w/Thing 1&2, #2050, 1960, (Dr. Seuss)	75
MK925	Fink Eliminator, #1310, 1965 (Ed Roth)	120
MK930	Flash Gordon and Martian, #1450, 1965	90
MK935	Flipper and Sandy, #1930, 1965	50
MK940	Game of the Yertle, #2100, 1960 (Dr. Seuss)	75
MK945	George Harrison, #1353, 1964	250
MK950	Gowdy The Dowdy Grackle, #2002, 1958 (Dr. Seuss)	60
MK952	Grickily The Gractus, #2005, 1959 (Dr. Seuss)	60
MK953	Grickily, Busby, and Rosco, #2081, 1960 (Dr. Seuss)	150
MK955	Horton The Elephant, #2052, 1960 (Dr. Seuss)	75
MK958	John Lennon, #1352, 1964	250
MK960	Mother's Worry, #1302, 1963 (Ed Roth)	55
MK962	Mr. Gasser, #1301, 1963 (Ed Roth)	60
MK965	Norval The Bashful Blinket, #2003, 1959 (Dr. Seuss)	60
MK967	Outlaw (Ed Roth)	50
MK970	Paul McCartney, #1350, 1964	200
MK972	Phantom And Witch Doctor, #1451, 1965	90
MK974	Ringo Starr, #1351, 1964	200
MK978	Robin Hood Fink, #1270, 1965 (Ed Roth)	175
MK980	Roscoe The Many Footed Lion #2004, 1959 (Dr. Seuss)	60
MK982	Scuz Fink, #1309	210
MK985	Superfink, #1308, 1964	185
MK987	Surfink, #1306, 1965	60
MK990	Tingo The Stroodle, #2001, 1958 (Dr. Seuss)	60
MK991	Tingo, Gowdy, And Norval, #2080, 1960 (Dr. Seuss)	150
MK995	Tweedy Pie w/Boss Fink, #1271, 1965 (Ed Roth)	90

See also: **Batman; Beatles; KISS; Star Trek; Star Wars**

MOVIE POSTERS   by Howard Lowery

From the earliest days of commercial film making in America, the poster has held a prominent place in movie advertising. Standardized at a width of 27" and height of 41" by the New Jersey-based Edison Studio in the early years of this century, the "one-sheet" poster has been the main "point-of-purchase" (box office) advertising medium, second only to the brightly-lit marquee for attracting movie-goers. It promoted current releases and tantalized audiences with coming attractions.

Circulation of these posters was until recent years controlled by regional and national poster exchanges and screen services. Theater owners were allowed to "rent" them for the run of the movie and were supposed to return them after the show closed. Many did not, and the posters that did not end up in the trash found their way into collections, closets, and garages.

The 1950s and 1960s represent a transitional period for

MK472

MK520

MK393

MK356, MK331, and MK512

115

Hollywood studios. A new generation of stars emerged: Elizabeth Taylor, Marlon Brando, Steve McQueen, Clint Eastwood, Sophia Loren, Audrey Hepburn, and others. Genre and cult films flourished, and studios continued to search for the ultimate spectacle and blockbuster. New technologies were developed to lure audiences into theaters: 3D, CinemaScope, Panavision, Cinerama, and many others.

Film posters are generally collected by film or genre, not by star. Important exceptions to this rule are James Dean and Marilyn Monroe. Science fiction, animation, horror/monster, western, and mystery films are very desirable; important, memorable films that were enormously popular or trend-setters are among the more sought after. In general, only posters produced for the film's initial release have significant value. Reissue posters (commonly designated by a capital "R" preceding the year) may be attractive, but are nowhere near as valuable.

Most of the posters listed in this section are one-sheets. A selection of other styles are included: three-sheets (41" x 81"), half sheets (22" x 28"), and inserts (14" x 36"). All prices quoted are from actual 1990-91 auction sales. Condition is important, and all posters listed are in fine or better condition. Listings are in alphabetical order. SF = science fiction.

MP180

MP260

One Sheets (27" x 41")

MP100	*African Queen, The* 1952, Bogart-Hepburn	1000
MP105	*Alice in Wonderland* 1951, Disney, on linen	300
MP110	*Attack of the Crab Monsters* 1957, SF	600
MP115	*Bedtime for Bonzo* 1951, linen-backed, Ronald Reagan classic	325
MP120	*Birds, The* 1963, Hitchcock classic	400
MP125	*Buster Keaton Story, The* 1957, Donald O'Connor	99
MP130	*Butch Cassidy and the Sundance Kid* 1969, linen-backed, Newman-Redford western	100
MP135	*Camelot* 1967, musical w/Richard Harris	83
MP140	*Casablanca* 1956, re-issue, Bogart	250
MP145	*Car of Tomorrow* 1951, MGM cartoon	450
MP150	*Cinderella* 1950, Disney animated feature	143
MP155	*Creature Walks Among Us, The* 1956, SF	425
MP160	*Diamonds Are Forever* 1971, Sean Connery	275
MP165	*Dr. No* 1962, 1st James Bond film	400
MP170	*Enforcer,The* 1976, Clint Eastwood	39
MP175	*ET* 1982, highest grossing film of all time	250
MP180	*Gentlemen Prefer Blondes*	750
MP185	*Gun Crazy* 1950, linen-backed	1600
MP190	*Hard Day's Night, A* 1964, Beatles' 1st film	350
MP195	*Help* 1965, Beatles' 2nd film	275
MP200	*High Noon* 1952, Gary Cooper western	550
MP205	*How to Dance* 1953, Disney's Goofy cartoon	650
MP210	*Invasion of the Body Snatchers* 1956, linen-backed, Don Siegel's SF classic	1000
MP215	*Invasion of the Saucer-Men* 1957, AI SF film	300

MP220	*Invisible Boy, The* 1957, Robbie the Robot	264
MP225	*Jaws* 1975, Steven Spielberg film	150
MP230	*Jet Pilot* 1957, John Wayne	110
MP235	*Jungle Book, The* 1967, Disney	248
MP240	*Lady and the Tramp* 1955, Disney	500
MP245	*Lawrence of Arabia* 1989, rare re-issue	150
MP250	*Long, Long Trailer, The* 1954, linen-backed, Lucille Ball-Desi Arnaz	325
MP260	*Love Me Tender*	600
MP265	*Niagara* 1953, Marilyn Monroe	600
MP270	*On the Waterfront* 1954, Marlon Brando	375
MP275	*Popeye Cartoon,* 1950, linen-backed stock	550
MP280	*Pluto's Party* 1952, Disney cartoon	600
MP285	*Psycho* 1960, Hitchcock's most famous film	275
MP290	*Quiet Man, The* 1952, John Wayne	700
MP295	*Raiders of the Lost Ark* 1981	125
MP300	*Rancho Notorious* 1952, M. Dietrich western	149
MP305	*Revenge of the Creature* 1955, SF-horror	715
MP310	*Revenge of the Jedi* 1982, unused teaser	220
MP315	*Sid & Nancy* 1986, Gary Oldman	125
MP320	*Singin' in the Rain* 1952, Gene Kelly musical	1700
MP325	*Sleeping Beauty* 1959, Disney	325
MP330	*Spare the Rod* 1954, linen-backed, Disney's Donald Duck cartoon	700
MP335	*Streetcar Named Desire, A* 1951, M. Brando	375
MP340	*Ten Commandments, The* 1956, DeMille's	550
MP345	*Terrytoons Cartoons,* 1957, linen-backed	250
MP350	*This Island Earth* 1954, SF	1320
MP355	*Trouble with Harry, The* 1955, Hitchcock	187
MP360	*2001: A Space Odyssey* 1968, 2 one-sheets in different styles	300
MP365	*Tobor the Great* 1954, Republic film	1000
MP370	*Uncle Donald's Ants* 1952, Disney's	650
MP375	*War of the Worlds* 1953, linen-backed	1200
MP380	Warner Brothers Cartoon, 1952, linen-backed	700
MP385	*West Side Story* 1961, road show, N. Wood	250
MP390	*Winnie the Pooh and the Blustery Day,* 1968 Disney animated short	121

Inserts (14" x 36")

MP430	*Alice in Wonderland* 1951, Disney	495
MP440	*An American in Paris* 1951, Gene Kelly	300
MP450	*Rebel Without A Cause* 1955, James Dean	550
MP460	*Shane* 1953, Alan Ladd western	600
MP470	*Singin' in the Rain* 1952	450
MP480	*Some Like It Hot* 1959, Jack Lemmon-Tony Curtis-Marilyn Monroe comedy	750
MP485	*Star is Born, A* 1954, Judy Garland musical	300
MP490	*Sunset Boulevard* 1950, Holden-Swanson	550

Half Sheets (22" x 28")

MP530	*It Came From Beneath the Sea* 1955, signed by Ray Harryhausen	143
MP540	*One Hundred and One Dalmatians* 1961, Disney animated feature	325
MP550	*Rebel Without A Cause* 1955, James Dean	450
MP560	*Some Like It Hot,* 1959	300
MP570	*Streetcar Named Desire, A* 1951	325

Three-Sheets (41" x 81")

MP610	*African Queen, The* 1952	600
MP620	*Alamo, The* linen-backed, John Wayne	800
MP630	*Dial M For Murder* 1954, Grace Kelly	375
MP640	*Limelight* 1952, linen-backed, Charles Chaplin	800
MP650	*Sleeping Beauty* 1959, linen-backed	475
MP660	*Time Machine, The* 1960, George Pal SF	325

Six-Sheets

MP720	*Barbarella* 1968, SF w/Jane Fonda	650
MP730	*James Dean Story, The* 1957, linen-backed	550
MP740	*Lolita* 1962, Peter Sellers	500
MP750	*Some Like It Hot* 1959, linen-backed	1000

Odd Size

MP820	*Batman* 1966, 60" x 40" poster for TV film	175

Foreign Language

MP900	*Adventures of Robin Hood* 1950s, linen-backed 43" x 29" Argentinian reissue	900
MP905	*Andy Warhol's Dracula* 1974, linen-backed 63" x 47" French	325
MP910	*Creature From the Black Lagoon* 1954, linen-backed 63" x 47" French	350
MP915	*Day the Earth Stood Still, The* 1953, linen-backed 33" x 24" Danish	750
MP921	*Forbidden Planet* 1956 22" x 14" Belgian	200
MP923	*Forbidden Planet* 63" x 47" French	3250
MP930	*400 Blows, The* 1959, linen, 63" x 47" French	600
MP935	*Jailhouse Rock* 1957, linen-backed 63" x 47" French, Elvis Presley	350
MP340	*Monkey Business* 1960s, linen-backed 63" x 47" French reissue of Marx Bros.	100
MP950	*Rebel Without A Cause* 1955, linen-backed 63" x 47" French	350
MP955	*Revenge of the Creature* 1955, linen-backed 54" x 38" Italian	350
MP960	*Star is Born, A* 1957, linen-backed, 33" x 47" German, Judy Garland	500
MP980	*Wild Bunch, The* 1969, 30" x 40" British	225

See also: **Beatles; Disney; Elvis; James Bond; Marilyn Monroe**

NON-SPORTS TRADING CARDS by Jim Buchanan

Non-sports trading cards are a good example of how a simple idea (marketing bubble gum) can be elevated to an art form. This collectible goes back at least to the 19th century, when cards were used to sell products like tobacco and were characterized by elaborate artwork and biting satirical humor.

Today there are literally thousands of sets to choose from. Unfortunately, economic reality has caught up with the business in the last 30 years. Many recent sets have been simple designs with photographed fronts. However, artwork is showing signs of making a comeback. Also appearing again is a type of humor that, while tame compared to a century ago, can nevertheless be refreshingly irreverent.

In addition to the gum cards there are many product premium cards which have been issued over the years. Most have been issued by candy, bakery, and cereal companies, and in recent years by the fast food establishments. Cards have been offered with such non-food products as tobacco, toys, comic books, clothing, and baking soda. These product or service cards are much scarcer than gum cards. Set size varies but most are smaller than gum issues. It remains to be seen if these special cards will demand as much interest with collectors in the future as gum cards have, but the future looks quite bright for these issues.

The most interesting recent trend has been the growing popularity in wrapper collecting. Some wrappers are among the fastest appreciating collectibles today. But there are dangers: large quantities of wrappers are occasionally discovered, especially for post 1960 card sets, so prices can fluctuate wildly. The most challenging collectible items are the display boxes.

The following sets are listed (when known) by name, size, company, and year. Values are for good to near mint condition. Prices for wrappers and boxes are shown when they are valuable. Occasionally a set may contain variations; all variations may not be shown due to space limitations. Some listings are test sets which did not see wide distribution, but are included because of their high value. Pre-1960 mint condition #1 cards of all sets sell for double value of the single card prices. Post -1960s cards #1's usually sell for 25%-50% more. Last cards in sets many times also bring a bonus price. Before the use of plastic card sheets the top and bottom card usually received most of the damage from handling and improper storage and therefore are much scarcer in mint condition.

Addams Family, 2-1/2" x 3-1/2" Donruss 1964
66 card set of b&w photos from TV series, large white caption area at bottom, wrapper is black with red print.

NS101	Set	150-300
NS102	Card	1-3
NS103	Wrapper	35
NS104	Box	50-75

Animals of the World, 2-1/8" x 2-5/8" Topps 1954
100 card set, continuation of "Bring Em Back Alive" set.

NS107	Set	250-500
NS108	Card	2-4
NS109	Wrapper	15-25

NS111

Antique Autos, 2-1/2" x 3-3/4" Bowman 1953
48 card set with 3-D backs.

NS110	Set	100-180
NS111	Card	2-3
NS112	3-D glasses	10-25

Batman, 2-1/2" x 3-1/2" Topps 1966
55 card set of color drawings of Batman & Robin in action with caption in black bat. Reverse is light orange with narrative & running Batman.

NS113	Set	75-150
NS114	Card	1-2
NS115	Wrapper	20-30
NS116	Box	100-200

NS114   NS118

Batman, 2-1/2" x 3-1/2" Topps 1966
44 cards numbered 1A to 44A (the "A Series") with caption in red bat. Puzzle piece and text on reverse.

NS117	Set	80-120
NS118	Card	1-2
NS119	Wrapper	20-30
NS120	Box, small sticker	125-250
NS121	Box, large sticker	150-275

NS124

Batman, 2-1/2" x 3-1/2", Topps 1966
44 cards numbered 1B to 44B (the "B Series") with caption in blue bat. Reverse was either text inside blue bat (the most difficult Batman cards to find) or puzzle/text combination.

NS122	Set, blue bat reverse	85-175
NS123	Set, puzzle/text reverse	85-175
NS124	Cards	1-2.75
NS125	Wrapper	20-30
NS126	Box	125-250

NS107

NS133   NS128

Batman, 2-1/2" x 3-1/2" Topps 1966

38 cards with color photo from movie, caption & riddle on reverse. Riddle decoder was in gum pack.

NS127	Set	85-180
NS128	Card	2-3
NS129	Decoder	5-8
NS130	Wrapper	20-30
NS131	Box	120-225

Batman, 2-1/2" x 3-1/2" Topps 1966

55 cards with color photo from 1966 TV show, either "Bat Laffs" or puzzle pieces on reverse.

NS132	Set	85-175
NS133	Card	1-2
NS134	Wrapper	20-30
NS135	Box	120-225

Battle, 2-1/2" x 3-1/2" Topps 1965

66 card set with great artwork depicting violent WWII war scenes in realistic detail. Also issued in each pack was a 2" x 3-5/16" cloth emblem.

NS136	Set (without emblems)	225-450
NS137	Card	2.50-5
NS138	Cloth emblems (24) - each	5-10
NS139	Cloth emblem checklist (no #)	15-25
NS140	Card checklist (#66)	15-30
NS141	Wrapper	50-100
NS142	Box	75-150

Beverly Hillbillies, 2-1/2" x 3-1/2" Topps 1963

66 card set of color photos from TV series, captions at bottom. Reverse is brown & gray with "Hillbilly Gags."

NS152	Set	200-300
NS153	Card	2-5
NS154	One cent wrapper	25-50
NS155	Five cent wrapper	75-150
NS156	Box	75

Brady Bunch, 2-1/2" x 3-1/2" Topps ©1969, rel. in 1971

88 card "regular" series of scenes from TV show.

NS157	Set	300-450
NS158	Card	2-5
NS159	Wrapper	25-50
NS160	Box	150-200

Brady Bunch, Topps ©1970

55 card test set, sometimes listed as a 2nd Series, are identical to 1969 series, only copyright date is different. This set is much harder to find than ©1969 series.

NS161	Set	500-1000
NS162	Card	15-25

NS164

Bring 'Em Back Alive, 2-1/8" x 2-5/8" Topps 1954

100 card set (also see "Animals of the World").

NS163	Set	200-375
NS164	Card	1.50-3
NS165	Wrapper	50-75

Dark Shadows, 2-1/2" x 3-1/2" Phil Chewing Gum Co. 1968-69

Two 66 card sets, based on popular TV series.

NS174	Pink border set	175-350

NS175	Green border set	175-350
NS176	Card	2.50-5
NS177	Wrapper	25-50
NS178	Box	75-150

NS181-82

Davy Crockett, 2-5/8" x 3-3/4" Topps 1956

Two 80 card sets. The second series (greenbacks) was sold in limited quantities as the Crockett fad faded.

NS179	Orange back set	150-300
NS180	Green back set	200-400
NS181	Orange back cards, #1-80	1.50-3
NS182	Green back cards, #1A-80A	2-4
NS183	Wrapper	40-80

NS185

Dinosaur Cards, 2-1/2" x 3-1/2" Nu-Card Sales 1961

80 card set of greenish-blue drawings, text on reverse. A mounting album was available as a mail premium.

NS184	Set	175-350
NS185	Card	3-4
NS186	Wrapper	15-30
NS187	Box	75-150

Elvis Presley, 2-1/2" x 3-1/2" Topps 1956   NS189

66 card set, most valuable of Elvis sets and one of only two produced in USA (other is 1978 Donruss). This set also issued in England. Topps name not on most cards.

NS188	Set	350-600
NS189	Card	5-10
NS190	Wrapper	75-150
NS191	Box	500+

NS212-13

Fight the Red Menace, 2-1/2" x 3-1/8" Bowman 1951

48 cards to capitalize on mood during the Korean War.

NS210	Set, gray backs	250-500
NS211	Set, white backs	300-600
NS212	Card, gray back	4-8
NS213	Card, white back	5-10
NS214	Special cards No. 2, 23, 24, 48	7.50-15
NS215	Wrapper	50-100

Fighting Marines, 2" x 3" Topps 1954

96 in set. For 2 card panels add 100% value.

NS216	Set	250-550
NS217	Card No. 1-48	2-4

NS217-18

NS218	Card No. 49-95	2.50-5
NS219	Special cards No. 74, 96	5-10
NS220	Wrapper	25-50

NS227

Firefighters, 2-1/2" x 3-3/4" Bowman
64 in set.

NS226	Set	400-600
NS227	Card	5-10
NS228	Wrapper	50-75

NS229   **NS412**

Flying Things, Irregular sizes, Topps 1965-1975
At least 48 in set issued a minimum of 5 different times. (Also see Marvel Flyers.)

| NS229 | Flying Thing | 15-20 |
| NS230 | Envelope | 10-25 |

NS231

Freedom War, 2-1/8" x 2-5/8" Topps 1950
203 in set, first 96 had both white and gray backs: titles on front with white back & titles on reverse with gray back. Cards 97-103 came die cut & not die cut. Two card panels are worth 100% more than single cards.

NS231	Set of 203 cards	750-1400
NS232	Cards #97-103 die cut	30-60
NS233	Cards #97-103 not die cut	50-75
NS234	Cards 1-96 gray back	1.50-3
NS235	Cards 1-96 white back	2-4
NS236	Other cards	.50-3.50
NS237	Wrapper	50-75

NS239

Frontier Days, 2-1/2" x 3-3/4" Bowman 1955
128 attractive cards with well designed obverses reprinted from set called "Wild West" but enlarged with white side panels; also issued in Canada.

NS238	Set	250-500
NS239	Card	2-3
NS240	Wrapper	50-75

NS251-52

Garbage Pail Kids, 2-1/2" x 3-1/2" Topps
This controversial set has become the largest and most profitable single theme set ever issued, with 15 sticker series, buttons, posters, and 3-D wall plaks released to date. Several cautions are in order: most series contain variations, such as two names for the same picture. Also, due to the poor initial response, large amounts of Series 1 stickers were never shipped. These are now finding their way into the market, so Series 1 prices can fluctuate greatly.

Series 1-88 stickers (includes 6 variations)

NS250	Set	50-125
NS251	Sticker	1.50-3
NS252	6 variation stickers, each	3
NS253	25 cent wrapper	1
NS254	No price wrapper	2
NS255	Box	5-10

Series 2-84 cards & 2 variations in 3 print runs

NS256	1st printing set	50-75
NS257	2nd printing set	25-50
NS258	3rd printing set	25-50
NS259	Sticker	.50-.75
NS260	Live Mike	25-50
NS261	Messy Tessy	50-75
NS262	Schizo Fran (1st two print runs only)	15-25
NS263	25 cent wrappers	.25-.50
NS264	No price wrappers	.50-1
NS265	Box	3-5

Series 3-88 stickers (includes 6 variations)

NS266	Set	10-15
NS267	Sticker	.25
NS268	25 cent wrappers	.25
NS269	No price wrappers	.50-1
NS270	Box	2-3
NS271	Series 4-15, set	10-15

Garbage Pail Kids Giant Stickers, 4-7/8" x 6-7/8" Topps
15 in first group are designed like advertising posters (except for #1); 39 in second are enlargements of regular Series 1 stickers.

NS275	1st group set	10-15
NS276	Sticker	.25-.50
NS277	Wrapper	.25-
NS278	Box	1-2
NS279	2nd group set (marked "1st Series Kids")	40-50
NS280	Stickers #1-4, 15-18, 29-35	.50-1
NS281	Sticker #8	3-4
NS282	Wrapper	.25
NS283	Box	1-2

Get Smart, 2-3/8" x 2-1/2" Topps 1966
66 b&w photo cards based on TV show, came as 2 card panels perforated in middle, 22 cards were double printed. 16 bonus Secret Agent Kits came with cards.

NS291	Card set	150-200
NS292	Secret Agent Kit set	80-160
NS293	Single print cards	1.50-3
NS294	Double print cards	1-2
NS295	Individual Secret Agent Kits	5-10
NS296	Panel with 2 single print cards	5-10
NS297	Panel with 2 double print cards	2.50-5
NS298	Wrapper	20-30
NS299	Box	75-125

Gilligan's Island, 2-1/2" x 3-1/2" Topps 1965
55 cards based on TV show, has b&w photo with white border, reverse has photos that resemble filmclips.

NS300	Set	200-400
NS301	Card	2.50-5
NS302	Wrapper	15-30
NS303	Box	75-125

NS305

Green Hornet, 2-1/2" x 3-1/2" Donruss 1966
44 cards based on TV show, color with white border, reverse is poster piece with caption.

NS304	Set	90-200
NS305	Card	1.50-3
NS306	Wrapper	20-40
NS307	Box	100-200

NS309

Green Hornet Stickers, 2-1/2" x 3-1/2" Topps 1966
44 based on TV show.

NS308	Set	125-250
NS309	Sticker	2-4
NS310	Wrapper	10-15
NS311	Box	50-100

Hee Haw, 2-1/2" x 3-1/2" Topps 1970
55 cards based on TV show, color with comic style word balloons, reverse is orange with joke in 3-D, rare test set.

| NS312 | Set | 500-1000 |
| NS313 | Card | 10-20 |

Hogan's Heros, 2-1/2" x 3-1/2" Fleer 1966
66 cards based on TV show, b&w photo with caption below, reverse of entire set forms giant poster. Difficult to find.

NS314	Set	300-600
NS315	Card	3-6
NS316	Wrapper	75-150
NS317	Box	150-300

Hopalong Cassidy, 2-1/8" x 2-5/8" Topps 1950 NS321

NS321	Set	600-1200
NS322	One color 8 sets (186)	2-4
NS323	Multi-color 2 sets (44)	3-6
NS324	Foil cards (8), each	50-75
NS325	Wrapper	40-80

Hopalong Cassidy, Post Cereal 1951
36 cards in set, color with information on reverse.

| NS326 | Set | 75-150 |
| NS327 | Card | 2-4 |

Horror Monster Series, 2-1/2" x 3-1/2" Nu-Cards '60-61
146 cards total in two series: green in "Horror Monsters"

NS327

NS332

wrappers & orange in "Movies Monsters" wrappers & "Shock Monsters" boxes. Was also an unknown number of slightly smaller blue cards (original issue?).

NS328	Green (1-66) set	125-250
NS329	Orange (67-146) set	125-250
NS330	Blue card	3-6
NS331	Green card	1.50-3
NS332	Orange card	1.50-3
NS333	Card #102 (with 100 wrapper bonus on reverse)	10-15
NS334	"Horror Monsters" wrapper	50-100
NS335	"Movies Monsters" wrapper	35-75
NS336	"Horror Monsters" box	75-150
NS337	"Movies Monsters" box	40-80

Howdy Doody Magic Trading Cards, 2" x 3"
Burry's Cookies
42 card set, Howdy Doody Cookies.

| NS338 | Set | 75-150 |
| NS339 | Card | 2-4 |

James Bond, 2-1/2" x 3-1/2" Phil. Chewing Gum Co 1965
66 cards with b&w photos from 3 Bond movies, description on reverse.

NS340	Set	100-200
NS341	Card	1.25-2.50
NS342	Wrapper	20-30
NS343	Box	40-80

James Bond, 2-1/2" x 3-1/2" Phil. Chewing Gum Co. 1965
66 cards based on movie "Thunderball," similar to 1st set but with "Code Quiz" and paper "Secret Decoder."

NS344	Set	125-250
NS345	Card	1.50-3
NS346	Decoder	5-10
NS347	Wrapper	15-30
NS348	Box	50-100

NS350-52

Jets, Rockets, Spacemen, 2-1/8" x 3-1/8" Bowman 1951
This 108 card set (& the Lone Ranger cards) are some of the best artwork ever produced on gum cards. Some interesting highlights: first time Bowman produced cards of this larger size & first set to utilize a continuing story format. Interestingly, the mid-range numbers are much harder to find (usually it's the high numbers). Difficult to find in near mint condition or better.

NS349	Set	900-2000
NS350	Cards #1-36, each	3-6
NS351	Cards #37-72, each	12-15
NS352	Cards #73-108, each	4-8
NS353	Wrapper	100-300
NS354	Box	500-750

Julia, 2-1/2" x 3-1/2" Topps 1968
33 b&w photo cards with facsimile autograph, only card number on reverse. Test issue, rare.

| NS357 | Set | 500-750 |
| NS358 | Card | 15-25 |

King Kong, 2-1/2" x 3-1/2" Donruss 1965
55 cards, b&w pictures based on original movie, but with

120

funny captions. Reverse of entire set forms picture of King Kong & girl.

NS359	Set	90-180
NS360	Card	1.50-3
NS361	Wrapper	20-40
NS362	Box	50-75

King Kong, 2-1/2" x 3-1/2" Topps 1976
55 cards & 11 stickers based on 1976 movie remake, color pictures with red borders & caption at bottom, reverse is 44 puzzle pieces & 11 "Movie Facts."

NS363	Set	10-15
NS364	Card	.25
NS365	Sticker	.75-1
NS366	Wrapper	1.50
NS367	Box	5-15

KISS, 2-1/2" x 3-1/2" Donruss 1978
132 color photo cards in 2 series: 1-66 has jagged corners on frame line & blue wrapper, 67-132 has rounded corners & red wrapper. After death of Peter Criss, 1st series was reprinted with 21 new photos. There's been a great increase in value of KISS cards in last 5 years due to large number of collectors & tight supply.

NS368	Set, Series I	20-30
NS369	Set, Series II	35-50
NS370	Card, Series I	.25-.50
NS371	Card, Series II	.50-.75
NS372	Corrected version set	50-75
NS373	Corrected version card	1-3
NS374	Wrapper (either color)	3-5
NS375	Box (either series)	15-25
NS376	Unopened box, Series I	150-175

Land of the Giants, 2-1/2" x 3-1/2" Topps
55 in set, color photo & caption. Reverse of 1-44 have narratives, 45-54 are poster pieces, 55 has checklist. Test issue, rare.

NS377	Set	1000-1500
NS378	Card	25-50
NS379	Wrapper	200-500
NS380	Box	500-1000

Laugh-In, 2-1/2" x 3-1/2" Topps 1968
77 cards in six formats (photo, knock-knocks, necklaces, finger puppets, door cards, foldees) plus 24 "Goldie's Laugh-ons" stickers, based on TV show.

NS385	Card set	100-175
NS386	Sticker set	75-125
NS387	Cards 1-45 (photos & knock-knocks)	2-3
NS388	Cards 46-77 (all others)	3-4
NS389	Sticker	3-4
NS390	Wrapper	20-30
NS391	Box	50-75

Look N See, 2" x 3" Topps 1953   NS93-97
135 cards in set, questions on back, answers revealed with red paper.

NS392	Set	500-950
NS393	Cards #1-75 (1st series)	2-4
NS394	Cards #76-135 (2nd series)	3-5
NS395	Card #15, Babe Ruth	50-75
NS396	Indian cards, each	5-7
NS397	President cards, each	5-7
NS398	Wrapper	20

Lost in Space, 2-1/2" x 3-1/2" Topps 1966
55 b&w captioned photo cards depicting the adventures of the "Space Family Robinson" with story on reverse.

NS401	Set	250-350
NS402	Card	2.50-5
NS403	Wrapper	50-75
NS404	Box	200-300

Mars Attacks, 2-1/2" x 3-1/2" Topps 1962
55 cards with sensational color artwork of graphic scenes, story on reverse. Clearly the most popular science fiction set although several cards were redone due to parental objections.

NS405	Set	800-1500
NS406	Card	10-20
NS407	Card #1	25-50
NS408	Card #55 (checklist)	75-100
NS409	Wrapper	150-300
NS410	Box	500-1000

Marvel Flyers, Irregular, Topps 1962
12 put-together super hero "flyers" based on earlier "Flying Things" set. Printed on thin Styrofoam.

NS411	Set	500-750
NS412	Flyer	25-50
NS413	Envelope	25-50
NS414	Unopened packs	75-125

Monkees, 2-1/2" x 3-1/2" Donruss 1966
44 cards of sepia-tone photos with facsimile autographs, puzzle pieces on reverse.

NS425	Set	75-150
NS426	Card	1-2
NS427	Wrapper	15-25
NS428	Box	50-75

Monkees, 2-1/2" x 3-1/2" Donruss 1966-67
3 color photo follow-on series of 44 cards each. A: white border & black panel, B: yellow border & red panel, C: deep pink frame lines on both sides.

NS430	Set (each series)	75-150
NS431	Cards	1-2
NS432	A series wrapper	10-15
NS433	B series wrapper	20-25
NS434	C series wrapper ("More of the Monkees")	5-10
NS435	A series box ("2nd Series" sticker)	50-75
NS436	B series box ("3rd Series" sticker)	50-75
NS437	C series box ("More of the Monkees")	35-50

Monkees Badges, 2-1/2" x 3-1/2" Donruss 1967
44 die cut badge-like front peel stickers with captions in the ribbon.

NS438	Set	100-200
NS439	Badge sticker	4-5
NS440	Wrapper	15-25
NS441	Box	50-75

Monkees Flip Movies, 2-7/16" x 3-1/2" Topps 1967
16 flip books of sequence photos, cover is photo in TV set.

NS442	Set	125-175
NS443	Movie flip book	10-15
NS444	Wrapper	25-50
NS445	Box	75-100

Monster Flip Movies, 2-1/2" x 4-3/4" Topps 1964
36 flip books of b&w photos from Universal Horror Films, 32 pages each.

NS446	Set	175-300
NS447	Movie flip book	5-10
NS448	Wrapper	25-50

Munsters, two sizes, Leaf 1964
72 b&w captioned photo cards & 16 unnumbered stickers based on TV show, "Munsters Mumbles" jokes on reverse.

NS450	Card set	250-450
NS451	Sticker set	50-100
NS452	Card	2-4
NS453	Sticker	3-5
NS454	Wrapper	20-30
NS455	Box	75-125

Outer Limits, 2-1/2" x 3-1/2" Bubbles (Topps) 1964
50 cards with captioned color drawings & story on reverse. Based on TV show. Black border makes finding complete mint

condition set very difficult. Was smaller English set.

NS465	U.S. set	250-350
NS466	English set	90-125
NS467	U.S. card	4-5
NS468	English card	1-2
NS469	U.S. wrapper	75-150
NS470	U.S. Box	175-350

Planes, 2-1/2" x 3-1/2" Topps
120 cards with reverse either blue or red.

NS471	Set, blue backs	175-300
NS472	Set, red backs	300-600
NS473	Cards #1-60, blue backs	.75-1.50
NS474	Cards #1-60, red backs	1.50-3
NS475	Cards #61-120, blue backs	1.50-3
NS476	Cards #61-120, red backs	2.50-5
NS477	Card #9 (scarce)	5-10
NS478	Checklist Card	7.50-15
NS479	Wrapper	15-30

Push-Pull, 2-1/2" x 4 -11/16" Topps 1965
36 cards, each with 2 pictures under a black shutter overlay, a picture becomes visible by moving the shutter up or down. Cards with baseball stars are most valued by collectors.

NS495	Set	150-300
NS496	Card #6, Mickey Mantle-Yogi Berra	10-30
NS497	Card #17, Lou Gehrig-Babe Ruth	10-30
NS498	Card #19, Casey Stengel Wins-Loses	8-15
NS499	Wrapper	125-150
NS500	Box	100-150

NS506-07

Rails & Sails, Topps 1956
200 captioned picture cards, reissued as Doeskin tissues premium, cards #1-130 are railroad, #131-200 are ships.

NS505	Set	500-700
NS506	Cards #1-80 & #131-150	1-2
NS507	Cards #81-130 & #151-200	3-4
NS508	One cent wrapper	15-30
NS509	Five cent wrapper	25-50

Robin Hood TV Scenes, 2" x 3-1/2" Johnson & Johnson Band Aids 1957
25 cards in set, most valuable of Robin Hood sets.

| NS515 | Set | 100-200 |
| NS516 | Card | 2-4 |

Rookies, 2-1/2" x 3-1/2" Topps
44 captioned color photo cards, test issue based on TV show. Reverse is puzzle picture area & narrative.

NS520	Set	450-900
NS521	Card	15-25
NS522	Wrapper	150-250

Room 222, 2-1/2" x 3-1/2" Topps 1969?
44 b&w photo cards, test issue based on TV show, facsimile autograph on all but three, reverse contains puzzle pieces.

NS529

NS525	Set	500-800
NS526	Card	15-20
NS527	Wrapper	125-175

Roy Rogers Pop-Outs, 2-1/4" x 3-1/4" Post Cereal 1950s
36 cards in set, most valuable of Roy Rogers sets. Prices listed are for cards with unpunched outer borders.

| NS528 | Set | 500-950 |
| NS529 | Card | 15-30 |

NS535-40

Scoops, 2-1/8" x 3" Topps 1954
156 cards in 2 series based on famous news headlines.

NS530	Set	750-1500
NS531	Cards #1-78-1st series	2-4
NS532	Cards #79-156-2nd series	3.50-7
NS533	Card #3-Lindbergh Flies Atlantic	5-10
NS534	Card #27-Bob Feller Strikeout King	20-40
NS535	Card #41-Babe Ruth Sets Record	50-75
NS536	Card #110-Notre Dame's 4 Horsemen	15-25
NS537	Card #128-Jesse Owens Races Horse	6-12
NS538	Card #129-Ben Hogan New Golf King	6-12
NS539	Card #130-Braves Go To Milwaukee	25-35
NS540	Card #154-26-Inning Tie Game	25-50
NS541	All boxer cards	10-20

NS543

Sgt. Preston Adventure Cards, Quaker Cereal 1956
36 cards of playing card size.

| NS542 | Set | 100-150 |
| NS543 | Card | 2.50-5 |

Shock Theater, 2-1/2" x 3-1/2" Topps 1975
51 captioned photo cards test issued in U.S., then marketed in England in 1976. In U.S., were two #17s and no #47. Reverse contains "Shocking Laffs" & narrative. Prices are for U.S. set.

NS550	Set	125-250
NS551	Card	2.50-5
NS552	Wrapper	25-50

NS555

Space Patrol Trading Cards, Rice/Wheat Chex 1950s
40 cards in set. With just one card per box of cereal, not many kids had a complete set.

| NS555 | Set | 500-1000 |
| NS556 | Card | 10-25 |

Spook Stories, 2-1/2" x 3-1/2" Leaf 1963-65
144 captioned b&w picture cards with "Spook Stories" on reverse. An unknown number of stickers was also issued. Wrappers & boxes for cards #1-72 said "Spook Theatre"; wrappers & boxes for #73-144 said "Son of Spook Theatre." Wrappers also differed in color, material and print.

| NS560 | Set, 1st series (#1-72) | 75-150 |
| NS561 | Set, 2nd series (#73-144) | 125-200 |

NS562	Card, 1st series	1-2
NS563	Card, 2nd series	2-3
NS564	Stickers	3-5
NS565	Wrapper, 1st series	
	Glossy paper, reddish-orange color	50-125
NS566	Wax wrapper, orange color	25-50
NS567	Wax wrapper, lavender color	25-50
	Wrapper, 2nd series	
NS569	Wax paper, lavender color	45-90
NS570	Wax paper, orange color	50-100
NS571	Lavender box	50-100
NS572	Orange box	50-100

Star Trek, 2-3/8" x 3-7/16" Leaf 1967

72 captioned b&w photo cards based on the original TV show with narratives on reverse. One of the most sought-after items by Star Trek & card collectors. Cards are rare because they were produced for only five weeks then withdrawn due to contractual problems.

NS573	Set	1500-2500
NS574	Card	15-25
NS575	Wrapper	125-175
NS576	Box	500-1000

Star Wars, 2-1/2" x 3-1/2" Topps 1977-78

330 photo cards and 55 stickers were issued in 5 series. Only one card is valuable: #207, the infamous "x-rated" C-3PO, created by a mischievous artist and issued by mistake. A corrected card was quickly reissued.

NS577	Set, 1st series	15-25
NS578	Set, 2nd series	10-20
NS579	Set, 3rd series	10-15
NS580	Set, 4th series	10-15
NS581	Set, 5th series	15-20
NS582	Card #207, x-rated	15-30
NS583	Card #207, reissued	5-10
NS584	Other cards	.25-.50
NS585	Stickers	.50-1
NS586	Wrappers (Series 1-5)	1-2
NS587	Boxes (Series 1-5)	5-10

NS582

Star Wars Sticker Set, 4-3/8" x 3-3/8" General Mills 1978

16 stickers packed in Frankenberry, Crazy Cow, Booberry, Cocoa Puffs, & Count Chocula cereals.

| NS588 | Set | 50-75 |
| NS589 | Card | 3-5 |

Super Hero Stickers, 2-1/2" x 3-1/2" Phil. Chewing Gum Co. 1967

55 picture stickers of super heroes with funny captions. Most were mis-cut.

NS590	Set	95-175
NS591	Sticker	2-3
NS592	Wrapper	15-20
NS593	Box	25-35

Tarzan & the She Devil, 2-5/8" x 3-3/4" Topps 1955

60 3-D picture cards, reverse is green.

NS594	Set	150-300
NS595	Card	2-4
NS596	3-D glasses	6-12

Tarzan's Savage Fury, Topps 1955

60 3-D cards, reverse is orange. Identical to above set.

| NS601 | Set | 225-450 |
| NS602 | Card | 3-6 |

NS594-604

NS606

| NS604 | 3-D glasses | 6-12 |

Television & Radio Stars of N.B.C., 2-1/2" x 3-3/4" Bowman 1952

36 picture cards, reverse is horizontal.

NS605	Set	150-275
NS606	Card	2.50-5
NS607	Wrapper	25-75

Terror Monsters, 2-1/2" x 3-1/2" Rosan 1963

130 b&w photo cards in two series. No. 1-64 had green borders & #67-132 had purple borders. Some photos are repeated in second series & there were two unnumbered bonus cards (#65 & 66?). Jokes were on reverse.

NS608	Set, 1st series (#1-64)	125-250
NS609	Set, 2nd series (#67-132)	125-250
NS610	Numbered cards	2.50-5
NS611	Bonus cards	15-30

Terror Tales, 2-1/2" x 3-1/2" Topps 1967

88 sickly green photos of horror movies, funny comment in word balloon. Reverse is purple with "Terror Tales" narrative. Wrapper & box are marked "Movie Monsters."

NS620	Set	225-500
NS621	Card	2.50-5
NS622	Wrapper	20-40
NS623	Box	50-75

NS629, NS627

Untouchables, 2-9/16" x 4-5/8" Leaf

16 8 page booklets, each with an "Official Eliot Ness Adventure Story." As bonus, one of 16 stickers with emblems of law enforcement agencies was included.

NS625	Booklet set	50-90
NS626	Sticker set	50-90
NS627	Booklet	4-6
NS628	Sticker	3-5
NS629	Wrapper	25-30
NS630	Box	50-75

Wacky Ads, 3-1/8" x 5-1/4" Topps 1969

NS633

Set of 36 postcard size cards and predecessor to the many "Wacky Packages" series. Satirized product can be removed, reverse is coated with water activated adhesive.

NS631	Set	150-200
NS632	Card #25	15-25
NS633	Other cards	4-7
NS634	Wrapper	15-25
NS635	Box	25-50

Wild Man, 2-1/8" x 2-1/2" Bowman 1950

72 picture cards in 2 series of 36 each.

NS646

PD156

NS640	Set	500-950
NS641	Card	4-8
NS642	Wrapper	50-75

Wild West, Bowman 1959
180 picture cards in 8 series, some are smaller versions of "Frontier Days" set.

NS645	Set	550-1100
NS646	Card, Series A to G	2-4
NS647	Card, Series H	4-8
NS648	Wrapper	50-75

World on Wheels, 2-5/8" x 3-3/4" Topps 1955 NS56-58
180 picture cards with transportation theme.

NS655	Set	500-750
NS656	Cards #1-160 - red back	.75-1.50
NS657	Cards #161-180 - red back	10-20
NS658	Cards #171-180 - blue back	10-20

Zorro, 2-1/2" x 3-1/2" Topps 1958
88 captioned picture cards of Disney's Zorro.

NS659	Set	150-275
NS660	Card	1.50-3
NS661	Wrapper	35-75

See also: **Baseball Cards; Batman; Beatles; James Bond; Disney; Elvis; Football Cards; KISS; Marilyn Monroe; Playboy; Star Trek; Star Wars**

PAPER DOLLS   by Mary Young

The exact origin of paper dolls is a mystery. Some think they began in Europe as "pantins"...cardboard dolls with arms and legs that moved in jumping jack fashion when their strings were pulled.

Advertising paper dolls were used by many companies in the late 19th century. Often a child could send away for a complete series after receiving the first doll with the product. Dolls for advertising purposes still appear today.

The most popular paper dolls have always been those modeled after celebrities. Famous dancers and opera stars were favorites during the 1800s. Movie stars have been very popular in this century. Celebrity dolls have always brought the highest prices. Perhaps that's because they always reflected a star's public image, accurate or not. Stories are told of Marilyn Monroe rejecting the artwork for her dolls because they didn't look thin enough. The art was returned a number of times for continued "slimming down" until they finally met with her approval.

Although the advent of television has caused a steady decline in the number of dolls produced, paper doll collecting has become increasingly popular since the 1960s. Most commonly produced in book form which feature dolls on the covers with their clothes on the inside pages, they also come in box form and inside women's and children's magazines.

The following is a list of the most valuable paper dolls produced in the post 1950s. Prices are for uncut books in excellent to near mint condition. Dolls are also collected in cut sets. For a cut set, the value is generally half the price if the set is complete and the dolls and clothes are in excellent condition. If dolls and outfits are missing, bent, or torn, the value decreases even more.

The dolls are listed with their book's original identifying number. Numbers are usually found at the top of the book in the right or left hand corner. Unless otherwise specified, the price applies to that number only. Many times the publisher would reprint a popular paper doll book under a new number. Sometimes the book would be copied exactly but in other cases fewer costume pages would be included and the cover would be on lighter paper. So generally the reprints are worth less.

Listings are in alphabetical order by either last name or the first key word. The manufacturer and year introduced are also listed. The four largest producers of paper dolls are listed by code: Saalfield (S), Whitman (W), Lowe (L), and Merrill (M) companies.

1950s

PD101	June Allyson, #1173, W, 1953	65-100
PD102	Pier Angeli, no #, Dell, 1955	85-150
PD103	Eve Arden, #4310, S, 1953	65-125
PD104	Gene Autry, #990, W, 1950	65-100
PD105	Gene Autry, #1184, W, 1951	65-100
PD106	Lucille Ball/Desi Arnez, #2101, W, 1953	55-90
PD107	Lucille Ball, Desi Arnez & Little Ricky, #2116, W, 1953	65-100
PD108	Ann Blyth, #2550, M, 1952	75-125
PD109	Ann Blyth, #2550, M (six page book)	50-80
PD110	Barbara Britton, #4318, S, 1954	65-125
PD111	Joan Caulfield, #2725, S, 1953	65-125
PD112	Cyd Charisse, #2084, W, 1956	65-125
PD113	Rosemary Clooney, #2569, L, 1956	65-125
PD114	Coronation Paper Dolls & Coloring Book, #4312, S, 1953	50-80
PD115	Arlene Dahl, #4311, S, 1953	65-125
PD116	Linda Darnell, #2733, S, 1953	65-125
PD117	Faye Emerson, #2722, S, 1952	55-100
PD118	June & Stu Erwin, #2735, S, 1954	55-100
PD119	Rhonda Fleming Paper Dolls & Coloring Book, #4320, S, 1954	55-100
PD120	Ava Gardner, #2108, W, 1953	75-125
PD121	Betty Grable, #1558, M, 1951	85-150
PD122	Betty Grable, #2552, M, 1953	85-150
PD123	Judy Holliday, #2734, S, 1954	55-100
PD124	The Honeymooners, #2560, L, 1956	100-300
PD125	Betty Hutton, #2099, W, 1951	65-100
PD126	Martha Hyer, #4423, S, 1958	65-100
PD127	Grace Kelly, #2049, W, 1955	75-125

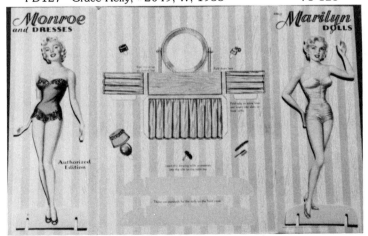

PD137

PD118

PD128	Grace Kelly, #2069, W, 1956		75-125
PD129	Hedy Lamarr, #2600, S, 1951		75-125
PD130	Piper Laurie, #2551, M, 1953		85-150
PD131	Janet Leigh, #2554, M, 1953		85-150
PD132	Janet Leigh, #2405, L, 1957		65-100
PD133	Virginia Mayo, #4422, S, 1957		80-140
PD134	MGM Starlets, #2060, W, 1951		75-150
PD135	Vera Miles, #2086, W, 1957		70-125
PD136	Carmen Miranda, #2723, S, 1952		75-140
PD137	Marilyn Monroe, #4308, S, 1953		125-300
PD138	Sheree North, #4420, S, 1957		70-120
PD139	Kim Novak Paper Dolls with Pictures to Color, #4409, S, 1957		75-140
PD140	Kim Novak, #4429, S, 1958		75-140
PD141	Ozzie & Harriet, #4319, S, 1954		75-140
PD142	Oklahoma, #438, Golden Press, 1956		75-120
PD143	Oklahoma, #1954, W, 1956		70-100
PD144	Patti Page, #2488, L, 1958		70-100
PD145	Debra Paget, no#, Dell, 1954		90-150
PD146	Jane Powell, all from 1950s		75-120
PD147	Debbie Reynolds, no#, Dell, 1953		90-150
PD148	Debbie Reynolds, all others from 1950s		75-125
PD149	Roy Rogers & Dale Evans, #988, W, 1950		75-135
PD150	Roy Rogers, all others		70-100
PD151	Dinah Shore, all from 1950s		70-100
PD152	Elaine Stewart, no#, Dell, 1954		125-175
PD153	Elaine Stewart, #2048, W 1955		75-125
PD154	Gale Storm, #117, Dell, 1957		90-150
PD155	Gale Storm, all others		75-125
PD156	Elizabeth Taylor, all from 1950s		75-125
PD157	Shirley Temple, #5110, S, 1958 (18" doll)		75-125
PD158	Shirley Temple, #4435, S, 1958 (8" dolls)		60-100
PD159	Shirley Temple Playkit, #9859, S, 1958 (9" & 5-1/2" dolls)		70-120
PD160	Esther Williams, #1563, M, 1950		85-140

PD161	Esther Williams, #2553, M, 1953 (paper doll/coloring book)	85-140
PD162	Natalie Wood, #1962, W, 1957	75-125
PD163	Natalie Wood, #2086, W, 1958	75-125
PD164	Joanne Woodward, #4436, S, 1958	75-125
PD165	Loretta Young, #4352, S, 1956	75-125

1960s

PD166	Beverly Hillbillies, #1955, W, 1964	35-50
PD167	Caroline (Kennedy), #109, Magic	
PD168	Wand Corp.	50-75
PD169	Angela Cartwright, #3450,	
PD170	Transogram Toy Co.	50-60
PD171	Finian's Rainbow, #4436, S, 1968	25-35
PD172	The First Lady (Jackie Kennedy) #204, Magic Wand Corp., 1963	75-100
PD173	The Flying Nun, #5121, S, 1968	30-45
PD174	Connie Francis, #1956, W, 1963	40-50
PD175	The Happiest Millionaire, #4487, S, 1967	30-45
PD176	Jackie & Caroline (Kennedy), #107, Magic Wand Corp.	65-85
PD177	Kewpie Kin, #4488, S, 1967	25-35
PD178	The Kewpies, #1332, S, 1963	35-45
PD179	Lucy, all from 1960s	40-65
PD180	Hayley Mills in "Summer Magic", #1966, W, 1963	35-45
PD181	Mod Fashions (Jane Fonda), #4469, S, 1966	30-40
PD182	The Munsters, #1959, W, 1966	35-45
PD183	My Fair Lady, #2060-5, Ottenhimer Pub. Inc., 1965	40-60
PD184	The Nutcracker Ballet, #1990, W, 1960	30-40
PD185	Petticoat Junction, #1954, W, 1964	40-50
PD186	The Quintuplets, #1352, S, 1964	35-45
PD187	Debbie Reynolds, all from the 1960s	60-80
PD188	Brenda Starr, 4438, S, 1964	75-150
PD189	The Wonderful World of the Brothers Grimm, #1336, S, 1963	35-45

1970s

PD190	The Brady Bunch, #1976, W, 1973	15-25
PD191	Susan Dey, #4218, S, 1972	15-20
PD192	Donnie & Marie, #1991, W, 1977	15-25
PD193	Hee Haw, #5139, S, 1971	15-20
PD194	Lost Horizon, #5112, S, 1973	20-35
PD195	Nanny & The Professor, #4213, S, 1970	15-25
PD196	Marie Osmond, #5225, S, 1973	15-25
PD197	The Partridge Family, #5137, S, 1971	15-25
PD198	Tricia (Nixon), #4248, S, 1970	15-25
PD199	The Waltons, #1995, W, 1975	15-25

PEANUTS   by Tom Tumbusch

In 1950, Charles M. Schulz began a comic strip about a boy and his dog. Originally named "Snoopy", the strip added characters and evolved into "Peanuts." The drawing style was looser than previous standards and it took several years for the strip to catch on. Merchandise began around 1955 and proliferated in the '70s. A unique licensing arrangement was established by United Media through 12 major licensees, which in turn approve sub-licenses. Hallmark, Schmidt, and Determined Productions produced the major variety of merchandise items while Hasbro, Kenner, and King Seeley Thermos turned out fewer products in mega volume. The abundance of Peanuts memorabilia has interested many people to collect Snoopy and the rest of the gang. The earlier, figural items find their way into this compilation of most valuable collectibles. These items have achieved greater value because of competition from toy, doll, and comic character collectors.

PE101	Schroeder w/piano (Hungerford Plastics Corp.) 1958	125-200
PE111	Charlie Brown nodder	50-75
PE112	Linus nodder	50-75
PE113	Lucy nodder	50-75

PD128

PEANUTS GANG TEA SET

PE133   PE111-16

PE201

PE192

PE114	Pig Pen nodder	50-75
PE115	Schroeder nodder	60-90
PE116	Snoopy nodder	60-100
PE120	Dancing Snoopy alarm clock	65-100
PE121	Snoopy "I'm Allergic to Mornings" alarm clock	75-125
PE130	Music Boxes, Anri, 1971, each	75-200
PE131	Limited Edition Schmidt Christmas music boxes, ea	75-200
PE132	Lucy at psychiatrist booth counciling Charlie Brown	250-500
PE133	Snoopy Red Baron music box, 1971	125-250
PE141	Christmas plate, (Schmidt) 1973	75-150
PE151	Schroeder's Piano (Child Guidance)	65-125
PE161	Sitting Snoopy 16" bank (Determined)	125-175
PE162	Snoopy Santa Claus bank	100-175
PE170	Skediddler Club House, Mattel,	50-150
PE171	Snoopy Skediddler & His Sopwith Camel in carrying case, Mattel	100-200
PE181	Snoopy Drive-In Movie Theater, Kenner	75-150
PE191	Snoopy Tea Set, Chein, 1970	125-165
PE192	Peanuts Gang Tea Set, Chein, 1970	150-200
PE201	Speak Up, Charlie Brown, talking book, Mattel	90-140
PE210	Super Cartoon Maker featuring Snoopy and his Peanuts Pals, Mattel	75-150
PE220	Talking Peanuts Bus, Chein	250-375
PE231	Snoopy Astronaut (Determined) 1977	100-200
PE232	Snoopy Magician (Determined) 1977	75-150
PE233	Snoopy Rock Star (Determined) 1977	70-140
PE241	Articulated ceramic Snoopy figurine (Determined)	75-225
PE250	Electric Toothbrush (Kenner) in box	60-75

PEZ DISPENSERS   by Maryann Kennedy
additional pricing information by P. David Welch

PEZ (short for the German word for peppermint, PfeffErminZ) started as a refreshing peppermint candy for adults as an alternative to smoking. PEZ was invented by Eduard Haas I, owner of Haas Trading Company in Linz, Austria, in 1927. Production was suspended in 1939 due to World War II.

It was reintroduced in 1949 with the first automatic plastic PEZ dispenser. The PEZ box resembled a Bic lighter and is referred to by collectors today as a "Regular" or non-head dispenser.

In 1952 PEZ-HAAS, Inc. was founded and PEZ was introduced into the United States. The first U.S. Patent for PEZ dispensers was issued in December 1952. About the same time, market research led to the introduction of fruit flavors and the addition of character heads on the dispensers. In 1974, PEZ built a factory in Orange, CT where candy is still manufactured, packaged and distributed to such outlets as supermarkets, drug stores, convenience stores, and toy chains throughout the U.S.

PEZ is marketed in over 45 countries around the world. The number of known dispenser designs exceed 200. They are manufactured in Austria, Hong Kong, Yugoslavia, Mexico, Hungary, and China. Although there may be some head variation from country to country, this does not substantially affect value. Plastic feet were added to dispensers in the U.S. in 1987.

PEZ dispensers are available in seasonal assortments (Christmas, Easter, Halloween, etc.) as well as non-seasonal assortments of both licensed (Disney, MGM, Warner, Universal Pictures) and non-licensed (animals, whistles, trucks) dispensers. Early variations of five dispensers were made with die-cut designs on the sides: Mickey Mouse, Donald Duck, Casper the Friendly Ghost, Bozo the Clown, and the Easter Bunny. Two full figured dispensers have also been made: a Santa (in the late 1950s) and a Space Trooper which came in several colors. Three PEZ guns were marketed between 1952 and 1982. These guns actually dispensed the candy.

All characters that are authorized by PEZ-HAAS, Inc., are not distributed in the USA. Some are created for special occasions and have limited distribution such as the Olympic dispensers from 1972, 1976, and 1984, and a lion created for the 1962 Lions Club International Convention in France. Some characters more popular in Europe, like the Asterix series, aren't sold in the U.S.

PZ115

Dispensers are currently packaged in blister packs or poly packs. Older styles include a cardboard vending pack with dispenser and extra packages of candy.

In the 1960s and 1970s PEZ promoted a PEZ Club concept with mail in proofs of purchase for premium offers. The last such offer was in 1982 for a collector's stand. Some of the premiums offered were Flashers, masks, glasses, balloons, coin holders, guns, Golden Glow (a gilded regular dispenser), and costume books. Package enclosures have included clickers, balloons, cardboard costumes or dresses, badges, tatoos, puzzles, and comics. Promotional tie-ins were also done with Ralston's Donkey Kong Jr. cereal, Cocoa Marsh syrup, and White Castle Hamburgers.

Other companies such as Totems, Yummies, and Smarties have copied the dispenser-with-head concept but none have approached the universal acceptance of PEZ.

The dispensers listed below have been graded according to scarcity and desirability. Only the most valuable are listed. Values are for dispensers in excellent condition - no cracks, broken heads, or other major damage. Defects such as missing pieces, melt marks, scuffs, excessive dirt, and cracks decrease value.

PZ176

PZ145

PZ101	Air Spirit, soft headed monster	50-75
PZ102	Alpine, 1972 Olympics	100-125
PZ103	Asterix	100-125
PZ104	Astronaut, small silver or white helmet	70-125
PZ105	Astronaut, white or green helmet	50-75
PZ106	Baseball Glove, 1 figure & 2 parts combinations w/ball	55-90
PZ107	Same as PZ106, w/home plate/bat/ball	100-125
PZ108	Batman w/cape	50-75
PZ109	Betsy Ross, Bicentennial	25-60
PZ110	Bozo the Clown	30-55
PZ111	Bozo the Clown die-cut, w/"Bozo/Butch"	50-75
PZ112	Bride w/white veil	100-125
PZ113	Brutus	65-100
PZ114	Bullwinkle Moose w/antlers	80-110
PZ115	Candy Shooter handgun, mail premium	90-125
PZ116	Captain, Bicentennial, round sticker on hat	30-75
PZ117	Casper the Friendly Ghost	35-75
PZ118	Casper die-cut, w/"Casper"	55-100
PZ119	Chick in egg w/out hat	30-70
PZ120	Cow, large nose, circular ears	50-75
PZ121	Cowboy , human face, brown hat	75-100
PZ122	Creature from the Black Lagoon green cartridge/head, UPCo licensed	85-110
PZ123	Same as PZ122, orange cartridge/dark green head, (also known as Fishman)	50-105
PZ124	Same as PZ122, black head, not licensed	70-105
PZ125	Daniel Boone w/coonskin cap	60-100
PZ126	Diabolic, soft headed monster	50-75

PZ127	Dog	50-75
PZ128	Donald Duck die-cut, w/3 nephews	60-100
PZ129	Donkey Kong, Jr., Ralston premium	100-125
PZ130	Dopey, from Disney	80-110
PZ131	Easter Bunny, thin straight ears	30-75
PZ132	Easter Bunny die-cut w/eggs	90-120
PZ133	Football Player	25-55
PZ134	Frankenstein	75-105
PZ135	Green Hornet man, green hat/mask	100-125
PZ136	Groom, black top hat & hat band	80-115
PZ137	Gun, Space, 1950s, planets & rockets	60-100
PZ138	Gun, Space, 1982, red/silver	30-65
PZ139	Indian Brave, one feather	50-75
PZ140	Indian Chief, full headdress	20-50
PZ141	Indian Squaw	20-50
PZ142	Joker from Batman, softhead	20-50
PZ143	Knight	35-60
PZ144	Lion's Club Lion from 1962 convention	100-125
PZ145	Make-A-Face (similar to Mr. Potato Head w/approximately 20 face pieces)	140-165
PZ146	Mary Poppins, lavender hat & large head	90-115
PZ147	Mickey Mouse, original, stencil cut mask face	50-75
PZ148	Mickey Mouse die-cut, w/"Minnie"	45-100
PZ149	Miraculix from *Asterix* comics	100-125
PZ150	Obelix from *Asterix* comics	100-125
PZ151	Olive Oyl from Popeye	70-105
PZ152	Pear w/visor	110-135
PZ153	Penguin from Batman, softhead	20-50
PZ154	Peter Pan	75-105
PZ155	Peter PEZ, clown w/"PEZ" on hat	50-75
PZ156	Pif Gardet, pug nosed molded dog	50-75
PZ157	Pineapple w/white sunglasses	110-135
PZ158	Pinocchio, original, eyes looking up, feather is part of hat	30-85
PZ159	Pinocchio, feather protrudes thru hat	50-75
PZ160	Popeye, original, hat cannot be removed	22-50
PZ161	Popeye, red or white removable hat	20-45
PZ162	Psychedelic Eye, hand holding eyeball	110-135
PZ163	Psychedelic Flower, eyeball in flower	110-135

PZ122   PZ134   PZ196
PZ182   PZ101   PZ191   PZ197   PZ187   PZ126

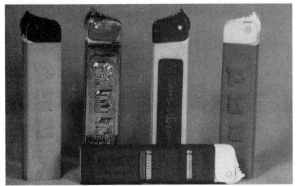

PZ170-71

Regular (no heads) and variations PZ170-76

PZ170	Arithmetic, mini slide rule	100-125
PZ171	Golden Glow, gold shiny finish, premium	35-100
PZ172	Personalized, has paper label on side	80-110
PZ173	Regular (resembles BIC lighter)	50-100
PZ174	Regular w/advertising	50-125
PZ175	U.S. Zone Germany markings	40-65
PZ176	Witch w/witch picture	120-145
PZ177	Robot, full body, 3 colors	65-105
PZ178	Sailor, full white beard w/blue hat	30-75
PZ179	Santa Claus, full body	50-75
PZ180	Santa Claus, molded face & beard same color	25-55
PZ181	Santa Claus, small head w/white beard	35-75
PZ182	Scare Wolf	50-75
PZ183	Snow White	35-75
PZ184	Spaceman, clear helmet	45-75
PZ185	Spaceman, clear helmet, "Cocoa Marsh"	45-75
PZ186	Snowman w/arms, 1976 Olympics	100-125
PZ187	Spook, soft headed monster	50-75
PZ188	Stand By Me, RCA promotional item	100-125
PZ189	Thor	30-70
PZ190	Tinkerbell	50-75
PZ191	Vamp, soft headed monster	50-75
PZ192	Witch, 1 piece orange head	60-100
PZ193	Wolf w/ski hat, 1984 Olympics	75-105
PZ194	Wolf w/bobsled hat, 1984 Olympics	75-105
PZ195	Wolf, hatless, 1984 Olympics	75-105
PZ196	Wolfman	85-110
PZ197	Zombi, soft headed monster	50-75
PZ198	Zorro, w/"Zorro"	35-75
PZ199	Zorro, plain	12-20

PICTURE DISCS by Carol Markowski

A picture disc is a phonograph record with a photo or graphic artwork sandwiched between two pieces of clear grooved vinyl. These discs come in 12", 10", 7", or die-cut shapes.

The earliest form of picture discs were in the late twenties and early thirties. they were one-sided grooved shellagh records with photos of a scene from the record's subject matter pasted on the other side. In the forties children's cardboard picture discs with vinyl coating or plastic lamination swept the USA. The laminated 10" discs of popular songs released by Vogue in the late forties and early fifties are the most sought after today.

The major boom of modern music picture discs began in 1976-78, with the die-cut shapes entering the scene in 1979.

PI110

PI360

PI310

Most record fanciers collect picture discs by size (the 12" being the most popular), by artist (there are more than 50 Elvis picture discs alone) or just by shape.

PI100	America on Parade	25-60
PI110	Nixon—cardboard speech	15-20
PI120	Styx—Rockin' the Paradise	15-20
PI130	Transformers, the Movie (soundtrack)	15-20
PI140	Toto—Rosana	20-25
PI150	Ray Parker—Ghostbusters	15-20
PI160	Rolling Stones—Brown Sugar	20-25
PI170	Boston	15-20
PI180	Bruce Springsteen (interview)	15-20
PI190	Rock Goddess—Hell Hath No Fury	15-20
PI200	Abba—Thank You For the Music	20-25
PI210	Rolling Stones—She Was Hot	25-30
PI220	Pink Floyd—Dark Side of the Moon	20-40
PI230	Elton John—Sad Songs	20-25

PI370

PI410

PI240	Tina Turner—Thunderdome	25-30
PI250	Blackfoot—Send Me an Angel	15-20
PI260	Survivors—Burning Heat	15-20
PI270	Bing Crosby—White Christmas	15-20
PI280	Prince—Girls and Boys	25-30
PI290	Monty Python—Galaxy Song	20-25
PI300	Neil Diamond—Heartlight	20-25
PI310	Elvis—Merry Christmas	30-35
PI320	Captain Midnight	75-80
PI330	Dracula (Orson Wells)	75-90
PI340	Laurel and Hardy	60-70
PI350	Joe Palooka	75-80
PI360	Reagan/Carter Fighting Clowns	20-25

PI240

PI280

128

PLAYBOY   by Bob Welbaum and Tom Tumbusch

Playboy magazine with its famous nude centerfold is generally credited with spearheading the sexual revolution in the U.S. The bunny empire was launched by Hugh Marston Hefner, the child of strict Methodist parents. Born in Chicago on April 9, 1926, Hefner was a shy adolescent with a high school talent for drawing cartoons. After serving in the Army and graduating from the University of Illinois, Hefner found himself writing subscription promotion copy for *Esquire* magazine in 1952. When *Esquire* wanted to move him from Chicago to New York but wouldn't meet his salary demand (they were $5 a week apart), Hefner left "to publish a magazine that would thumb its nose at all the phony puritan values of the world." Financing came from all the money he could scrape together plus sale of $10,000 worth of stock to friends. His original title choice was *Stag Party*, but when *Stag* magazine objected the name *Playboy* was adopted. The first issue appeared in October 1953, featuring Marilyn Monroe on the cover and her famous nude calendar photo inside. The entire press run of 54,000 copies was sold at 50 cents each. This financed the second issue and *Playboy* was on its way. Hefner's success was merchandised in the magazine, with features on his Chicago mansion and aboard his Playboy jet.

The magazine's most famous feature, "Playmate of the Month" was born in 1956 when Hefner persuaded subscription manager Janet Pilgrim to pose nude. Hefner's master promoting led to an empire that at its zenith included publishing, two resort hotels, Playboy Clubs, gambling operations, TV production, and limousine services. These are mostly gone, and a leaner Playboy Enterprises is operated by Hefner's daughter Christie, with Hefner still handling editorial matters.

The clubs proliferated in the early sixties to major cities around the world. Waitresses, called Bunnies, were chosen to match the Playboy image and often appeared unclad in the magazine. The price of a membership automatically provided a pass to mix with the jet set. When too many members didn't fit the image, the clubs failed. During the club years Playboy gift

PL360

PL101

PL300

PL175

PL320

items reached their peak. They were sold at club gift shops and by mail via ads in *Playboy*. Ashtrays and china from the clubs are among the most often seen items. Femlins, the black and white female figure appearing on the joke page, and high ticket logo jewelry are among the rarest found.

The first magazine issue is sought after by Playboy and Marilyn Monroe collectors. Other early issues and ones featuring Marilyn Monroe, Jayne Mansfield, or unique contents have special value.

Other highly collectible artifacts include garters from Playboy Club Bunnies, early calendars in their original sleeves, canned puzzles, and club merchandise.

The following collectibles are taken from items recently offered for sale to the general public. Values are for excellent to near mint condition.

Playboy Magazines

PL101	#1 w/Marilyn Monroe cover	600-1500
PL102	#2-12, ea	50-125
PL113	Remaining 1954-59 issues, ea	10-50
PL150	1960-1962, ea	5-20
PL175	1962-1980, ea	1-4
PL205	1982-1990, ea	1-2

Merchandise

PL300	Femlins, 4 different, ea	350-700
PL310	Club garter	25-50
PL320	The Best From Playboy #1	20-30
PL333	"Granny '72" red, white, blue button with cartoon Granny in Uncle Sam hat	10-25
PL340	1962 Wall Calendar in envelope	50-75
PL350	1967 Wall Calendar	25-50
PL360	Playboy Playmate jigsaw puzzles, packaged in 4" cans w/mini centerfold insert, ea	8-22

ROBOTS   by Robert Lesser

The word "robot" comes from a 1921 story entitled R.U.R. (Rossum's Universal Robots) by Karel Capek. The word means "worker" in the author's native Czechoslovakian, but in the English translation the word remained "robot." The world has been fascinated with the concept of mechanical creatures ever since. The first robot toys were made in Japan in the '30s, but they didn't proliferate until the post-war science fiction boom of the '50s.

Why are robots so valuable today? Are there reasons for the tremendous increase in this collector obsession? Yes, there are two. They could be called "cemetery values". The tin plate method of manufacturing is dead. It's no longer legal because the sharp edges cut children, nor is it economical to produce. Today's robots are all plastic. The second cemetery value is pre-solid state electronic devices. This also is a never again process. Today's robot is all plastic with solid-state micro-chip technology. The robots of the '50s and '60s, almost all manufactured in Japan, were really based on technology of the '20s and '30s, i.e., punch presses, break forming, and printing on

RO205

RO203,
RO204

RO208,
RO210

RO213,
RO201

RO207

metal. The people are dead, the technology is dead.

But the desirability of robots is much more subjective. It is based upon the visual appeal of its sculpture and mechanical design. Many of the robots are visually descended from the Samurai warriors. Faces are almost identical to the masks used in Kabuki theater·and the amazing Japanese puppet theater of Bunraku. Japanese see and understand this historical continuity and images. Another attraction is the imaginative mechanical and electrical plays they enact. The Robot X-70 tells a complete story in action. Its flower-petal head opens in sections to reveal a rotating TV camera taking pictures of a strange planet and relaying them back to a delighted 7-year-old sitting next to his Christmas tree. These toys were made for children!

Is it any wonder that almost all of the collectors of these marvelous space demons are graphic designers, commercial and fine artists? They have "The Third Eye!"

Robots today are in fantastic demand and the prices are extremely high. The market is mint in the box! Mint in the box! Mint in the box! Your chances are very, very good in finding a rare robot because they were mass produced. Almost all were exported to the United States. Many were bought by Sears, Roebuck for large quantity mail order distribution and their mechanisms can quite easily be restored. All you need to know is the top ones and what they are worth. Here we go, fellow hunters. May the Goddess of Good Luck shine down upon you in full color! The prices are mint in box.

RO201	Robby Space Patrol		25,000
RO202	Cragstan Mr. Atomic	RO206	15,000
RO203	Machine Man		25,000
RO204	Musical Drummer Robot		25,000
RO205	Lilliput		12,000
RO206	Target Robot		15,000
RO207	Radicon Robot		17,000
RO208	Jupiter Robot		15,000
RO209	Super Cycle		20,000
RO210	Diamond Planet Robot		15,000
RO211	Mechanized Robot (Robby)		3,500
RO212	Red Rosco Astronaut		7,500
RO213	Cragstan Astronaut, large size		7,500
RO214	Lavender Robot		7,500
RO215	Thunder Robot		12,000
RO216	Mechanical Moon Robot		6,500
RO217	"Topolino" Radar Robot		10,000
RO218	Gold Robot		5,500
RO219	Cocaine Robot ("blows powder through his nose")		5,000
RO220	Tremendous Mike (orange)		5,000

130

RO221	High Bounce Moon Scout	3,000
RO222	Mighty Robot	4,000
RO223	Rocketman (must have 2 rockets and	
	yellow radar spinner on top)	5,000
RO224	Moon Explorer	3,000
RO225	Missile Robot	3,000
RO226	Smoking Spaceman	7,000
RO227	Mr. Mercury - 3 versions (gold body)	2,500
RO228	Chief Smoky	3,000
RO229	Astroman (Dave from *2001*)	2,500
RO230	Fireman	4,000
RO231	Atomic Robotman	1,200
RO232	X-70	6,000
RO233	Mighty Robot 8	2,500
RO234	Space Explorer (red)	2,000
RO235	Cragstan Great Astronaut	2,000
RO236	Door Robot	3,800
RO237	(Dino) Robot	1,800
RO238	Super Space Giant, silver	2,000

STAMPS   by Stuart J. Morrissey

All great...and not so great... "finds" in the history of stamp collecting are just that: someone took the time to look more closely than anyone else did, perhaps had a little additional bit of knowledge, and came away with something quite valuable.

Even at a garage sale you can come upon something that will delight you and your checkbook. As an example, in about 1986, as the story goes, a sheet of current $1 stamps was purchased for use in the headquarters of the Central Intelligence Agency (CIA) in Washington, D.C. Why the stamps were purchased has never been noted, for the CIA does not need stamps for its "official" mail, which goes with the same type of indicia as your annual IRS notice or a Social Security check.

Nevertheless, this particular sheet had one worthwhile characteristic: one of the colors was printed upside down. This error was not noticed until about five or so of the stamps were used. The remainder of the sheet has garnered national attention, and currently those individual stamps are being offered at $15,000 each. One of the five used ones, if they still exist, would be worth at least that much. How easily we overlook the obvious.

Another example: the 1969 commemorative stamp honoring Professional Baseball is without its black ink. The wording "1869-1969," "United States 6¢," and "Professional Baseball" all are omitted. That anomaly, a bit easier to spot on sight than the "CIA $1" stamp, retails in the $1200 range.

Another point to watch for are two stamps with no perforations between them. When you see this, do nothing until you have had it inspected by a stamp dealer or knowledgeable collector. If it actually is an "imperforate between " variety, you have made a minor find that could net you upwards of $50, with the actual amount dependent on the stamp issue involved.

Not all "finds" revolve around printing errors. One of the more popular stamp collecting areas right now is U.S. coil stamps with tiny plate numbers at the center bottom. These numbers appear at set intervals, such as every 52nd stamp, but this varies depending on the printing press used. For the most part, the numbers you will see are very common and have a "premium" of a penny or so over the value of a stamp without a number.

But...and this is the good part...there are known stamp-and-number combinations that will net you into the hundreds of dollars. How do you know which are valuable? The most available guide is the annual *Specialized Catalogue of United States Stamps*, published by Scott Publishing Co., Sidney, Oh. All of the other items noted here are listed along with many, many more examples of recent stamps that may surprise you.

Literally billions of U.S. stamps are printed and sold each year. Most have no premium value to a collector because they are so readily available. There are those few, however, that are valuable. But someone has to find them. Happy hunting!

STAR TREK   by T.N.Tumbusch

In 1963, Gene Roddenberry conceived the Star Trek series as a method of confronting modern-day issues against a background of science fiction. The show communicates its messages through its characters — the crew of the deep space-exploration vessel Enterprise — whose five-year mission is "to explore strange new worlds, to seek out new life forms and new civilizations, to boldly go where no one has gone before." The members of the crew come from different racial, cultural, gender, and ethnic backgrounds. Working together, they learn and promote values such as justice, racial tolerance, morality and peace among themselves and the beings they encounter.

The Star Trek ideal has been shared in a unique way by many fans, sometimes referred to as "Trekkies" or "Trekkers." Trek enthusiasts played an active role in preventing the cancellation the original TV show, and have since swelled in size. The official fan club alone numbers 35,000 people. National and regional conventions are held regularly.

Despite its short initial life span as a television series, Star Trek has maintained its popularity for more than twenty years. A few items were produced during the early days of the show, but the major surge in licensed merchandise began in 1973. With the arrival of movies and a new television series, the popularity of the Star Trek genre has continued to grow and produce new collectibles.

Fans and fan/dealers have also been the source of numerous "fanzine" publications and unlicensed Star Trek merchandise—mainly uniforms, tribbles, insignia pins, buttons, reproductions of props, garage kits, posters, T-shirts and other artifacts. Most of this material remains available at conventions or by mail.

Space Adventure Collectibles includes a more detailed Star Trek section, as well as information on 19 other categories of Space Adventure, supplemented by more than 2,000 b&w and color photos. See page 150 for ordering information.

For simplification, several common designations have been abbreviated in the following list. These include the original television show (TV), *Star Trek: The Motion Picture* (STTMP), *Star Trek II: The Wrath of Khan* (STII), *Star Trek III: The Search for Spock* (STIII), *Star Trek IV: The Voyage Home* (STIV), *Star Trek V: The Final Frontier* (ST5) and "Star Trek: The Next Generation" (NG).

MF506-61	Mego Figures *See: Mego Figures—p. 110*	
ST115	Animation Cels. The average cel commands $100-$150, but choice items with original backgrounds must be judged on an individual basis.	
ST125	Film crew jackets, ea	100-300
ST150	Utility Belt, including disk-shooting phaser, tricorder, and communicator	30-100
ST155	Reversible belt w/coin buckle	35-50
ST160	Binoculars (Larami)	45-75
ST165	Punch Out and Play Album (Saalfield, 1975)	30-60

ST115

ST165   ST450

ST326　　　　　　　　ST414　　　ST600

ST200	Saurian Brandy bottle	50-150
ST201	Spock decanter (Grenadier)	10-35
ST210	Star Trekulator (Mego)	35-50
ST220	Alarm clock (Zeon, 1984)	25-50
ST221	Enterprise clock	20-35
ST230	Enterprise coin (1974)	25-50
ST231	10th Anniversary coin (1976)	30-75
ST232	Silver coins, Kirk or Spock, (Rarities Mint, 1989), ea	40-50
ST233	Same as ST3252, but gold	150-400

Costumes and Play Outfits ST301-04

ST301	Mr. Spock (Ben Cooper, 1967)	60-120
ST302	Kirk (1976)	25-50
ST303	Spock (1976)	25-70
ST304	Klingon (1976)	25-70
ST315	Large cloth Kirk (Knickerbocker, 1979)	10-40
ST316	Large cloth Spock (Knickerbocker, 1979)	10-40
ST317	Kirk porcelain doll (Hamilton Collection)	50 -100
ST318	Spock porcelain doll (Hamilton Collection)	50-100
ST325	Board game (Ideal, 1967)	60-125
ST326	Board game (Hasbro, 1974)	15-50
ST327	Phaser battle game (Mego)	20-65
ST328	Phaser II target game (Mego, 1976)	20-65
ST332	Arcade game, 2 sizes (Sega), ea	400-1000
ST350	Helmet (Enco)	30-75
ST375	Spock bop bag (AHI, 1975)	20-45
ST400	Adult Spock mask	25-50
ST412	Tracer scope (1966)	20-65
ST414	Projection Phaser	50-150
ST416	Phaser Saucer gun (AHI, 1975)	15-35
ST418	Phaser Ray gun	15-35
ST420	"U.S.S. Enterprise" water gun	15-35
ST422	STTMP Dual Phaser II set (South Bend)	20-45
ST424	STTMP Signal gun	20-45
ST426	STTMP water pistol	20-40
ST450	Telescreen Console playset (Mego)	50-135
ST451	Transporter Room playset (Mego)	50-135
ST452	Command Communications Console (Mego, 1976)	75-150

Posters-Film ST500-505

ST500	Star Trek: The Motion Picture	20-40
ST501	Star Trek II: The Wrath of Khan	18-35
ST502	Star Trek III: The Search For Spock	15-30
ST503	Star Trek IV: The Voyage Home Teaser	15-30
ST504	Star Trek IV: The Voyage Home	15-30
ST505	Star Trek V: The Final Frontier	10-25
ST600	Tricorder, w/cassette (Mego, 1976)	50-100
ST650	Tribble (Mego)	50-75
ST700	Controlled Space Flight Enterprise (Remco, 1976)	35-75
ST705	Dinky Enterprise (Micano)	30-50
ST710	Small Dinky Enterprise (1979)	30-50
ST711	Dinky Klingon Battlecruiser	30-50
ST712	STTMP Electronic Enterprise (Milton Bradley/Southbend, 1979)	40-80
ST713	Action Fleet Mobile (unpunched)	10-35
ST715	STII Mini Enterprise (Corgi)	35-75
ST720	STII Klingon ship (Corgi)	35-75

ST725	STIII die cast Enterprise	35-75
ST726	STIII die cast Excelsior	35-75
ST727	STIII die cast Klingon Bird of Prey	35-75
ST740	Pewter Enterprise	150-250
ST800	Communicator set (Mego, 1974)	50-100
ST803	STTMP Wrist Communicators	35-85
ST805	Working comunicators (1989)	30-40
ST820	TV wastebasket	20-50
ST821	STTMP wastebasket	10-30

See also: **Autographs; Comic Books; Lunch Boxes; Mego Figures; Model Kits;**

STAR WARS　　　　　　by T.N.Tumbusch

Star Wars was a surprise smash hit which set new quality standards for special effects and space adventure. Despite a slow start, merchandise was produced in enormous quantities and revolutionized the action figure industry. Approximately 80% of the original items were manufactured by Kenner products.

Initially, there were complications. The original 12 action figures were not available in time for Christmas in 1977. To fill the demand, Kenner quickly produced "early bird" kits. The kits came in a large cardboard envelope which contained the following items: a cardboard display stand with detachable cards, a sheet of stickers, and the early bird certificate. This last item was mailed to Kenner. In return, the company promised to send four of the original figures (Luke Skywalker, Princess Leia, Chewbacca, and R2-D2) "as soon as they are ready!", and plastic pegs to complete the display stand. The sets were mailed between Feb 1 and June 1. The gambit paid off, and a flood of *Star Wars* merchandise followed which dominated toy stores for the next six years.

The *Star Wars* logo was regularly updated to that of the most recent film or figure series. High-end values always assume the figure or playset is packaged with its original logo.

Action figures and related accessories are rated in three condition categories (see the Action Figure section on page 5 for a complete explanation). The remaining prices are listed as a range from Fine to Mint condition. Items not in their original package, missing parts, or worn from play bring substantially lower values.

Space Adventure Collectibles includes a more detailed Star Wars section, as well as information on 19 other categories of Space Adventure, with more than 2,000 b&w and color photos. See page 150 for ordering information.

SW505

SW131   SW138

SW143

SW201

SW210

	CNP	MIP	MMP
SW099 Early Bird kit	100	250	400
SW100 Early Bird figures in mailing box w/12 pegs	-	200	300

Original 12 Action Figures (SW101-04 comprised the "early bird" set), 1977 on *Star Wars* cards.

SW101 Chewbacca	5	50	65
SW102 Luke Skywalker	5	50	65
SW103 Artoo-Detoo (R2-D2)	5	50	65
SW104 Princess Leia Organa	5	70	90
SW105 Han Solo	5	50	65
SW106 See-Threepio (C-3PO)	5	50	65
SW107 Stormtrooper	5	50	65
SW108 Darth Vader	5	50	65
SW109 Ben (Obi-Wan) Kenobi	5	50	65
SW110 Jawa	5	60	75
SW111 Sand People (Tusken Raider)	5	50	65
SW112 Death Squad Commander (later called Star Destroyer Commander)	5	50	65

Later *Star Wars* figures (1978-79)

SW120 Boba Fett (Star Wars card)	5	65	75
SW121 Boba Fett w/working Rocket Launcher (mail offer)	100	125	150

***Return of the Jedi* (1983)**

SW125 8D8	5	15	20

Star Wars—The Power of the Force

SW130 EV-9D9	5	40	60
SW131 Artooo-Detoo w/pop-up ligtsaber	10	60	75
SW132 Han Solo in Carbonite Chamber	25	75	95
SW133 Same as SW130, tri-logo	25	60	70
SW134 Luke Skywalker (Imperial Stormtrooper outfit)	22	50	75
SW135			
SW136 A-Wing Pilot	10	45	60
SW137 Amanaman	10	45	60
SW138 Yak Face	28	100	125

***Star Wars* accessories (1977-79)**

SW140 *Millennium Falcon* Spaceship	30	65	125
SW141 Death Star Space Station	75	95	125
SW143 Cantina Adventure Set (Sears)	100	175	350
SW145 Sonic Land Speeder (Penney's)	100	200	300
SW146 Land of the Jawas Playset	50	85	125
SW147 Action display stand, store box	25	75	95

***The Empire Strikes Back* accessories (1980-82)**

SW151 Turret and Probot playset (Penny's)	25	80	100
SW152 Rebel Command Center	125	225	300
SW156 Cloud City playset (Sears exclusive)	100	250	375
SW157 Ice Planet Hoth playset	50	85	125

***Return of the Jedi* accessories (1983+)**

SW161 Jabba the Hutt Dungeon (Sears exclusive) w/EV-9D9, Amanaman, and Barada (green background)	20	65	85
SW162 Jabba the Hutt Dungeon (Sears exclusive) w/Klaatu, Nikto, and 8D8 (yellow background)	20	85	95
SW163 A-Wing Fighter	50	75	90
SW164 One-Man Sand Skimmer	20	75	95
SW165 Imperial Sniper	20	75	95
SW166 Security Scout	20	75	95
SW167 Droids Tatooine Skiff	25	75	100

Large figures SW200-12

SW200 C-3PO	60	100	150
SW201 Ben Kenobi	75	145	200
SW202 Jawa	75	125	175
SW203 R2-D2	45	75	95
SW204 Darth Vader	75	100	150
SW205 Princess Leia	75	100	150
SW206 Chewbacca	60	100	150

	SW145		SW156	

SW207	Luke Skywalker	100	200	250
SW208	Stormtrooper	100	200	250
SW209	Han Solo	120	225	300
SW210	Boba Fett	95	175	225
SW211	Boba Fett, *Empire Strikes Back* box	95	150	200
SW212	IG-88	75	275	400
SW250	Animation Cels—The average commands $100-$150, but items must be judged on an individual basis.			
SW275	Crew jackets			25-100
SW280	ESB promotional art portfolio			25-50
SW290	R2-D2 ceramic bank			25-40
SW291	Darth Vader ceramic bank			25-40
SW292	C-3PO ceramic bank			25-40
SW293	Darth Vader anodized silver plated bank (Leonard Silver, 1981)			40-70
SW299	Chewbacca/Darth Vader bookends (Sigma)			30-60

Books

SW300	The Art of Star Wars, hardcover (1979)	25-35
SW301	The Art of Star Wars, softcover	20-25
SW302	Art of The Empire Strikes Back (Ballantine, 1980)	15-35
SW303	Art of Return of the Jedi (Ballantine, 1983)	15-25

Bisque figures SW320-31 (Towle/Sigma, 1983)

SW320	Han Solo	20-50
SW321	Luke Skywalker	20-50
SW322	Princess Leia	20-50
SW323	C-3PO/R2-D2	25-55
SW324	Darth Vader	20-50
SW325	Klaato	20-50
SW326	Bib Fortuna	20-50
SW327	Gammorean Guard	20-50
SW328	Wicket W. Warrick	20-50
SW329	Lando Calrissian	20-50
SW330	Boba Fett	20-50
SW331	Galactic Emperor	25-55
SW428	Electronic Laser Battle game	50-75
SW429	Electronic Battle Command game	30-100
SW430	X-Wing Aces target game	150-300
SW445	SW arcade game	500-700
SW446	Similar to SW445, cockpit style	700-1000
SW447	ESB arcade game	400-600
SW449	ROTJ arcade game	400-600
SW500	Han Solo Laser Pistol, Star Wars sticker (1977)	25-40
SW503	3-Position Laser Rifle	50-150
SW505	Electronic Laser Rifle (1980)	20-40
SW508	Biker Scout Laser Pistol	10-30
SW530	Luke and Tauntaun teapot set	25-50
SW550	Inflatable lightsaber (1977)	75-125
SW551	Star Wars lightsaber	30-75
SW552	"The Force" lightsaber (1980)	25-50
SW553	Droids battery-operated lightsaber (1985)	30-65
SW600	Darth Vader helmet	75-125
SW603	Chewbacca mask	60-120
SW604	Tuskin Raider mask	50-100
SW605	Cantina Band Member mask	50-100

SW700-02

Micro Collection Sets

SW676	Death Star Trash Compactor	20-30
SW677	Death Star World (includes SW675 & SW676)	35-70
SW678	Hoth Ion Cannon	15-25
SW679	Hoth Turret Defense	10-20
SW680	Hoth Wampa Cave	10-30
SW681	Hoth Generator Attack	25-60
SW682	Hoth World (includes SW678, SW679 and SW680)	50-100
SW683	Bespin Gantry	10-25
SW684	Bespin Freeze Chamber	10-30
SW685	Bespin Control Room	10-25
SW686	Bespin World (includes SW683, SW684 and SW685)	50-100

Tankards SW700-02 California Originals

SW700	Darth Vader	50-75
SW701	Obi Wan Kenobi	50-75
SW702	Chewbacca	50-75
SW945	Star Wars Duel Racing set (Lionel, 1978)	45-120
SW950	Luke Skywalker AM headset	85-250

Star Wars soundtrack recording

SW959	Reel-to-reel boxed set: Star Wars soundtrack/Story, w/book	30-75
SW960	Radio-controlled R2-D2	40-95
SW961	Radio-controlled Jawa Sandcrawler	75-175
SW965	Darth Vader speakerphone (ATC, 1983)	70-110
SW975	Millennium Falcon, diecast	35-100
SW978	Twin TIE Bomber, diecast	300- 600
SW995	Speeder Bike pedal vehicle	400-800

See also: **Cereal Boxes; Cookie Jars; Model Kits; Watches**

THEATRE WINDOW CARDS   by Tom Tumbusch

Movie posters are printed by the thousands and have reached the hands of collectors for as long as there have been movies. Until 1970 it was difficult to obtain promotional material for a Broadway musical or play. Often less than 300 were silk screened before the fate of the show was known. The producers, publicity agents, members of the cast and backers usually could get a standard size window card (14" X 22") as a keepsake, but none were made available to the public.

Artcraft Printing and Lithographing Co, Inc., owned by Harold Friedlander, printed virtually all theatrical posters for several generations. These are identified by a union bug and the 491 shop number. Most of these posters were not available to the public...this I.D. can signal a more valuable poster.

Around 1970, Roger Puckett, owner of the Triton Gallery in New York, convinced producers and press agents there was a commercial market for these posters and they were made available for sale. Printing of larger quantities opened up the business to more printers.

Some public relations firms did sell them during the 1960s,

TH535   TH649   TH325

TH605   TH250   TH320

but it wasn't common knowledge. Before then, you knew someone or simply grabbed one on display.

Once posters were promoted they became collectible and were sold in theatres in New York and wherever a traveling company was playing.

Collectors prefer original design, original cast posters, but other factors contribute to value. The artist, the star(s) of the show, the composer or writers, design appeal, or other special factors go into the desirability of each poster. Naturally, the rarity of posters printed before 1970 is a factor.

The biggest market for collectible theatrical posters is New York City, but there are collectors throughout the country.

Posters for *My Fair Lady*, *The Music Man*, and several others from the Artcraft era have been reproduced. The poster board is thinner, white on the reverse rather than gray, and reference to Artcraft has been deleted.

Musicals

TH120	All American	250-450
TH126	Anyone Can Whistle	350-700
TH130	Apple Tree, The (A)	200-400
TH131	Apple Tree, The (B)	175-350
TH150	Bajour	225-450
TH160	Bells Are Ringing	400-600
TH175	Boy Friend, The (Julie Andrews)	450-700
TH190	Bye Bye Birdie (Dick Van Dyke)	250-500
TH200	Cabaret (original 1966 cast)	200-400
TH205	Camelot (Andrews, Burton)	500-700
TH210	Can-Can	300-600
TH215	Carnival	250-500
TH250	Damn Yankees	400-650
TH260	Dear World	275-500
TH300	Fade Out, Fade In (A) (withdrawn at the request of Carol Burnett)	800-1100
TH305	Fanny	250-500
TH320	Fiddler on the Roof	225-450
TH325	Fiorello	200-500
TH350	Flora the Red Menace	300-600
TH355	Flower Drum Song	250-500
TH360	Follies	100-225
TH380	Funny Girl (Barbra Streisand)	300-600
TH383	Funny Thing Happened on the Way to the Forum, A	250-500
TH405	Golden Apple, The	400-600
TH408	Golden Boy	200-400
TH415	Goldilocks	300-600
TH425	Grease	75-160
TH430	Guys and Dolls	300-650
TH440	Gypsy	300-600
TH450	Hair	150-300
TH457	Half a Sixpence	200-400
TH465	Hello Dolly (silk screened)	300-600
TH480	How Now, Dow Jones	250-500
TH482	How to Succeed in Business Without Really Trying	250-500
TH495	I Do! I Do!	200-450
TH497	Irma La Douce	100-250
TH499	It's a Bird, It's a Plane, It's Superman	750-1000
TH525	King and I, The	300-600
TH528	Kismet	250-500
TH535	Li'l Abner	350-700
TH540	Little Mary Sunshine	200-400
TH560	Mame	150-300
TH565	Man of La Mancha	100-200
TH570	Most Happy Fella, The	250-500
TH575	Music Man, The (silk screened)	500-1000
TH576	Music Man, The	275-550
TH577	Music Man, The (repro)	6-15
TH580	My Fair Lady	300-600
TH581	My Fair Lady (repro)	6-15
TH590	Oliver	75-150
TH594	On a Clear Day You Can See Forever	100-200
TH596	Once Upon a Mattress	100-200
TH604	Paint Your Wagon	200-400
TH605	Pajama Game, The	250-500
TH610	Peter Pan (Mary Martin)	400-600
TH622	Pleasures and Palaces	800-1000
TH630	Promises, Promises	95-180
TH640	Redhead	200-450
TH642	Roar of the Greasepaint, The Smell of the Crowd, The	175-350
TH649	Rothchilds, The (gold foil stamped red flocked board)	300-600
TH650	1776 (parchment on board)	250-500
TH651	1776 (printed)	150-300
TH658	She Loves Me	200-450
TH662	Skyscraper	250-500
TH670	Sound of Music, The (Rogers, Martin & Hammerstein)	750-1000

TH300   TH130   TH131

TH480   TH350   TH415

TH670	TH590	TH700

TH120	TH210	TH360

TH671	*Sound of Music, The* (instruments)	150-300
TH675	*Stop the World-I Want to Get Off*	175-350
TH680	*Sweet Charity* (Gwen Verdon)	95-180
TH690	*Threepenny Opera, The*	400-600
TH700	*Unsinkable Molly Brown, The*	200-400
TH725	*West Side Story* (A)	400-600
TH726	*West Side Story* (B)	500-800
TH735	*Wildcat* (Lucille Ball)	300-550
TH745	*Wonderful Town*	200-400

Plays

TH810	*Any Wednesday*	75-125
TH820	*Auntie Mame*	200-400
TH822	*Autumn Garden, The*	250-500
TH825	*Barefoot In the Park*	100-200
TH828	*Bell, Book and Candle*	200-400
TH832	*Caine Mutiny Court Martial, The*	250-500
TH835	*Come Back, Little Sheba*	250-500
TH836	*Come Blow Your Horn*	150-300
TH839	*Crucible, The*	225-450
TH842	*Daphne in Cottage D*	75-150
TH845	*Diary of Anne Frank, The*	250-500
TH850	*Grass Harp, The*	250-500
TH855	*Homecoming, The*	150-300
TH878	*Luther*	75-150
TH880	*Matchmaker, The*	150-300
TH888	*Murat/Sade*	200-400
TH896	*No Time for Sergeants*	200-400
TH904	*Oh, Dad, Poor Dad, Mamma's Hung You in the Closet and I'm Feelin' So Sad*	150-300
TH906	*Once More, With Feeling*	175-375
TH907	*One Flew Over the Cuckoo Nest*	75-125
TH910	*Picnic*	250-500
TH914	*Play It Again, Sam*	100-175
TH920	*Rhinoceros*	175-400
TH925	*Romanoff and Juliet*	225-450
TH928	*Rosencrantz and Guildenstern Are Dead*	60-90
TH932	*Shot in the Dark, A* (Julie Harris & William Shatner)	100-150
TH937	*Star Spangled Girl, The*	75-100
TH943	*Teahouse In the August Moon*	225-450
TH947	*Thousand Clowns, A*	100-225
TH960	*Visit to a Small Planet*	200-425
TH970	*Who's Afraid of Virginia Woolf?*	100-200
TH972	*Witness for the Prosecution*	200-400

Revues

TH995	*Beyond The Fringe*	100-200
TH997	*New Faces of 1952*	150-300

TOP CAT by Jeff Stewart

"Top Cat" was the second Joe Barbera creation to premiere on prime time. This Hanna-Barbera cartoon aired on Wednesday evening from 8:30 to 9:00 pm beginning September 27, 1961 on ABC. Although the sophisticated humor of these alley cats was aimed at adults, it also appealed to children and the network moved these feline inhabitants of trash cans on Mad Ave. to Saturday mornings (11:30-12:00) in October of 1962 through March of 1963. In April of 1965,

the show moved to NBC on Saturday mornings (9:00-9:30). The last appearance of "Top Cat" was on May 10th, 1969, on NBC.

In 28 episodes, Top Cat and his gang Benny the Ball, Choo-Choo, Brain, Fancy Fancy and Spook (with appearances by Pierre, Honey Dew, and Goldie) aspired to become rich and remove themselves from their trash can domain through some hair-brained, con-artist, mad cap scheme only to be foiled by the mild mannered Officer Dibble of the 13th precinct.

TC100	Animation cel, 1960s	250
TC170	Book, Top Cat punch out book	60
TC200	Clock, Top Cat wall (boxed), 1988 England	100
TC250	Costume, Halloween, 1961 Ben Cooper	150
TC300	Dolls, 1964 Ideal series, ea	50
TC350	Game, Shoe Toss, 1960s Marx	80
TC360	Game, Top Cat, 1962 Whitmans	200
TC450	Choo Choo's Choo Choo, Movie, 8mm	50
TC500	Top Cat vs Ariswald, Movie, 8mm	40
TC550	Pitcher's rubber, 1960s Renzi	80
TC750	Ramp walker (boxed) 1962 Marx, ea	75
TC800	Record album, original TV sound track, 1962 Colpix	50
TC875	Telephone, child's plastic, 1960s	40
TC900	TV, Tinytoons (boxed) 1961 Marx, ea	50

TOY TRAINS by Ron Barrow

Over the years these iron horses in miniature have been produced in many different sizes, gauges, and types. Two of the major producers were the Lionel Corporation and the A.C. Gilbert Company (American Flyer). Both were founded by inventors. Joshua Lionel Cohen (later Cowen), was the inventor of the flash powder used in the early days of flash photography. A. C. Gilbert invented enamel coated wire. Gilbert also invented the famous "Erector" set.

The Gilbert Company entered the model train market in 1936 when it purchased the American Flyer line. Gilbert introduced a new dimension to the industry by using a two rail track rather than the three rail track Lionel and others employed.

The 1950s saw rapid growth in the HO scale (1/87) trains. This smaller size had first appeared in the U.S. about 1930, being imported from Great Britain under such names as Hornsby and Tricks. The first American set was a Hudson Steamer marketed by Gilbert around 1938. Since the post-

TR115

TR116

TR121

World War II average suburban home was smaller, standard gauge layouts took too much room. Thus the increased desire for smaller trains.

With the 1960s came a reversal of fortunes. The A.C. Gilbert Company fell and Lionel was sold to Fundimensions, a division of General Mills. The model train market ground to a virtual halt, especially for scales larger than HO. However, there were several encouraging developments. The MPC line was born and Lionel started to take on a new face. After purchasing the rights to American Flyer, Lionel reintroduced the American Flyer line in 1979.

The late 1970s also witnessed the appearance of the G or "Large Scale" sets. First introduced by a German company, LGB, this scale is much like the original standard gauge produced by Lionel in the 1930s, except the major material is plastic, the sets run on DC current, and the track is two rail and is usually made of brass. Purchased by avid collector Richard Kuhn in 1986, Lionel is now reproducing many of the older items from the early and mid 19th century. Lionel has also reintroduced the standard gauge line and many new items are now being made with metal parts and bodies.

Common brand names for HO scale are Tyco, Bachmann, Mantua, Fox, Atlas, Varney (kits), Life-Like, Bowser, and Athearn.

In general, the most valuable items to the collector since 1950 are the Lionel and American Flyer items made during the fifties and early sixties. Complete sets made from the 1940s to the early 1960s have done well, especially circus, military, space, and specially built items. Retail prices have increased significantly since the early 1970s.

Listed below are examples of the higher valued items. An item found in its original box in mint condition, or a complete set found in the original set box can increase the value by two to three times.

The listings are by manufacturer and gauge. The manufacturer's number and year(s) of availability are given when known. Prices are for good to excellent condition. Scale sizes are also noted as a convenience. To illustrate, standard gauge is 1/26 scale, which means one inch of the model is equal to twenty-six inches of the prototype. "Steamer," "switcher," and "diesel" are locomotive categories. The three sets of numbers (4-8-4) are the wheel arrangements for steam-powered locomotives: the number of pilot, drive, and trailing wheels.

LIONEL
TR126

Standard Gauge-1/26 scale

TR101	390E steamer, 13100, 1988	525-600
TR102	Set of 3 passenger cars, 13400/01/02	530-625
TR103	Passenger Station, 13800, 1988	1280-1350
TR104	1-381E steamer with 3 passenger cars, 13102, 1989	2400-2600
TR105	#200 Trolley (powered), 13900, 1989	315-375
TR106	#201 Trolley (dummy), 13901, 1989	210-250
TR107	440N signal bridge, 51900, 1989	300-350
TR108	Blue Comet set, 13103, 1990 Steamer & passenger cars, 13408	2500-3000
TR109	"Old No. 7" steamer, 13104, 1991	835-900
TR110	Set of 3 passenger cars, 13412, 1991	835-925
TR111	Runabout boat, 13802, 1991	475-500

O & O27 Gauge-1/48 scale

TR112	AEC switcher, 57, 1959-60	100-350
TR113	N & W steamer 4-8-4, 746, 1957	200-600
TR114	Steamer 4-6-4, 773, 1950	300-750
TR115	Set: Lady Lionel for Girls (pink, blue, yellow, lilac), 2037, 1957	400-1200
TR116	Virginian, 2331, 1955-58	200-500
TR117	Penn GG-1, 2340, 1955	150-400
TR118	JC Trainmaster, 2341, 1956	200-400
TR119	West PAC F-3 AA, 2345, 1952	200-550
TR120	C & O GP-7, 2347, 1965	250-850
TR121	Can Pac F-3 AA, 2373, 1957	250-600
TR122	Milw. Road F-3 AB, 2378, 1956	200-500
TR123	Passenger cars (3) 2481/82/83, 1950	100-300
TR124	Pullman cars (3), 2625/27/28, 1946-50	125-350
TR125	WP boxcar, red lettering, 6464, 1953	200-600
TR126	Erie bay window caboose, 6517-75, 1966	75-275
TR127	New York Central boxcar, 6464-510, 1957	75-275
TR128	Great Northern snowplow, 58, 1959	100-300
TR129	Great Northern EP-5, 2358, 1959-60	100-300
TR130	G N steamer 4-8-4, 3100, 1981	500-625
TR131	Lionel wood side reefer, 5712, 1982	200-350
TR132	N & W diner, 7203, 1984	250-450
TR133	S P daylight diner, 7204, 1984	250-450
TR134	CL steamer 4-6-4, 8006, 1980	600-1100
TR135	N & W steamer, 8100, 1981	1000-1525
TR136	S P F-3 dummy unit, 8261	500-900
TR137	S P steamer 4-8-4, 8307, 1983	1500-2400
TR138	TCA gold bullion car, 9319, 1979	175-350
TR139	Snow White Hi-Cube boxcar, 9667	275-550
TR140	Mickey Mouse 50th Anv. box, 9672	300-600

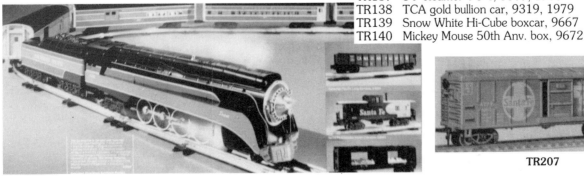

TR207

TR137

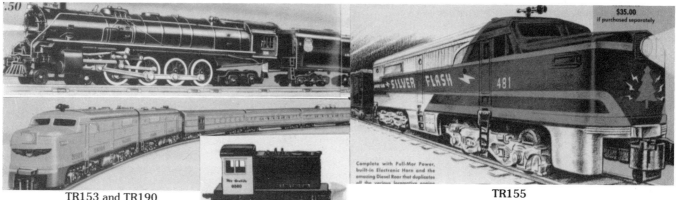

TR153 and TR190

TR149

TR155

TR141	Complete Disney set, 1970s, engine, 14 cars, caboose	650-1250
TR142	Erie magnetic crane, 12700, 1987	125-200

HO Gauge-1/87 scale

TR143	Wabash GP-9, 0580	50-125
TR144	UP Alco diesel, 0568	25-75
TR145	Exec. inspection car, 0068	25-75
TR146	Cop & Hobo car, 0357	25-75
TR147	Gantry crane, 0282	25-75
TR148	FP Pacific with whistle tender, 0646	50-100
TR149	D & RG snow plow switcher, 0560	50-150
TR150	Virginian rectifier, 0590	50-150
TR151	CNW ABA diesel, 0500/10/20	75-200
TR152	Penn passenger cars (4), 0708/09/10/11	80-200

A. C. GILBERT (American Flyer)

S Gauge-3/16 scale

TR153	Northern steamer 4-8-4, 336, 1953-56	100-275
TR154	Switcher engine 0-8-0, 346, 1955	125-325
TR155	Silver Flash diesel, 481, 1955	500-1500
TR156	Northern Pacific diesel, 490/491/493, 1956	200-750
TR157	New Haven electric engine, 499, 1956-57	100-400
TR158	Keystone Line boxcar, 24067, 1960	500-1250
TR159	Switcher steamer 0-6-0, 21005, 1957-58	100-300
TR160	Northern steamer 4-8-4, 21140, 1960	250-750
TR161	C & O diesel, 21234, 1961-62	125-500
TR162	Seaboard diesel, 21925/21913-1, 1958	125-500
TR163	Gabe the Lamp Lighter, 23780, 1958-59	100-500
TR164	MKT boxcar, 24016, 1958	100-650
TR165	Planters Peanuts boxcar, 24068, 1961	250-3500
TR166	Northern Pacific reefer, 24409, 1958	200-750
TR167	NW reefer, 24416, 1958-59	300-900
TR168	BAR reefer, 24425, 1960	100-400
TR169	Union Pacific AA diesel 21925/21925-1	200-400
TR170	Union Pacific passenger cars (4), 24837/38/39/40, 1959-60	400-1000
TR171	MP passenger cars (4), 24856/59/65/66, 1963-64	500-1200
TR172	Hudson steamer 4-6-4, 21129, 1958	150-650
TR173	MP diesel, 21920/21920-1, 1958	200-600
TR174	B & M GP-7 diesel, 8350, 1983	175-300
TR175	Erie PB diesels, 8153/8253, 1982	150-250
TR176	B & O ABA diesels, 8153/54/55, 1981	200-325
TR177	B & O GP-20 diesel, 8459, 1985	150-250
TR178	Santa Fe GP-20 diesel, 8551, 1986	150-225
TR179	New York Central GP-9 diesel, 8552, '86	150-225
TR180	Set of 4 SP passenger cars, 9500/01/02/03, 1981	200-325
TR181	Set of 4 Erie passenger cars, 9504/05/06/07, 1982	150-275
TR182	B & M flatcar, 9002, 1983	35-75
TR183	B & M tanker, 9104, 1983	35-75
TR184	B & M hopper car, 9203, 1983	35-75
TR185	B & M boxcar, 9703, 1983	50-75
TR186	B & M caboose, 9402, 1983	30-65

TR187	Wabash PA's diesel, 48100/8101, 1988	250-350
TR188	C & O PA's diesel, 48102, 1989	250-300
TR189	A F RailScope PA's diesel, 48104, 1989	300-425
TR190	Union Pacific passenger set, 49600, AA's and 4 cars, 1990	475-600
TR191	Union Pacific passenger car, 48905, 1990	50-125
TR192	Union Pacific Vista Dome car, 48906, '90	50-125

HO Gauge-1/87 scale

TR201	City Service tank car, 33314	300-500
TR202	Sohio tank car, 33315	300-400
TR203	New Central Hudson steamer/whistle, 31006	250-300
TR204	Set: "Northern Pacific Passenger" F7 diesel, L1000-1; C-1000-2/3/4	600-800
TR205	Set: "Franklin" 35099, 31088, 33720 (2), (made by Mantua for Gilbert)	500-700
TR206	Northern Pacific Pig Palace, 33004	150-175
TR207	Santa Fe boxcar 33012	100-150
TR208	Canadian Pacific Xmas tree car, 33544	100-150
TR209	New Haven trap rock gondola, 33121	75-100
TR210	Erie work caboose, 33626	45-60
TR211	CD&Q covered hopper, 33220	150-200
TR212	Set: "The Eagle" 3 car passenger set with diesel engine, 30742	700-800
TR213	Pacific Fruit Express reefer, 33504	75-100
TR214	Denver and Rio Grand Western boxcar, 523	35-50
TR215	LACKAWANA diesel F7, 420, (Varney)	75-100
TR216	Whistling Station, 259	100-150
TR217	Inspection car, 35105	300-500

MARX

027 Gauge-1/48 scale

TR218	Steamer 4-6-2 (die cast), 333	15-60
TR219	Penn Central diesel, 4000	50-200
TR220	Cape Canaveral Express, 1798	25-75
TR221	Mickey Mouse Meteor Set, engine & 3 cars	250-750
TR222	Crook's Civil War Set	50-150
TR223	Plastic military cars	20-75
TR224	Erie flat cars with 2 farm tractors, 4528	20-50

HO Gauge-1/87 scale

TR225	NYC F-7 diesel, 4000	20-60
TR226	Hudson steamer, 6096	20-50
TR227	WFLX log unloading car, 6194	20-50
TR228	Santa Fe passenger cars (3)	30-75
TR229	Sanding tower, 6490	20-40

MISCELLANEOUS HO

TR255	Disneyland RR set, TYCO	350-500
TR265	AEROTRAIN set, Varney	125-250

See also: **Disney**

WATCHES, CHARACTER   by Hy Brown

The first comic character watch is generally assumed to be the 1933 Mickey Mouse. Between the years 1933 to 1939 when watch production ceased because of World War II, there were only 15 significant character wrist watches produced. Production began again in 1946 and continued unabated until 1958 when production again stopped because of over-supply.

WA815   WA260   WA110   WA441   WA559

WA221   WA366

WA195

WA591   WA431

WA575

Major production began once more in 1968 and continued to 1972 when Bradley Watch Company obtained the license for Disney and changed the marketing theory for watches. In 1985 Seiko Lorus obtained the license from Disney and the fifth era of watches began.

The following prices are for watches in extra fine condition to mint condition with the original mint box. The manufacturer is listed when known.

WA105	Alice in Wonderland, 1954,	100-400
WA110	Alice in Wonderland, 1958, coming out of flower	130-500
WA121	Andy Panda 1971, red face	100-300
WA131	Annie Oakley 1951, moving gun	300-800
WA141	Ape-George of the Jungle 1971, Jay Ward	250-500
WA151	Bamm Bamm 1971, small, Prince Robale,	100-400
WA165	Barbie, 1963 facing left	100-300
WA170	Barbie, 1964 facing right, red rim	100-300
WA175	Barbie, 1971 facing right, blue rim	100-250
WA191	Batman 1966, plastic, Gilbert	300-700
WA201	Boris 1971, Jay Ward	250-500
WA211	Bugs Bunny 1951, Bugs in center w/carrot hands	300-800
WA221	Bullwinkle 1971, Jay Ward	250-500
WA231	Captain Liberty 1954, embossed airplanes on band	300-700
WA241	Cat in the Hat 1972, see-through back	100-450
WA255	Cinderella, 1950	100-300
WA260	Cinderella, 1958, castle at 12	100-300
WA281	Cool Cat 1971, Sheraton	200-600
WA305	Daffy Duck, 1971, Sheffield	250-700
WA310	Daffy Duck, 1971, Sheraton	200-600
WA320	Dale Evans 1957 rectangle	150-500
WA331	Davy Crockett, 1951, moving knife, Muros	300-700
WA335	Davy Crockett, 1954, green plastic	150-600
WA339	Davy Crockett, 1956, yellow, Tonneau	200-600
WA340	Davy Crockett, 1956, yellow, rectangle	200-600
WA365	Dudley Do-Right 1971, Ward, hand-painted	300-700
WA366	Dudley Do-Right 1971, Jay Ward	250-500
WA381	Elmer Fudd 1971, Sheraton	200-600
WA391	Felix the Cat	300-800
WA401	Flash Gordon 1960s, Sutton Time	200-600
WA411	Fred Flintstone 1971, animated hands, Prince Robale	100-350

WA421	Gene Autry 1951, moving gun	400-800
WA431	George of the Jungle 1971, Jay Ward	200-500
WA441	Goofy backwards, Helbros	300-1000
WA451	Hoopity Hoop 1971, Jay Ward	250-500
WA461	Hopalong Cassidy 1950 large	130-500
WA485	Howdy Doody, 1954, w/friends, Tonneau	200-700
WA486	Howdy Doody, 1954, large, moving eyes	300-700
WA490	Howdy Doody, 1971, animated hands	100-350
WA501	Huckleberry Hound 1966, Bradley	150-400
WA511	Li'l Abner, 1951 moving mule	400-800
WA512	Li'l Abner, 1951 moving flag front view	400-800
WA513	Li'l Abner, 1951 flag side view, salute	400-800
WA521	Little King 1971, O. Soglow	200-500
WA531	Little Nell 1971, Jay Ward	250-500
WA541	Merlin the Magic Mouse 1971, Sheffield	200-600
WA555	Mickey Mouse, 1971, Elgin electric	200-450
WA556	Mickey Mouse, 1971, Helbros	200-400
WA557	Mickey Mouse, 1971, Helbros electric	200-450
WA559	Mickey Mouse, 1971, Timex electric	200-450
WA575	Minnie Mouse, 1971, Timex	200-400
WA576	Minnie Mouse, 1971, Helbros	250-500
WA591	Natasha 1971, Jay Ward	300-600
WA601	Pebbles 1971, small, Prince Robale	100-300
WA615	Popeye, 1966, Bradley	200-400
WA618	Popeye, 1971, animated arms, Sheffield	400-800
WA625	Porky Pig, 1971, Sheffield	400-700
WA626	Porky Pig, 1971, Sheraton	300-600
WA641	Quick Draw McGraw 1966, Bradley	250-500
WA651	Road Runner/Wile E. Coyote 1971, revolving disc	200-500
WA661	Road Runner 1971, Sheffield	300-700
WA675	Robin Hood, 1956, rectangle	300-700
WA678	Robin Hood, 1958, round	300-700
WA691	Rocky 1971, Jay Ward	250-500
WA701	Rocky Jones 1954, rectangle	200-700
WA721	Roy Rogers, 1951, on Trigger	150-500
WA725	Roy Rogers, 1957, rectangle, green	150-500
WA726	Roy Rogers, 1957, green, Tonneau	150-500
WA741	Scooby Doo 1971, 21 jewels, w/date	200-600
WA751	Shep 1971, Jay Ward	250-500
WA761	Smokey Bear 1971, Hawthorne	100-350
WA771	Smokey Stover 1971, Hi Time	100-350
WA781	Snidely Whiplash 1971, Jay Ward	250-600
WA805	Snoopy, 1968, on dog house, Timex	100-400
WA807	Snoopy, 1969, yellow background	100-350
WA808	Snoopy, 1969, black background	100-350
WA815	Space Patrol	60-600

WA821	Super Chicken 1971, Jay Ward	250-600
WA835	Superman, 1955, bolt hands, green face	300-700
WA840	Superman, 1962, flying, Bradley	200-450
WA845	Superman, 1968, Revolving disc	300-500
WA861	Sylvester 1971, Timesetters	200-400
WA861	Tom Corbett 1951, Tonneau	250-700
WA871	Tweety 1971, Timesetters	250-600
WA881	Wile E. Coyote 1971, Sheraton	250-600
WA891	Woody Woodpecker, 1950, rectangle	250-700
WA899	Woody Woodpecker, 1972, revolving disc, Rouan	200-450
WA921	Yogi Bear 1971, Prince Robale	300-500
WA931	Zorro 1950, black face	100-350

See also: **Batman**

WESTERN HEROES — by Ted Hake

Adventures set in the Old West have struck a responsive chord in the American psyche since the earliest days of one-reel movies.

When television sets became available to most families in the early 50s, the films of Hopalong Cassidy, Roy Rogers, and Gene Autry were one of the largest programming sources. The Long Ranger made an easy transition from radio to round out the big four. Many other western film stars such as Gabby Hayes, The Cisco Kid, Hoot Gibson, Bob Steele, Lash LaRue, and others received TV exposure, but failed to be as extensively merchandised as the big four. The radio success of Tom Mix and Straight Arrow also carried over into the 50s for a few notable collectibles.

Wild Bill Hickok was a product of TV in the mid-50s, but the prime time westerns headed by *Gunsmoke; Bonanza; The Rifleman; Have Gun, Will Travel; Maverick; Bat Masterson; Wagon Train; The Life and Legend of Wyatt Earp; Cheyenne; Sugarfoot; Bill Powell's Zane Grey Theater; Wells Fargo; Lawman; Wanted - Dead or Alive; The Texan; Yancy Derringer; Bronco; Johnny Ringo; The Virginian; Laredo; Branded;* and many more started to appear in 1957 and lasted thru most of the 1960s before TV network programmers decided the format was tired and worn. Prime time shows never produced the quantity of merchandise as did the big four, but were the source of isolated items on the "most valuable" list.

Prices are for items in fine to excellent condition. Excellent condition items must be close to perfect. Fine condition items may show some minor wear or aging, but no serious defects.

The Cisco Kid
WH125	Secret Compartment Picture Ring	450-1000
WH129	Range War Game, TV premium	45-100

Davy Crockett
WH150	Marked Coon-skin Hat, real fur	75-125
WH155	Leather Sign	300-500
WH160	Outfit (Cooper-Iskin, Inc.)	90-150
WH161	Outfit (L.M. Eddy Mfg. Co.)	100-200

WH165	Bow & Arrow Set (Rollin Wilson), 1956	35-75
WH170	Marionette (Peter Puppet Playthings), 1955	50-100
WH175	Wood Guitar in cardboard case	100-250
WH176	Uke-Guitar w/crank, in box	75-125
WH185	Rifle	40-80

Gabby Hayes
WH225	Shooting Cannon Ring (Quaker)	60-200
WH228	Western Wagon Collection (Quaker)	30-60
WH230	"Cottontail" Rocking Horse	60-125

Gene Autry
WH250	Plastic Guitar, cardboard case (Emenee)	50-100
WH255	Double Gun Holster Set (Leslie-Henry Co)	75-150
WH260	American Eagle Ring (Dell)	50-150
WH261	American Flag Ring (Dell)	50-150
WH263	Bread End Seal Map/Poster, complete	20-60
WH266	Gene Autry and Champion School Bag	50-125
WH270	Western Outfit (guns, spurs & cuffs)	150-275

Hopalong Cassidy, 1950-51
WH300	Alarm Clock (U.S. Time)	125-250
WH302	Bar 20 Ranch Portrait Badge on card	25-50
WH303	Hopalong Cassidy Bank, removable hat	20-40
WH305	Bar 20 Ranch Punch-Out Book (Whitman)	50-100
WH306	Official Bar 20 TV Folding Chair,	75-150
WH307	Cloth Doll, 22", stuffed, w/child-like face, "Hopalong Cassidy" name on hat band	75-150
WH308	Ear Muffs, portraits on tin oval inserts	75-150
WH309	Latex Face Mask, 1950s	35-75
WH312	Hopalong Cassidy & Topper Figures (Ideal)	35-75
WH315	Glass, 4-3/4", "Cowboy Branding Irons"	35-70
WH316	Hair Trainer bottle	15-30
WH318	Clothing Hamper, 23", pressed steel	75-150
WH320	Cookie Corral Ceramic Cookie Jar	150-300
WH322	Hopalong Cassidy/Topper Child's Cowboy Jeans, blue denim (Lurrie-Pizer)	35-75
WH324	Gun & Holster Night Light (Aladdin Lamps)	75-150
WH325	Ballpoint Pen, 3-D head on end (Parker)	25-50
WH327	Pillow Cover, "Good Luck From Hoppy"	20-45
WH328	Hopalong Cassidy Pocketknife (Hammer)	25-50
WH330	Potato Chip Tin Canister (Kuehmann Foods)	75-150
WH335	Compass Hat Ring w/hat	75-200
WH338	Topper Rocking Horse (Rich Toys)	100-200
WH339	Roller Skates w/Spurs (Rollfast)	100-200
WH340	Automatic Television Set (Automatic Toy)	75-150
WH343	Wallet, black vinyl w/zipper	20-35
WH344	Waste Can, steel w/embossed paper	75-150
WH346	Copper Gulch Television Book	25-50

Lone Ranger
WH505	Lone Ranger w/Tonto Packaged Figures, bag w/25 additional western figures (Marx Toys)	60-125
WH508	Signal Siren Flashlight	20-40

WH518

WH950

WH340

WH760

WH176

WH320

WH725

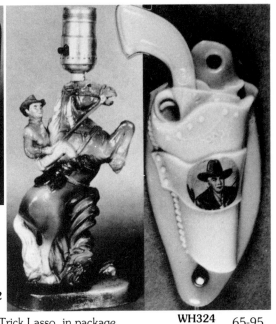

WH732

WH324

WH510	Guitar, 30", wood & cardboard	30-60
WH515	Official Outfit w/mask, key ring, belt, badge, & silver bullet (Esquire Novelty Co.)	55-85
WH518	Silver Bullet Pen Set, in box	100-150
WH519	Hand Puppet	30-60
WH522	Hand Puzzle w/metal balls	15-30
WH524	Magic Lasso w/badge (Round-Up Products)	150-300
WH525	Rodeo Playset, 1952, Marx Toy Set #3696	100-200
WH528	Lone Ranger Boxed Playsuit (Herman Iskin)	40-80
WH540	Flashlight Gun w/Secret Compartment	55-175
WH541	Movie Film Ring, w/8mm Marine Corps film	50-100
WH542	Shirt & Mask Neckerchief	30-90
WH544	Safety Club Kit, (Merita), letter, photo & card	40-95
WH547	Filmstrip Saddle Ring, w/16mm Lone Ranger film used to expose glow-in-dark images	40-150
WH549	Lone Ranger Cut-Outs (Merita)	50-225
WH551	Life Size Posters of Lone Ranger & Tonto, pair	150-400
WH553	Movie Ranch Wild West Town Plastic Figures	50-150
WH555	Target Pistol and Targets	25-75
WH560	Round-Up Snow Dome	30-60
WH562	Official Lone Ranger Tent w/box (H. Wenzel Tent & Duck Co.), 1958	50-100
WH564	Lone Ranger Inflatable Vinyl Toy (Plinno)	35-75

Rin Tin Tin

WH600	Cavalry Gun & Holster	45-100
WH601	Stereo Card Viewer	50-120
WH602	Pennant	25-75
WH606	Stuffed "Rinty" Dog	100-200
WH607	Cavalry Hat w/logo	30-100
WH610	Hard Plastic Figure of Rin Tin Tin	35-75
WH612	Belt w/Rinty and Rusty on foil buckle, 1956	25-50
WH615	Paint by Numbers set (Transogram)	30-60

Roy Rogers 1950-57

WH700	Roy & Dale Statuette Dolls Album (Whitman)	35-75
WH701	Bank, bronzed white metal boot (Alman)	25-50
WH705	Roy & Trigger China Bank, 7" tall	40-75
WH707	Bedspread, 55" x 69" beige cotton	60-125
WH710	Child's Belt, tan leather w/tooled floral design, metal bullets & cut glass stones	30-60
WH712	Binoculars, metal & plastic w/color decals	50-100
WH715	Child's Boots, black leather	75-150
WH720	Flash Camera (Herbert George Co.)	20-45
WH725	Animated Alarm Clock, Roy on Trigger (Ingraham)	75-150
WH730	Trigger Horse Trailer w/Nellybelle Jeep and Pat Brady Figure (Ideal Toy)	60-125
WH731	Western Gloves, leather w/pictures on cuffs	35-75
WH732	Roy Rogers on Trigger Lamp, 11" tall painted plaster (Plasto Mfg. Co.)	75-150
WH734	Hand Puppet, fabric w/soft rubber head	40-75
WH738	Paint-By-Numbers Set (Post premium)	25-75
WH740	Double R Bar Ranch (Post premium)	40-90
WH741	Raincoat, oilcloth w/portraits on pockets	50-100

WH742	Trick Lasso, in package	65-95
WH743	Shoot'n Irons, boxed	75-150
WH745	Rodeo Ranch, boxed playset (Marx)	100-200
WH746	"Happy Trails", 45 Record Player (RCA)	125-250
WH750	Trigger Child's Rocker Toy	100-200
WH752	Child's TV Seat, leather saddle seat on 3 wood legs	100-200
WH753	Trigger Play Horse on wheels	150-275
WH754	Nellybelle Jeep Pedal Car	150-350
WH755	Child's Slippers	25-50
WH756	Spurs (Classy Products Corp.), 1954	35-75
WH760	Fix-It Stagecoach, boxed (Ideal Toy), 1965	100-200
WH761	Roy Rogers/Trigger/Trigger Jr./Trailer Van w/Dodge Cab (Marx)	125-250
WH770	Woodburning Set	100-225

Straight Arrow 1950-53

WH800	Mystic Wrist Kit, plastic bracelet w/gold arrowhead & cowry shell	75-195
WH801	Tribal Shoulder Patch	30-75
WH804	Golden Nugget Ring w/picture	65-150
WH810	Game	30-65
WH811	Rite-A-Lite Arrowhead	80-200

Tom Mix

WH830	Magic-Light Tiger-Eye Ring, plastic	85-250
WH835	Ralston 50th Anniversary Watch, 1982	95-300

TV & Movie Western Heroes

WH900	Annie Oakley Plasysuit, boxed (Iskin)	20-40
WH910	Bat Masterson Figure, boxed (Hartland)	125-200
WH912	Bat Masterson Playsuit (Ben Cooper)	25-50
WH920	Gunsmoke Child's Slipper Boots	50-100
WH925	Have Gun, Will Travel Gun & Holster Set (Halco)	75-150
WH926	Paladin Small Figure w/Horse (Hartland)	50-100
WH928	John Wayne Color Book (Saalfield), 1951	25-50
WH930	Ponderosa Ranch Weapons Set, rifle, pistol, knife & accessories (Marx)	100-200
WH940	Red Ryder Corral Marble Game (Gotham), 1950	25-50
WH945	Branded, Cheyenne, & Sugarfoot Gun & Holster Set (Daisy)	75-175
WH950	Rifleman "Flip Special" (Hubley)	65-200
WH955	Tales of Wells Fargo Badge, on card, 1959-60	15-25
WH960	Wagon Train Covered Wagon w/box (Marx)	50-100
WH965	Wanted: Dead or Alive Rifle, on card, "Mares Laig" rifle (Marx)	100-200
WH970	Wyatt Earp Gun & Holster Set	60-125

See also: **Autographs; Bicycles; Cereal Boxes; Watches, Character**

WHERE TO BUY AND SELL

Many readers may find items listed in this book they wish to sell. The best way to realize full value is to find a collector-buyer. This can be accomplished by taking a space at a popular collectibles flea market or buy giving a dealer friend a small commission to sell it for you. Dealers purchasing items for resale can usually only pay 35 to 50 percent of the retail value due to ever increasing travel, exhibiting, and other costs.

Special mention of the dealers and collectors who have been helpful to Tomart Publications in publishing this book is due.

Those listed are by no means the total number of dealers or collectors buying or selling items listed. Many were approached. These are, however, the ones who spent the time to share their expertise for this book.

Tomart asked only reputable collectors and dealers to participate. They are well known in their fields and were highly recommended. Since they provided service above the ordinary for us, it seems likely they would do the same for anyone wishing to buy or sell.

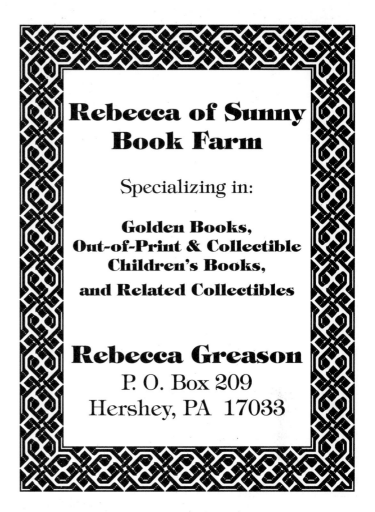

HOWARD LOWERY
GALLERY

© Disney

Walt Disney Studio, *Lady and the Tramp*, 1955, 11 x 8, cels of Lady, Si and Am with a master background painting from Disney's animated feature film. To be offered in our April 1992 auction.

FINE ANIMATION ART & RELATED ITEMS

1992 Schedule of Auctions

April	•	Fine Animation Art & Related Items
June	•	Comic Art & Cinema Collectibles
August	•	Fine Animation Art & Related Items
September	•	Disneyana & Related Items
November	•	Fine Animation Art & Related Items

For information please contact

HOWARD LOWERY • 3818 W. MAGNOLIA BLVE. • BURBANK, CA 91505 (818) 972-9080

California Auction License A2219

Learn More From the Experts

Tomart Photo Price Guides™ offer the most complete source of information available on Disneyana, Space Adventure Collectibles, Golden Books®, Character and Promotional Glasses, Action Figures, and other contemporary collectible subjects. Each Book contains thousands of color and black and white photos...a photo for approximately 85% of all listings.

Knowing the most valuable items from 1950-1990 is a big advantage, but they are only a beginning for the hot collectible fields covered. Tomart's definitive guides fill this void with comprehensive coverage of items, values, and important background information.

Tomart photo price guides are available from any bookseller. If you have difficulty finding any of our titles, write to Tomart Publications, P.O. Box 292102, Dayton, OH 45429. Titles may be ordered direct if not available at your bookstore. *Please try your bookseller first! They can special order if the book is not in stock. Add $2.75 postage and handling for the first book, and 75¢ for each additional book.*

McDONALD'S HAPPY MEAL Collectibles
All premiums, boxes, bags, translites, and displays connected with McDonald's Happy Meal promotions are pictured with 1992 value estimates. Included are all regional and test sets known to the author, Meredith Williams, publisher of the McDonald's Happy Meal Collector's newsletter. Available February 1992. Write Tomart Publications for details.

Tomart's DISNEYANA Series
The most complete resource on Disney collectibles available. Over 20,000 color and black and white photos of Disney items in the 4 volume series, plus hundreds of facts to help date Disneyana. complete list of U.S. licensed manufacturers up to 1987. "Mickey may be the leader of the club, but Tomart's Illustrated Disneyana Catalog & Price Guides are the leader of the definitive guidebooks on Disneyana"—Collector's Showcase Magazine.
$24.95 per volume

Condensed Edition
The index and price update edition to Volumes One through Four. Additional information on animation cels, watches, Disneykins, and over 100 other categories. 23 new color pages, "Where to Buy and Sell" section, updated collector information. Postage and Handling free if ordered with Volumes 1-4.   **$19.98**

Tomart's ACTION FIGURE DIGEST
Keep current on prices and the most valuable new action figure collectibles with Tomart's *Action Figure Digest* magazine. This bi-monthly publication updates *Tomart's Price Guide to Action Figure Collectibles* with the latest information on recent finds. Read what's happening with G.I. Joe, Star Wars, Star Trek, Super Heroes, Teenage Mutant Ninja Turtles, and hundreds of other Action Figure collectibles. Learn how to buy the most valuable figures before the toy stores sell out.

Annual subscription for 6 issues is $25 in the US, $30US in Canada, and $40US via airmail worldwide.

Become an Expert Yourself

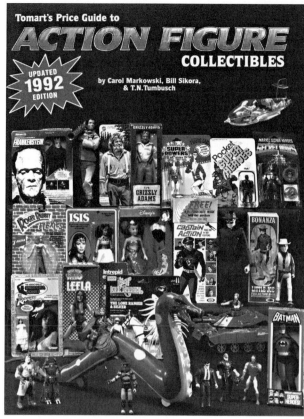

ACTION FIGURE Collectibles

Complete guide of superheroes, G.I. Joe, Mego's, Captain Action, Star Wars, Star Trek, TV and film characters Disney, fantasy, science fiction, monsters, Marx ... over 300 action figure issues. Even the latest Turtles, Toy Biz Marvel superheroes, and Swamp Thing releases. Nearly 4,000 color and b&w photos, 272 pages, hardbound.   **$34.95 + P&H**

RADIO PREMIUM & CEREAL BOX Collectibles

All the rings, badges, decoders, secret code manuals and other amazing gadgets which thrilled over 2 generations '30s-'60s... the golden age of character premium giveaways. Up to date values for Capt. Midnight, Lone Ranger, Shadow, Superman, Roy Rogers, Dick Tracy, Jack Armstrong, Orphan Annie, Tom Mix and 100's of other champions of BLB, comic book, and early TV fame. Soft cover, 176 pages.   **$22.95 + P&H**

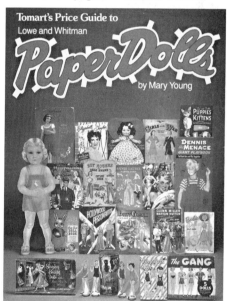

SPACE ADVENTURE

Twenty categories including 2001, Buck Rogers, Flash Gordon, E.T., Space Patrol, Alien, Dune, V, Star Wars, Star Trek, Planet of the Apes and Battlestar Galactica. Complete price guide, 1911-1990, 7" x 10", over 2,000 b&w and color photos. This one is a must.   **$19.95 + P&H**

CHARACTER & PROMOTIONAL GLASSES

Complete collector price guide to the mushrooming hobby of glass collecting. Photos of 3,000 glasses. Over 100 Disney issues; Coke, Pepsi, superheroes, sports, cartoon, McDonald's and other fast foods. 1930-1992. 8-1/2" x 11" w/color.   **$24.95 + P&H**

Lowe and Whitman PAPER DOLLs

An all-new book on Lowe and Whitman Paper Dolls, including Movie and TV Stars, toy/comic characters, western heroes, and others. 8-1/2" x 11" w/thousands of color and b&w photos, 168 pages.   **$24.95 + P&H***

151